DICTIONARY OF
LITERARY TERMS

COLES EDITORIAL BOARD

Bound to stay open

Publisher's Note

Otabind (Ota-bind). This book has been bound using the patented Otabind process. You can open this book at any page, gently run your finger down the spine, and the pages will lie flat.

ABOUT COLES NOTES

COLES NOTES have been an indispensible aid to students on five continents since 1948.

COLES NOTES are available for a wide range of individual literary works. Clear, concise explanations and insights are provided along with interesting interpretations and evaluations.

Proper use of COLES NOTES will allow the student to pay greater attention to lectures and spend less time taking notes. This will result in a broader understanding of the work being studied and will free the student for increased participation in discussions.

COLES NOTES are an invaluable aid for review and exam preparation as well as an invitation to explore different interpretive paths.

COLES NOTES are written by experts in their fields. It should be noted that any literary judgement expressed herein is just that – the judgement of one school of thought. Interpretations that diverge from, or totally disagree with any criticism may be equally valid.

COLES NOTES are designed to supplement the text and are not intended as a substitute for reading the text itself. Use of the NOTES will serve not only to clarify the work being studied, but should enhance the readers enjoyment of the topic.

ISBN 0-7740-3703-2

© COPYRIGHT 2000 AND PUBLISHED BY
COLES PUBLISHING COMPANY
TORONTO - CANADA
PRINTED IN CANADA

Manufactured by Webcom Limited
Cover finish: Webcom's Exclusive **DURACOAT**

A

Abbey Theatre: See **Celtic Renaissance**.

ABC (Absey): A poem in which the successive lines or stanzas begin with the successive letters of the alphabet.
For example:

> *A*fter the sun has set,
> *B*ehind the clouds at rest
> *C*lose to the horizon
> *D*rift the whitecaps.

The above example is a line ABC. An example of the stanzaic ABC is the 119th Psalm.
An ABC (or absey) poem is also known as an abecedarius.

Abecedarius: See **ABC**.

Abridge: To reduce in scope; to shorten by omission of words without sacrificing the sense. (See **Digest**.)

Absolutism: In literary criticism, the principle that there are definite, basic, unchanging standards by which a work of art can be judged.

Abstract: A brief statement of the essential thought of a book, article or speech; to abstract is to summarize briefly the essential thoughts of a work. Usually the word refers to a concise summary of a critical work. That is, one *summarizes* or *paraphrases* a novel or poem, but one *abstracts* a critical work about the novel or poem. (Compare with **Paraphrase** and **Summary**.)

Abstract Terms: Words or phrases referring to ideas or qualities; terms that describe that which is not concrete. For example, while *sugar*, *people* and *rock* are concrete, *sweetness*, *humanity* and *hard* are abstract. (See **Concrete Terms**.)

Academies: Associations of literary, artistic or scientific men and women who work together for the advancement of culture and learning within their special fields of interest. The term is derived from "the olive grove of Academe" where Plato taught in Athens.
In many countries, certain academies have official or national responsibilities. The Royal Society of England, for example, advises the British government on scientific problems. L'Académie française focusses on maintaining the purity and eloquence of the French language.

Acatalectic: See **Catalexis.**

Accent: In versification, accent is stress given to certain syllables according to a metrical pattern. The regular, orderly repetition of accent contributes to the poetic quality of writing and fixes the rhythm of the line. The following illustrates the relation of accent to meter and versification:

Ĭ cōme | frŏm haūnts | ŏf cōot | ănd hērn.

(See **Ictus, Quantity** and **Scansion.**)

Accentual-syllabic Verse: Referring to the rhythm of a piece of verse; verse that depends on both the number of syllables to the line and the pattern of accented and unaccented syllables.

Accidence: The part of grammar dealing with those changes in words that show case, number, tense and other non-essential qualities.

Acephalous Line: A headless line. (See **Truncation.**)

Acmeism: A movement in twentieth-century Russian poetry that rejected the symbolist movement and favored the definite and concrete. To the acmeist, the poet was not a seer or prophet, but a craftsman.

Acroama: (1) An entertainment, usually a musical or dramatic recital, presented during a meal. (2) A lecture or discourse given by a learned authority to a group that has been instructed in the subject discussed.

Acronym: A word formed from the initial letters or syllables of other words; for example, *radar* (*ra*dio *d*etecting *a*nd *r*anging).

Acrostic: Usually verse, though sometimes prose, arranged so that certain letters form a word or phrase which is often the name or title that is the subject of the composition. The simplest acrostics use the first or last letter of each line. For example, the following is an acrostic for *news*:

*N*orth
*E*ast
*W*est
*S*outh

Acrostics are often used as memory devices. The first letter of each word in the following sentence, for example, is helpful in remembering the names of the planets and their relative position with the sun: *M*ary's *v*iolet *e*yes *m*ake *J*ack *s*tay *u*p *n*ights *p*erhaps (Mercury, Venus, Earth, Mars, Jupiter, Saturn, Uranus, Neptune and Pluto). (See **Conundrum**.)

Action: The events that take place in a work of literature. In drama, *stage action* refers to any event that occurs on the stage (e.g., the actual physical movements of the actors).

The action of a novel, short story or narrative poem is usually both external and internal. *External action* comprises those physical events that actually occur in relation to the characters, actions that affect them or in which they participate. *Internal action* refers to a character's thoughts and feelings as they are reported by the author.

Acts: Divisions of plays or operas. On the contemporary stage, the three-act play is most common.

In Greek drama, the major parts were distinguished from each other by the appearance of the chorus. The Latin plays of Seneca were divided into five acts, a plan followed by Shakespeare and most Elizabethan dramatists. In some cases, the division into five acts corresponds to the five main divisions of the action. (See **Dramatic Structure**.)

After 1880, the conventional five-act play gradually gave way to plays of fewer acts. At about the same time, playwrights began to write one-act plays and these are now recognized as a separate genre.

Acyrology: An extreme form of euphemism. An example would be to refer to *teeth* as *the furniture of the mouth*. (See **Euphemism**.)

Adage: A proverb or wise saying made familiar by long use. Example: *A fool and his money are soon parted*. (See **Proverb**.)

Adaptation: The rewriting of a work to fit another medium. Novels, for example, are frequently adapted to the form of screenplays, appropriate for filming.

Addisonian: In the style of the English writer, Joseph Addison (1672-1719). Addison's essays were poised, lucid, urbane, judicial, good-natured and, at times, somewhat condescending. They appeared regularly in the English periodicals *The Tatler* (1709-1711) and *The Spectator* (1711-1714). *The Tatler* was started by Richard Steele (1672-1729), who later became Addison's partner in the publication of *The Spectator*.

Address: A speech or written statement, serious in intent and

3

somewhat formal in style. Frequently, for example, the political head of a nation gives an address to the country's citizens.

Adonic Verse: A verse form associated with Greek and Latin prosody. The meter of Adonic verse consists of a dactyl and a spondee, as $-\upsilon\upsilon\,|\,--$. This meter was used in the verses mourning the death of Adonis, a mythological young man who was loved by Venus, the goddess of love and beauty.

Adynaton: A form of hyperbole in which an actual event or emotion is magnified by reference to an impossibility. The following lines, by Robert Burns, are an example:

> As fair art thou, my bonnie lass,
> So deep in luve am I,
> And I will luve thee still, my dear,
> Till a' the seas gang dry.

(See **Hyperbole**.)

Aeolic: The Aeolic dialect was one of the three great dialects in the Greek language and was used by the poets, Sappho and Alcaeus. By extension, the term is applied to a meter in which dactyls ($-\upsilon\upsilon$) or iambs ($\upsilon-$) are combined with trochees ($-\upsilon$) in a verse. The resulting metrical foot is known as a choriamb ($-\upsilon\upsilon-$).

Aesthetic Distance (or **Psychical Distance**): The distance that, according to some critics, ought to exist between the perceiver and the work of art. By maintaining that distance, the reader gains the advantage of viewing the work as an object of art and not as an extension of his personal life. In not keeping the aesthetic distance, the reader's own fears and anxieties could be a disadvantage to him by interfering with his interpretation and enjoyment of the work.

Aestheticism: (1) The belief in beauty as the basic standard of value in human life, underlying all moral and other considerations. (2) Great love for and sensitivity to beauty and the arts.

The term was loosely applied to an English literary movement of the second half of the nineteenth century. The roots of the movement lay in the reverence for beauty instilled by Keats and the Pre-Raphaelites. (See **Pre-Raphaelitism**.)

Aesthetics: The science or study of the beautiful. There are two major approaches to aesthetics, the philosophical and the psychological. The philosophical approach has attempted, by logical reasoning, to establish the nature of art and beauty, their relationship to truth and goodness, etc. The psychological approach has emphasized the study of the process of creation in the artist and of appreciation in the beholder.

Affectation: Using a style or method that is not suitable to the subject or occasion. More specifically, the term is applied to an assumed elegance or an artificial pretence designed to produce an effect that has no basis in reality.

Affective Fallacy: The critical error of evaluating a work in terms of the results it has on the mind and emotions of the reader or audience rather than on more formalistic criteria. The term was defined by W. K. Wimsatt, Jr. and Monroe C. Beardsley in *The Verbal Icon* (1954). An example of affective fallacy would be the criticism that *Hamlet* was a poor play because it made one believe in ghosts.

Afflatus: See **Divine Afflatus**.

Age of Reason: A term frequently applied to the Restoration and Augustan periods (the final decades of the seventeenth century and the first half of the eighteenth century). During that period, rationality, refinement and judgment were greatly admired, and the literature reflected classical qualities. Among the important English writers of the period were Dryden, Pope, Swift, Addison, Steele, Johnson and Goldsmith.

Agon: That part of a Greek drama in which two characters, each one aided by half of the chorus, engage in verbal conflict.

Alazon: An impostor or braggart in Greek comedy.

Alba: See **Aubade**.

Alcaics: Verses written in the manner of the odes of the Greek lyric poet, Alcaeus; that is, a four-stanza poem, each stanza composed of four lines, each line having four stresses.

Since the pattern is classical, based on quantitative measures, the verses can only be imitated in English; exact English Alcaics are practically impossible.

Alexandrine: A verse line with six iambic feet (iambic hexameter). An iamb consists of an unaccented and an accented syllable. The following Alexandrine lines are found in Robert Browning's *Fifine at the Fair*:

If hunger, proverbs say, allures the wolf from wood,
Much more the bird must dare a dash at something good.

In the Spenserian stanza, the Alexandrine is used in the final line after eight pentameter (five iambic feet) lines.

In general, the English Alexandrine has proved too unwieldy for continuous use in a long work.

Allegory: Prose or verse in which the objects, events or people are presented symbolically, so that the story conveys a meaning other than and deeper than the actual incident or characters described. Often, the form is used to teach a moral lesson.

Fables and parables are common forms of allegory. Examples in literature are John Bunyan's *The Pilgrim's Progress* and Edmund Spenser's *The Faerie Queene.*

Alliteration: The repetition of the initial letter or sound in two or more closely associated words or stressed syllables. An example of alliteration through the repetition of initial letters is found in Gray's *Elegy Written in a Country Churchyard*:

The *p*lowman homeward *p*lods his *w*eary *w*ay.

The use of similar sound for alliterative effect is evident is these lines from Tennyson:

The *m*oan of doves in i*mm*e*m*orial elms,
And *m*ur*m*uring of innu*m*erable bees.

Alliteration is not restricted to poetry. Frequently, it occurs in popular expressions such as: *bag and baggage, fire and flood* and *thick and thin.*

Alliterative Romance: A romantic tale written in alliterative verse, especially one of those produced during the fourteenth-century revival of interest in alliteration. Examples are *William of Palerne, Sir Gawain and the Green Knight* and *Le Morte d'Arthur.*

Alliterative Verse: Those verse forms, usually Germanic in origin, in which the division of lines and the general metrical structure were based on periodic and regular repetition of certain initial letters or sounds within the lines.

A characteristic example of alliterative verse appears in *Piers Plowman*:

And *Piers* was *proud* there-of/and *putte* hem alle to swynke,
And yaf hem *mete* and *monye*/as they *myght* deseruen.

Allonym: (1) Someone else's name, assumed by a writer; a pseudonym or pen name. (2) The work published under such a name. (See **Pseudonym**.)

Allusion: A figure of speech making casual reference to a famous historical or literary figure or event. For example:

I know not where is that *Promethean heat*
That can thy light relume.

SHAKESPEARE

Almanac: In medieval times, an almanac was a permanent table showing the movements of the heavenly bodies, from which calculations for any year could be made. Later, almanacs or calendars were prepared for calculating and recording shorter time spans.

During the sixteenth century, forecasts, first, of the weather and, later, of such human misfortunes as plagues and wars, were added. As the form evolved, useful information — especially for farmers — was included. More recently, in works such as the *World Almanac*, the almanac has become a storehouse of historical and statistical information.

The almanac figures but slightly in literature. Spenser's *Shepheardes Calender* (1579) consists of twelve poems under the titles of the twelve months and has some seasonal implications. In the eighteenth century, Benjamin Franklin's *Poor Richard's Almanack* (1732-1757) was partly inspired by the English comic almanac, *Poor Robin*.

Altar Poem: Also known as pattern poetry; a poem in which the lines are arranged so that they form a design resembling the shape of the subject of the poem. The following stanza from George Herbert's (1593-1633) *Easter Wings* is an example.

Lord, who createdst man in wealth and store,
Though foolishly he lost the same,
Decaying more and more,
Till he became
Most poore:
With thee
O let me rise
As larks, harmoniously,
And sing this day thy victories:
Then shall the fall further the flight in me.

Alternate Rhyme: Lines with an *abab* rhyme scheme. (See **Rhyme**.)

Ambiguity: The expression of an idea in such a way that more than one meaning is possible.

Ambiguity can be intentional. (See Juliet's replies to her mother in Shakespeare's *Romeo and Juliet*, Act III, Scene 5.)

Unintentional ambiguity is often due to inexact pronoun references, poor punctuation, faulty or inverted word order, undue brevity and compression of statement, and the use of a word having two or more meanings.

American Language: A term used to designate certain idioms and forms peculiar to English speech in America. According to the *Encyclopaedia Americana*, these differences are usually due to one of the following: some forms originate in America independent of English speech (*gerrymander*, for example); some expressions, once native to England, have been brought to America and lived on after they had died out in England (*fall* for *autumn*); and certain English forms have taken on modified meanings in America (*store* instead of *shop*).

H.L. Mencken, in *The American Language*, points out six other respects in which American expression differs from English: syntax, intonation, slang, idiom, grammar and pronunciation.

Amerind Literature: The body of writing and oral tradition developed by the aboriginal tribes of America. The term is a combination of syllables from *American* and *Indian*.

Since much of the literature developed through the rhythmic accents of the ceremonial drum, it has a regularity of metric pattern that gives it the quality of poetry. Another part of the literature evolved through the recounting of events and has taken the form of prose.

Most of the Amerind literature known today is confined to a few types: the epic, the folk tale, the drama, ritualistic and ceremonial exercises, and narratives of adventure.

Ampersand: The symbol "&," meaning "and." The ampersand is primarily used in business correspondence, in reference works and in the names of companies.

Amphiboly (-e; -ogy; -ogism): An ambiguity induced either by grammatical looseness or by the double meanings of words. Prophecies with double meanings, such as those made by the witches to Macbeth, may also be called amphibolies. (See **Ambiguity**.)

Amphibrach: A metrical foot in verse, consisting of three syllables, the first and last unaccented, the second accented. An example is: ar range ment.

Amphigory or **Amphigouri:** Verse that contains little or no sense or meaning.

Amphimacer: A three-syllable metrical foot with a short middle syllable and a long first and third syllable, as in *summertime*. The amphimacer is the opposite of the amphibrach, which is also explained in this dictionary.

Amphisbaenic Rhyme: Backward rhyme. Named after an ancient serpent said to have a head at each end and capable of moving in either direction.

Amplification: A technique in which expressions likely to be ignored or misunderstood are emphasized through restatement with additional detail. The device is used in music, oratory and poetry. Misused, amplification can rob a statement of its original meaning.

Ana: A collection of scraps of information about people, places or events. During the seventeenth century, English readers delighted in this type of collection. Ana is also used as a suffix, as in Goldsmith*iana*, where it denotes a collection of miscellaneous information about Goldsmith.

Anabasis: The rising of an action to its climax.

Anachronism: Assignment of an event, a person, an object, language — anything, in fact — to a time when that event, person or object was not in existence. Numerous anachronisms occur in Shakespeare's plays. For example, cannons are placed in *King John*, a play set in a time many years before cannons were used in England. Humorists sometimes use anachronisms as a comic device.

Anaclasis: The substitution of a ditrochee or two trochees for an ionic, so that the second and third of the four syllables interchange length. The rhythmic movement is, therefore, upset by this irregularity, while the other parts of the line remain unaltered. (See **Ditrochee, Ionic, Rhythm** and **Trochee.**)

Anacoluthon: A change, accidentally or deliberately, from one grammatical construction to another within the same sentence. Used accidentally, anacoluthic writing is grammatically incorrect and confusing to the reader. Used deliberately, an anacoluthon can be effective, especially in oratory.
    The term is also applied to units of composition larger than the sentence when there is within the unit an obvious incoherency among

the parts. The following stanza from Robert Browning's *A Toccata of Galuppi's* illustrates this type of anacoluthon:

> Ay, because the sea's the street there; and
> 'tis arched by . . . what you call
> . . . Shylock's bridge with houses on it,
> where they kept the carnival:
> I was never out of England — it's as if I saw it all.

Anacreontic Poetry: Verse in the mood and manner of the lyrics of the Greek poet, Anacreon; that is, poems characterized by an erotic, amatory or Bacchanalian spirit. The characteristic Anacreontic stanza consists of four lines rhyming *abab*, each line composed of three trochaic feet with one long syllable added at the end of the line: $- \cup \mid - \cup \mid - \cup \mid -$.

Anacrusis: A term denoting one or more extra unaccented syllables at the beginning of a verse before the regular rhythm of the line begins. R. M. Alden cites the third verse of this stanza from Shelley as an example:

> What thou art we know not;
> What is most like thee?
> *From* rainbow clouds there flow not
> Drops so bright to see,
> As from thy presence showers a rain of melody.

Anadiplosis: Repetition in which the word(s) at the end of one clause recur at the beginning of the next.

Anagnorisis: A term used by Aristotle in the *Poetics* to indicate the moment of recognition in which a character moves from ignorance to knowledge.

Anagram: A word or phrase made by transposing the letters of another word or phrase, as *cask* is an anagram of *sack*. Usually, anagrams are a kind of word puzzle. In addition, however, writers have used anagrams in their work to conceal proper names or messages. Samuel Butler's *Erewhon* (nowhere) is an example of an anagram as a book title.

A variety of anagram, the palindrome, is an arrangement of letters that gives the same meaning when read forward or backward. A well-known palindrome involves the words Adam might have used in introducing himself to Eve: "Madam, I'm Adam." A longer palindrome is attributed to Napoleon, who said, "Able I was ere I saw Elba."

10

Analecta (Analects): Excerpts, selections or fragments from long pieces of writing; for example, *Analects from Confucius*.

Analogue: This word, meaning something that is similar to something else, has two special applications in literature: (1) a cognate or a word in one language corresponding to one in another language. Usually, the two words have a common origin. For example, the English word *mother* is an analogue of the Latin word *mater*; (2) in literary history, two versions of the same story may be called analogues. Thus, the story of the pound of flesh in *Gesta Romanorum* may be called an analogue of the similar plot in *The Merchant of Venice*.

Analogy: A comparison of two objects that are essentially different but have at least one common quality. Analogy is often used to explain an unfamiliar idea or concept in terms of a similar and familiar one.

    In logic, analogy is also used as a means of argument. For example, if A produces certain results, B, which is like A in some respects, will produce the same results. This type of analogy, however, should be used with care, since few *different* objects or ideas are essentially the *same* to more than a superficial observer or thinker.

Analysis: See **Synthesis**.

Ananym: A word or name written backward. For example, Blake, in some poems, used Los (Sol, the sun, spelled backward) as the name of the creative spirit.

Anapest: A three-syllable poetic measure comprising two short or unaccented syllables followed by a long or accented one ($\cup \cup -$). The following lines from Shelley's *The Cloud* are anapestic:

> Lĭke ă chīld frŏm thĕ wōmb, lĭke ă ghōst frŏm thĕ tōmb,
> Ĭ ărīse, ănd ŭnbuīld ĭt ăgaīn.

Anaphora: A term associated with the device of repetition, in which the same expression (word or words) is repeated at the beginning of two or more lines, clauses or sentences. (See **Repetition**.)

Anastrophe: Inversion of the usual, normal or logical order of the parts of a sentence. Anastrophe is used to secure rhythm or for emphasis and euphony. For example:

> Not fierce Othello is so loud a strain
> Roar'd for the handkerchief that caus'd his pain.
> ALEXANDER POPE

Anathema: A formal and solemn denunciation, particularly as pronounced by the Greek or Roman Catholic Church against an individual, an institution or a doctrine.

Anatomy: Originally a medical term meaning "dissection," the word anatomy was used figuratively in Aristotelian times to describe a logical dissection or analysis. In England, during the late sixteenth century, the term came to be used for any kind of analysis. Burton, for example, explained that his *Anatomy of Melancholy* (1621) discusses: "What it [melancholy] is, with all the kinds, causes, symptoms, prognostickes, and severall cures of it." Burton's and other anatomies anticipated the characteristics of the essay, and the philosophical and scientific treatises of the seventeenth century.

Ancients and Moderns, Quarrel of the: In literary history, the complicated controversy that took place during the late seventeenth and eighteenth centuries over the relative merits of classical and contemporary thinkers, writers and artists.

In France, the cause of the moderns was vigorously advocated by Charles Perrault, whose position was supported by Fontenelle, Thomas Corneille and others. Perrault, in his *Parallèle les anciens et les modernes* (1688-1697) and Fontenelle in his *Digression sur les anciens et les modernes* (1688) maintained that, in art and poetry, the efforts of the moderns were superior in taste and polish to those of the ancients.

In England, the controversy (known as "the battle of the books") began with the publication of Sir William Temple's essay, *Of Ancient and Modern Learning* (1690). Temple praised the ancients at the expense of the moderns. He was answered in 1694 by William Wotton, whose *Reflections upon Ancient and Modern Learning* found the moderns superior to the ancients in most, though not all, branches of learning.

Probably the most important literary work produced as a result of the controversy was Jonathan Swift's satirical *The Battle of the Books* (published in 1704), in which Swift upheld the cause of the ancients, although his satire was not altogether one-sided.

Anecdote: A short narrative detailing the particulars of an episode or event. Most frequently, the term refers to a narrated incident in the life of an important person.

The anecdote differs from the short story in that it lacks a complicated plot and is restricted to the relation of a single episode.

Anglicism: A peculiarity of expression or idiom characteristic of the English language; any form or expression peculiar to the British. For example, *lift* for *elevator* and *lorry* for *motor truck* are Anglicisms.

Anglo-Catholic Revival: See **Oxford Movement**.

Anglo-French (Anglo-Norman): Applied to the French language as used in England in the period following the Norman Conquest (ca. 1100-ca. 1350) and to the literature written in Anglo-French. Anglo-French literature flourished under the patronage of the Norman and early Plantagenet kings, particularly Henry II. French-English relations were so close at the time that it is difficult to be certain whether a given writer is to be classed as Anglo-French (Anglo-Norman) or simply as French. Many pieces of English literature (such as *The Lay of Havelok the Dane*) are English versions of Anglo-French writings.

Anglo-Irish Literature: Literature written in English by Irish writers, especially those living in Ireland who use Celtic material in their work.

Anglo-Latin: The learned literature written in Latin by inhabitants of England during the Middle English period. Most Anglo-Latin literature is prose, though light verse, as well as hymns, prayers and religious plays were also written.

Anglo-Norman: See **Anglo-French**.

Anglo-Saxons: A Germanic people who lived in England during post-Roman times. In the fifth and sixth centuries, the Angles and Saxons from the area now known as Schleswig-Holstein, together with the Jutes, invaded and conquered Britain. The name England (Angle-land) came from the Angles.

  The language of Anglo-Saxon England is sometimes called Anglo-Saxon, but the term Old English is usually preferred by literary scholars. (See **English Language** and **Old English**.)

Animal Epic: See **Beast Epic**.

Anisometric: Verse consisting of lines of unequal length.

Annal: A narrative of historical events recorded year by year. In the seventh century, Anglo-Saxon monks developed another sort of annal by recording important events of the year in ecclesiastical calendars. This practice developed into such records as the *Anglo-Saxon Chronicles*.

  More recently, the term has been used for historical narrative, and for digests and records of scientific and artistic organizations, such as *Annals of Music* and *Annals of Mathematics*. (See **Chronicles**.)

Annotation: A textual comment in a book. Annotations may range from a reader's pencilled comments in the margins of a page to an editor's printed notes, which clarify the meaning of the text.

Annuals: Books published in successive numbers at one-year intervals, usually reviewing the events of the year within a specific field of interest, such as high-school annuals. During the early twentieth century, books such as *The Boy's Own Annual* were popular. They were issued around Christmastime each year and contained prose, poetry and illustrations.

Antagonist: From the Greek *antagonistes*, meaning an opponent. In fiction or drama, the character who is directly opposed to the protagonist. (See **Protagonist**.) In Shakespeare's *Othello*, for example, Othello is the protagonist and Iago is the antagonist.

Antepenult: The third syllable from the end of a word. For example, the *nal* of *analogy* is the antepenult.

Anthem: A song of praise, rejoicing or reverence, as a national anthem or a religious anthem. In a more restricted sense, an anthem is an arrangement of selections from the Bible, usually from the Psalms, used in church services. Originally, the music was arranged for responsive singing, by two parts of a choir or by a priest and a choir. (See **Hymn**.)

Anthology: A group of selections, either prose or poetry, from the writing of one or more authors. Selections in an anthology are often grouped according to a particular subject or interest. Palgrave's *Golden Treasury* is a standard anthology of English poetry.

Anthropomorphic: Attributing human form or qualities to gods or animals. Homer's gods and goddesses in the *Iliad* and the *Odyssey* are anthropomorphized deities. (See **Personification**.)

Antibacchius: A foot of three syllables, of which the first two are long and the last one is short. The accent is on the first long syllable, as in *grandfather*.

Anticlimax: An abrupt descent from the important to the less important in a series of statements. When anticlimax is used intentionally, the effect is surprise and humor. An example of deliberate anticlimax is found in Pope's *The Rape of the Lock*:

> Not youthful kings in battle seized alive,
> Not scornful virgins who their charms survive,

> Not ardent lovers robbed of all their bliss,
> Not ancient ladies when refused a kiss,
> Not tyrants fierce that unrepenting die,
> *Not Cynthia when her manteau's pinned awry*,
> E'er felt such rage, resentment, and despair,
> As thou, sad Virgin! for thy ravished Hair.

The effect of unintentional anticlimax is bathos. (See **Bathos.**)

Antihero: A central character in a drama or novel who has none of the qualities traditionally associated with heroes. Willy Loman, in Arthur Miller's play, *Death of a Salesman* (1948), and Jimmy Porter, in John Osborne's play, *Look Back in Anger* (1956), are examples of antiheroes. (See **Antinovel.**)

Antilogy: A contradiction in ideas or terms; an illogicality.

Antimasque: A grotesque, usually humorous dance, interspersed among the beautiful and serious actions and dances of a masque. Often performed by professional actors and dancers, the antimasque served as a foil to the masque proper, performed by courtly amateurs.

    The development, and possibly the origin, of the antimasque is due to Ben Jonson. (See **Masque.**)

Antinomy: A conflict or contradiction between two principles that seem equally logical and true. For example, in ethics, two almost universal principles are that one should not lie and that one should try to help someone in need. It is not difficult to think of a situation in which it would be easy to help someone in need by lying either to that person or to whomever is causing the problem for that person. Both principles are valid but, in this case, they conflict. Usually, this conflict can be reconciled by appealing to a third, more important, principles or by deciding each case individually, on its own merits.

Antinovel: A piece of fiction that does not follow the traditional structure, form or methods of the novel. Frequently, there is no recognizable plot, and character development is minimal.

    The beginning of the modern antinovel is apparent in James Joyce's *Ulysses* and Virginia Woolf's *The Waves*. Nabokov in *Pale Fire* and Samuel Beckett in *Molloy* and *Murphy* contributed to the form. The novels of the French authors Camus, Sarraute and Robbe-Grillet are often termed antinovels.

    Dramatic works that do not follow traditional conventions are called antiplays. An example is Ionesco's *The Bald Soprano*. (See **Theater of the Absurd.**)

Antiphrasis: The satirical or humorous use of a word or phrase to convey an idea exactly opposite to the word's real meaning. In Shakespeare's *Julius Caesar*, Antony uses antiphrasis when he refers to Caesar's murderers as "honourable men."

Antiplay: See **Antinovel**.

Antiphon: A psalm or hymn sung or chanted in alternate parts of statements and responses; verses sung or chanted in response during a church service. (See **Hymn**.)

Antiquarianism: The study of old times through any available relics, especially literary and artistic.

Antiquarianism, as an organized effort in England, is associated with the sixteenth century. Much of the literature of the Renaissance, such as the chronicles, history plays and patriotic epics (for example, Spenser's *The Faerie Queene*), reflects the antiquarian movement.

During the Romantic Movement, the Gothic romances and the historical novels of Sir Walter Scott were the result of the antiquarian impulse.

Antistrophe: One of three divisions in Greek choral odes, the others being the strophe and the epode. While singing the strophe (the first part of the ode), the chorus moved from right to left on the stage. During the antistrophe, which followed, the movement was reversed, and the chorus circled from left to right. For the epode, the chorus moved to the center of the stage, standing motionless as they chanted.

The strophe and antistrophe were identical in meter, while the epode had a different metrical structure.

In modern free verse, strophe is sometimes used to designate a group of lines within a poem.

Antithesis: A literary technique in which opposite or strongly contrasting statements are balanced against each other for emphasis. Numerous examples of antithesis can be found in Pope's *The Rape of the Lock*. "Man proposes, God disposes" is one example.

Antonomasia: From the Greek, "to call by another name"; a figure of speech in which: (1) a title or epithet is used instead of a person's name (i.e., "the Bard" for Shakespeare); or (2) a proper name is used instead of a common noun (i.e., "a Machiavelli" for a crafty, unscrupulous politician).

Antonyms: Words in the same language with opposite meanings. For example, *up* and *down* are antonyms. (See **Synonyms**.)

Aphaeresis: Elimination of the first letter or syllable of a word, as in *phone* for *telephone*. If the omission occurs gradually, as the language develops, it is called aphesis. (See **Aphesis** and **Apocope**.)

Aphesis: The omission, as a language develops, of a short, unaccented letter or syllable from the beginning of a word. The word *down*, for example, was originally *adown*. (See also **Aphaeresis**.)

Aphorism: A brief statement, usually expressed in a single concise sentence, of an important truth. In its strict meaning, an aphorism is based on personal experience.

Loosely, the term is used interchangeably with proverb, apothegm, or maxim. However, a proverb is usually an anonymous expression; an aphorism can be attributed to an author. An apothegm is likely to be more practical in nature than an aphorism, which states an abstract, general truth. Finally, an aphorism differs from a maxim in that the former is not necessarily directed toward improving moral conduct.

In Shakespeare's *Hamlet*, Polonius used maxims in his advice to Laertes; Hamlet uttered an aphorism, from his own experience, when he said, "One may smile, and smile, and be a villain." (See **Proverb**.)

Apocalyptic Literature: Literature of disclosure or revelation, especially of the future. The last book of the New Testament (the *Revelation of St. John*) and Blake's *Jerusalem* are two examples.

Sometimes, apocalyptic literature predicts doom and destruction, warns of man's sinfulness and forecasts the end of the world.

Apocopated Rhyme: A rhyme in which the end of one rhyming word is cut off, as is *morn'* for *morning* in the following:

A song was born in early morn'.

Apocope: The dropping of a final letter, syllable or sound in the development of a word. For example, *curio* from *curiosity*. (See **Aphaeresis**.)

Apocrypha: Works of doubtful or unknown authorship. Apocrypha usually refers to Biblical books not regarded as inspired, and therefore excluded from the sacred canon. (See **Canon**.)

Apollonian: Theoretical; rational; well-ordered. The word is derived from Apollo, the Greek god of the sun, prophecy, music, medicine and poetry. The opposite of Apollonian is Dionysian. (See **Dionysian**.)

Apollonian and Dionysian were terms used by Friedrich Nietzsche in *The Birth of Tragedy out of the Spirit of Music* (1872), to contrast reason and instinct, culture and primitive nature, and other related ideas. Nietzsche argued that these poles formed a unity in Greek tragedy, with its rational (Apollonian) dialogue and its dithyrambic (Dionysian) music of the chorus.

Apologue: A fable with a moral. For example, Aesop's fables are apologues.

Apology: In literature, a defence or explanation; no admission of wrongdoing or expression of regret is involved. An example is Sir Philip Sidney's *An Apologie for Poetrie*.

The Latin form, *apologia*, is used in Cardinal Newman's autobiographical *Apologia pro Vita Sua*.

Apophasis: A statement that makes an assertion while seeming to deny it. For example, *If I did not know you were honest, I would say you stole that money yourself.*

Aposiopesis: The deliberate failure to complete a sentence. Frequently, the form is used to convey an impression of extreme exasperation, or to imply a threat, as, *If you do that, why, I'll* . . . Aposiopesis differs from anacoluthon in that the latter completes a sentence in irregular structural arrangement; the former leaves the sentence incomplete.

Apostrophe: Words addressed to an absent person as if he were present, or to a thing or idea as if it could appreciate them. In poetry, characteristic examples are found in invocations to the muses, as in Milton:

> And chiefly Thou, O Spirit, that dost prefer
> Before all temples the upright heart and pure,
> Instruct me, for Thou know'st.

The form is frequently used in patriotic oratory.

Apothegm: See **Aphorism**.

Apotheosis: Glorification or deification of a human to the rank of a god. For example, in ancient Rome the apotheosis of the emperors was customary.

Apron Stage: The apron is that part of the stage that projects beyond the proscenium arch. Any stage that consists primarily or entirely of an apron and on which the action is not seen as framed within the proscenium may be called an apron stage.

Arcadian: Arcadia, a picturesque plateau region in Greece, was pictured by pastoral poets as a land of ideal rural peace and contentment. Arcadian suggests an idealized rural simplicity and happiness, such as was exhibited by shepherds in conventional pastoral poetry. Sometimes the word is used as a synonym for bucolic or pastoral. (See **Bucolic, Eclogue, Idyll** and **Pastoral**.)

Archaism: (1) A word or expression no longer in general use. For example, *in sooth*, meaning *in truth*, is an archaism. (2) Outdated style or manner in art or literature.

Archetype: An original pattern from which copies are made, or a model from which later forms develop. A literary archetype is a basic, universal theme, situation or character that recurs in life and is reflected in the literature of all ages and languages. According to the Swiss psychologist, C. G. Jung (1875-1961) mankind's earliest experiences are stored in an individual's "collective unconscious." The artist unconsciously draws on this inherited memory as a pattern for his material. The quest or search is an example of a recurring archetypal theme.

The theory of the archetype has been developed and explored by such writers as J. G. Frazer in *The Golden Bough* (1915), Maud Bodkin in *Archetypal Patterns in Poetry* (1934) and J. Campbell in *The Hero with a Thousand Faces* (1949).

Architectonics: The structural qualities of proportion, unity, emphasis and scale that make a piece of writing proceed logically and smoothly from beginning to end. The requirements of architectonics, a term borrowed from architecture, are fulfilled when a piece of literature impresses a reader as being carefully planned and constructed.

Critics cite the novels of Thomas Hardy and Sir Walter Scott as noteworthy in their regard for architectonics.

Areopagus: The "hill of Ares [Mars]," the seat of the highest judicial court in ancient Athens. By association, the name has come to represent any court of final authority. In this sense, Milton used the term in his *Areopagitica*, addressed to the British parliament, on the question of censorship and the licensing of books.

Argot: The jargon or slang used by a particular class of persons; for example, sailors or thieves. (See **Jargon** and **Slang**.) Generally, the term argot can be used synonymously with jargon.

19

Argumentation: One of the four chief "forms of discourse." (Compare with **Description, Exposition** and **Narration**.) The purpose of argumentation is to convince a reader or listener by establishing the truth or falsity of a proposition.

Arsis: In prosody, both the stressed syllable and the emphasis given to the syllable. In the following line, the second, fourth, sixth, eighth and tenth syllables are, under the first meaning, arses:

The cŭr | fēw tŏlls | thĕ knēll | ŏf pārt | ĭng dāy.

Under the second meaning, the same syllables may be said to receive the arsis. (See **Ictus.**)

Art Ballad: A term used to distinguish the modern or literary ballad of known authorship from the early ballads of unknown authorship. Examples of the art ballad are *La Belle Dame sans Merci* by Keats and *Sister Helen* by Rossetti. A famous poem imitating the ballad manner is *The Rime of the Ancient Mariner* by Coleridge.

Art Epic: A term employed to distinguish an epic, such as Milton's *Paradise Lost* or Virgil's *Aeneid*, from so-called "folk epics," such as *Beowulf*, the *Iliad* or the *Odyssey*. The folk epic deals with traditions closely associated with the people or "folk" for whom it was written. The art epic is more sophisticated, more highly idealized and more consciously moral in purpose than is the folk epic. (See **Epic.**)

Arthurian Legend: The legendary deeds of King Arthur and the Knights of the Round Table came to represent all that was best in the age of chivalry. Whether King Arthur actually existed is moot. However, for centuries stories about him and his followers have been a seminal source of artistic inspiration.

The popularity of the Arthurian tradition reached a climax in medieval English literature in Malory's *Le Morte d'Arthur* (printed 1485). Spenser used an Arthurian background for his romantic epic, *The Faerie Queene* (1590). In the nineteenth century, Tennyson used Arthurian legend as the basis of his *Idylls of the King*.

Article: (1) A literary composition, complete in itself, but forming part of a magazine, newspaper or book. The article, in this sense, is usually impersonal and factual. (See **Essay.**) (2) A clause in a contract, treaty or statute. (3) A particular item or thing on a list. For example, *Her shopping list includes five articles*. (4) One of the words *a, an* or *the*. *A(n)* is the indefinite article; *the* is the definite article.

Artificial Comedy: A term sometimes used (as by Lamb) for comedy reflecting an artificial society. For example, Congreve's *The Way of the World* and Goldsmith's *She Stoops to Conquer* could be termed artificial comedies. (See **Comedy of Manners**.)

Artificiality: In criticism, a term characterizing writing that is consciously and deliberately artistic, as opposed to natural. In general, writing that is highly conventional, elaborate, ornate, courtly, affected or self-conscious is called artificial. The work of such writers as Lyly and Donne is often termed artificial, for example, in comparison with the work of other writers, such as Fielding and Burns.

Art Lyric: The art lyric is characterized by a restrictedness of subject, delicacy of touch, perfection in phrasing, artificiality of sentiment and formality. It differs from the ordinary lyric in the degree to which the poet's self-conscious struggle for perfection of form dominates the spontaneity of his emotion.

In English literature, Elizabethan and seventeenth-century poets (for example, Herrick, Lovelace, Jonson and Herbert) made much of the art lyric, polishing and perfecting their song. In the work of Shelley and Keats, the art lyric began to include abstract ideas.

Arts, the Seven Liberal: See **Seven Arts**.

Art Theater: See **Little Theater Movement**.

Ascending Rhythm: See **Rising Rhythm**.

Aside: A remark made by a character in a play and intended to be heard by the audience but not by the other characters on stage. An aside is a theatrical convention used especially, but not exclusively, in comedy and melodrama.

Assonance: Resemblance or similarity in sound between vowels in two or more syllables. Related to rhyme, assonance is only an approximate resemblance of sound, where rhyme is an exact correspondence. Used in the strict sense, assonance demands that the sound similarity occur within the vowels, not the consonants, and only in accented syllables.

Love and *dove* are perfect rhymes; *lake* and *fate* are examples of assonance.

Poe and Swinburne are examples of poets who relied largely on both rhyme and assonance for their musical effects. Assonance is also used effectively in prose, particularly in prose that is poetic in quality. (See **Dissonance**.)

Asyndeton: A form of condensed expression in which words or short

21

phrases, usually joined by conjunctions, are presented in a series, separated only by commas.

Atmosphere: The mood or feeling evoked by a piece of writing. Atmosphere differs from setting and local color in that the latter elements are largely physical and geographic, while atmosphere is the intangible, subjective quality that involves the tone of the work, the effect that the writing has on the reader. Critics speak, for example, of the "weird" atmosphere of a Dunsany story and the "romantic" atmosphere of a Stevenson novel.

Atonic: A term used to describe the unaccented syllable(s) of a word or a foot of verse. In the word *medalist*, for example, *al* and *ist* are atonic syllables. The syllable most heavily stressed (in this case, *med*) receives the *tonic* accent.

Attic: Writing characterized by a clear, simple, polished and witty style. Attica was formerly one of the ancient Greek states. With Athens as its capital city, Attica was famed for its culture and art. Attic came to denote grace, culture and the classic in art. Addison may be said to have written attic prose.

Attic Salt: *Salt*, in this use, means *wit*. Attic salt is writing distinguished by its classic refinement of wit. (See **Attic.**)

Aubade: A song greeting the new day and often expressing the regret of lovers who must part at daybreak. The Spanish term for this type of lyric is *alba*.

Augustan: This term refers to the age of Emperor Augustus of Rome (ruled from 27 B. C. to A. D. 14), but, since this age was notable for the progress in writing and learning, the term has also been applied to other ages when literary culture was high. As Virgil and Horace made the Augustan age of Rome, so Addison and Steele, Swift and Pope are sometimes said to have made the Augustan age of English letters.

Autobiography: An account of a person's life written by that person. As a division of literature, autobiography is usually so loosely defined as to include memoirs, diaries and even letters, as well as more formal narrative chronicles. (See **Biography.**)

Avant-garde: In literature, a term designating new writing that contains innovations in form or technique.

Awakening, The Great: A phrase applied to a revival of emotional religion that took place in the United States about 1735-1750. The movement was at its height from 1740 to 1745 under the leadership of Jonathan Edwards.

The revival began as an effort to reform religion and morals. Many of the meetings were marked by emotional manifestations, such as trances, shouting, tearing of garments and fainting. The conservatives, representing the stricter Calvinists, protested against the emotional excess of the movement. Even Edwards opposed the more extreme exhibitions of emotionalism and, by 1750, a reaction was under way. (See **Calvinism, Deism** and **Puritanism**.)

Axiom: A statement that is held to be true without formal proof; a self-evident truth.

B

Bacchic (or Bacchius): A metrical foot composed of one short and two long syllables. The accent is on the first long syllable. The name is derived from Bacchus, the Greek god of wine. The bacchic foot was prevalent in the hymns in honor of Bacchus.

Background: A term borrowed from art, where it signifies those parts of a painting against which the principal objects are portrayed. In literature, the term can specify either the physical setting of a piece of writing or the tradition and point of view from which the author presents his ideas. Thus, one might speak either of the Russian background (setting) of *Anna Karenina*, or of the background of education, philosophy and convictions from which Tolstoy wrote the novel.

Baconian Theory: The theory, now generally discredited, that the plays of William Shakespeare were written by Francis Bacon.

Balance: In rhetoric, that structure in which parts of a sentence — words, phrases or clauses — are set off against each other in position, to emphasize a contrast in meaning. For example:

> The memory of other authors is kept alive by their works;
> but the memory of Johnson keeps many of his works alive.
> MACAULAY

As a critical term, balance characterizes the proportion among the various elements of a piece of writing. A story, for example, in which setting, characterization and action are carefully planned, with no undue emphasis on any element, might be said to have fine balance.

Ballad: A form of verse, adapted for singing or recitation, which presents a dramatic or exciting episode in simple narrative form. In most cases the so-called "popular ballad" belongs to the early periods before written literature was highly developed. In almost every country, the folk ballad is one of the earliest forms of literature. A one-volume collection of ballads is *The Oxford Book of Ballads*, edited by Sir Arthur Quiller-Couch.

Ballade: A popular artificial French verse form. The ballade should not be confused with the ballad, which is usually folk poetry. The ballade is essentially more sophisticated.

In early ballades there were usually three stanzas and an envoy, though the number of lines to the stanza and the number of syllables to the line varied. Typically, the refrain carried the motif of the poem and recurred at the end of each stanza and of the envoy. The envoy, a climactic conclusion, was often addressed to a high member of the court or to the poet's patron. A frequent rhyme scheme was *ababbcbc* for the stanza and *bcbc* for the envoy. An example of early use of English ballade form is Chaucer's *Balade de bon conseyl*.

Modern ballade form most commonly presents three-, eight- or ten-verse stanzas with an envoy of four or five lines.

Ballad Opera: A kind of burlesque opera that flourished on the English stage following the appearance of John Gay's *The Beggar's Opera* (1728), a well-known example of the type. Modelled on Italian opera, which it burlesques, the ballad opera included songs set to old tunes, and appropriated various elements from farce and comedy. (See **Comic Opera** and **Opera**.)

Ballad Stanza: A stanza form characterized by four lines, the first and third lines having eight syllables each, and the second and fourth lines six syllables each. The rhyme scheme is *abcb*. The meter is usually iambic. The following, from *Sir Patrick Spens*, is an example:

Whare will I get a bonny boy
Will take thir sails in hand,
That will gang up to the top-mast,
See an he ken dry land?

Barbarism: See **Solecism**.

Bard: Historically, a poet who recited verses, usually glorifying the deeds of heroes and leaders, to the accompaniment of a musical instrument, such as the harp. In modern use, a bard is a poet.

Baroque: A term applied to the architectural style that succeeded the classical style of the Renaissance and flourished, in varied forms, in different parts of Europe, from the late sixteenth into the eighteenth century. The baroque style stressed movement, energy and realistic treatment. In attempting to avoid the effects of repose and complacency, the baroque sought to startle by the use of the unusual and unexpected.

In literature, the age of baroque included the late sixteenth, seventeenth and early eighteenth centuries. The broken rhythms of Donne's verse and the verbal subtleties of the English metaphysical poets are called baroque elements.

Basis: From the Greek, meaning "step." In literary usage, a verse, containing two feet, recited to the choric dance in Greek drama. In general usage, the foundation or principal ingredient.

Bathos: The effect of unsuccessfully straining to achieve dignity, pathos or elevation of style; an unintentional anticlimactic dropping from the sublime to the ridiculous. An example of bathos is in Temple's lines:

> Advance the fringed curtains of thy eyes,
> And tell me who comes yonder.

The term is sometimes applied to the deliberate use of anticlimax for satiric or humorous effect.

Battle of the Books, the: See **Ancients and Moderns, Quarrel of the**.

Beast Epic: A popular medieval literary form, consisting of a series of linked stories grouped around animal characters, and often presenting satirical comment on contemporary life by attributing human qualities to beast characters. The best known of the beast epics is the French *Roman de Renart*. Chaucer's *The Nun's Priest's Tale* in *The Canterbury Tales* is another example. More recent beast fables include Kipling's *Jungle Books* and *Just So Stories*, as well as George Orwell's barnyard fantasy, *Animal Farm*.

Beast Fable: See **Fable**.

Beat: The metrical emphasis in music and verse. Often, beat and stress are used interchangeably. (See **Stress**.)

Beginning Rhyme: See **Rhyme**.

Belles-lettres: Literature, comprising drama, poetry, fiction, criticism and essays, that endures because of inherent imaginative and artistic characteristics, rather than scientific or intellectual qualities. Lewis Carroll's *Alice in Wonderland*, for example, belongs to the province of belles-lettres, while the mathematical works of the same man, Charles Lutwidge Dodgson (his real name), do not.

Bestiary: A type of literature, particularly popular during the medieval centuries, in which the habits of beasts, birds and reptiles were made the text for allegorical and mystical Christian teachings. The bestiaries were designed to moralize and to expound church doctrine. The natural history employed is fabulous rather than scientific, and has helped to make popular in literature such abnormalities as the phoenix, the siren and the unicorn. Many of the qualities literature familiarly attributes to animals owe their origin to the bestiaries.

Bible: Derived from a Greek term meaning "little books," Bible is now applied to the collection of writings known as the Holy Scriptures, the sacred writings of the Christian religion. Of the two chief parts, the Old Testament consists of the sacred writings of the ancient Hebrews, and the New Testament consists of the writings of the early Christian period. The Jewish Scriptures include three collections — The Law, The Prophets, and Writings — written in ancient Hebrew at various dates in the pre-Christian era. The New Testament books were written in the Greek dialect used in Mediterranean countries about the time of Christ.

Bible can also mean any book or collection of religious writings received by its adherents as a divine revelation. The Koran is the Bible of the Moslems.

Bibliography: (1) A list of books, articles, etc. about a particular person or subject. (2) A list of works by a person, country, printer, etc. (3) A study of the history of book publication — writing, illustrating, printing, binding and publishing.

In an annotated bibliography, some or all of the items are followed by brief descriptive or critical comments.

Bildungsroman: A novel describing the development of the hero or heroine from youth to maturity. The term is derived from the German, meaning "formation novel." Dickens' *David Copperfield* and Joyce's *A Portrait of the Artist as a Young Man* are examples.

Billingsgate: Vulgar, violent, abusive language. The term is derived from the reputation of the fishers' wives in Billingsgate fish market (in London) for the vulgarity of their language.

Biography: The history of the life of a particular person written by someone else.

Early biographies were written to glorify and commemorate heroes. William Roper (1496-1578) wrote what is now often referred to as the first English biography, his *Life of Sir Thomas More*. In the same century, George Cavendish wrote *Life of Wolsey*. Both authors used anecdotes and fairly vivid dialogue.

In the eighteenth century, James Boswell's *Life of Dr. Johnson* presented its subject "warts and all." Boswell used humor, anecdote and a wealth of detail from which readers could make their own deductive analyses. Commemorative elements were subordinated; didactic qualities minimized.

The Victorians, on the whole, restricted the freedom Boswell had brought to biography. Religious orthodoxy, piety and moral judgments were again in vogue.

However, the first quarter of the twentieth century saw biographers again shake off this scrupulous morality. Giles Lytton Strachey's *Eminent Victorians* and *Queen Victoria* are examples of the biography of the period.

Biography today may be defined as the accurate presentation of the life history of an individual. The conscientious biographer makes an honest effort to interpret the facts of the life in such a way as to offer a unified impression of the character, mind and personality of the subject.

Black Comedy: Drama based on the belief that human beings exist in a purposeless universe in which they are subject to forces beyond their understanding or control. Moral and ethical values, therefore, are meaningless, and life is, in Ionesco's phrase, "a tragic farce." Examples of black comedy are Pinter's *The Homecoming* (1965) and Orton's *Entertaining Mr. Sloane* (1965).

Elements of black comedy are also apparent in many modern novels. Joseph Heller's *Catch-22* (1961) and Mordecai Richler's *St. Urbain's Horseman* (1966) are "darkly" comic.

Some of Shakespeare's plays, such as *All's Well that Ends Well* and *Measure for Measure*, have been called black or dark comedies. (See **Theater of the Absurd.**)

Black Humor: Humor based on cruelty or a reversal of customary ethical values. Black humor is sometimes found in light verse, as in these lines by Lewis Carroll:

Speak roughly to your little boy,
And beat him when he sneezes.
He only does it to annoy,
Because he knows it teases.

It is also the basis of certain jokes: *And apart from that, Mrs. Lincoln, how did you like the play?*

In addition, black humor is an element of black comedy. (See **Black Comedy.**)

Blank Verse: Unrhymed verse, usually with lines of ten syllables each, the second, fourth, sixth, eighth and tenth syllables bearing the accents (iambic pentameter). The form is used in English drama and poetry. Marlowe, Shakespeare and Milton used blank verse extensively.

More recently, the term has been extended to include almost any metrical unrhymed form.

Bloomsbury Group: A group of writers and artists who lived in the Bloomsbury area of London, England, during and after World War I. The group included Virginia and Leonard Woolf, Lytton Strachey, Clive Bell, Roger Fry, John Maynard Keynes, David Garnett and E.M. Forster.

Blue Book: An inexpensive novel, so named for its blue cover, which was popular at the end of the eighteenth century and the beginning of the nineteenth century. Blue books were usually crudely written and dealt with sensational topics. (See **Penny Dreadful.**)

Blues: An Afro-American folk song developed among the Negroes of the southern United States. Blues are characteristically short (three-line stanzas), melancholy in tone and marked by frequent repetition.

Bluestockings: Intellectual, bookish women. The term gained currency about 1782, when it was applied to a group of women of literary and intellectual tastes, who held assemblies in London to which men of letters were invited. The group's activities were directed toward encouraging an interest in literature and fostering the recognition of literary genius. Their meetings were the English equivalent of the French *salons*.

Blurb: A brief description, usually enthusiastic, which appears on the dust jacket of a book and which recommends it to prospective readers.

Boasting Poem: A poem in which the speaker boasts about his exploits. The epic, *Beowulf*, contains such poems.

Bombast: Ranting, insincere, extravagant language; grandiloquence. Elizabethan tragedy, especially early Senecan plays, contains much bombastic style, marked by extravagant imagery. An example appears in Shakespeare's *Hamlet* (Act II, Sc. 2):

> Roasted in wrath and fir,
> And thus o'er-sized with coagulate gore,
> With eyes like carbuncles, the hellish Pyrrhus
> Old grandsire Priam seeks.

Bon mot: A witty repartee or statement; a clever saying. From the French, meaning literally "good word."

Boulevard Drama: Originally, the body of plays produced in the late nineteenth century for the major theaters of Paris by such writers as Labiche and Halévy. The term is now applied, for the most part, to sophisticated comedies, designed for commercial success.

Bourgeois Drama: A term applied to plays in which the life of the common people rather than that of the courtly or the rich is depicted. The term is used for such widely differing kinds of plays as Heywood's *Interludes*, Dekker's *The Shoemaker's Holiday* and Lillo's *The London Merchant*.

Bourgeois Literature: Literature written primarily to appeal to the middle-class reader. Compare with **Bourgeois Drama**, where bourgeois describes the social sphere of the play's action and not the class of readers or audience.

Bowdlerize: To omit all offensive, indecorous passages from a book or piece of writing. Named after Thomas Bowdler, an English physician who published (in 1818) an expurgated edition of Shakespeare.

Brachiology: Condensed, brief expression.

Braggadocio: The braggart who is generally a coward at heart; a stock character in drama and other literary forms.

Breviary: A book of prescribed prayers to be said each day by Roman Catholic priests and members of religious orders.

Brief: A short, concise statement; a résumé of the main arguments or ideas presented in a speech or piece of writing. In legal practice, a formal summary of laws and authorities bearing on the main points of a case. In church history, a papal letter less formal than an official order.

British Museum: A museum and library containing more than five million volumes, as well as collections of antiquities, drawings and prints. Founded in 1753, through a bequest from Sir Hans Sloane, the British Museum is located on Great Russell Street, in Bloomsbury, London. It is particularly wealthy in its collection of valuable manuscripts, including a series of documents from the third century to the present. Under British copyright law, the Museum receives a free copy of every copyrighted publication. It also houses an assortment of items from North American, Chinese, Oriental, Hebrew and Slavonic literatures. The result is a comprehensive collection of the learning and literature of the world.

Broadside Ballad: Soon after the development of printing in England, ballads were prepared for circulation on folio sheets, printed on one side only, two pages to the sheet, and two columns to the page. These were termed "broadsides." The ballads ranged from reproductions of old ballads of real literary distinction to semiliterate pieces of writing with little poetic quality. Subjects included accidents, dying speeches of criminals, miraculous events and religious and political harangues. They were often satirical in nature and frequently personal in invective.

Brochure: See **Pamphlet.**

Brook Farm: A communal experiment in the United States, growing out of certain aspects of New England transcendental thought. The farm, located in West Roxbury, Massachusetts, nine miles from Boston, was taken over in 1841 by a joint stock company, headed by George Ripley. The full name of the organization was The Brook Farm Institute of Agriculture and Education. The scheme was intended to provide residents with an opportunity for cultural pursuits and leisure at little cost. The farm was supposed, through the rotation of labor among the members, to support the residents, who would then be free to attend lectures, read, write and discuss intellectual problems. However, by 1846 the project had failed. Two major reasons for its failure were insufficient soil fertility and dissension among the members. (See **Transcendentalism.**)

Bucolic: A term used to characterize pastoral writing, particularly poetry, concerned with shepherds and rural life. The treatment is usually rather formal and fanciful. The plural, bucolics, refers collectively to the pastoral literature of writers such as Theocritus and Virgil.

Burden: The theme or principal idea of a song; the refrain, chorus or repeated verse.

Burlesque: A form of comic art characterized by ridiculous exaggeration. The essential quality of burlesque is the discrepancy between subject matter and style. A style ordinarily dignified may be used for nonsensical matter, or a nonsensical style may be used to ridicule a dignified subject. Burlesque, as a form of art, occurs in sculpture, painting and architecture, as well as in literature.

The term has been broadened to include musical plays that are light in nature, though not essentially burlesque in tone or manner.

Burletta: A term used in the late eighteenth century for a variety of musical dramatic forms. (See **Extravaganza, Opera** and **Pantomime.**)

Burns Stanza: This is a six-line stanza used by the Scottish poet, Robert Burns. The rhyming scheme is *aaabab*, a rather unusual pattern, in which the fourth and sixth lines have two stresses, while the other lines have four stresses.

Buskin: A boot, thick-soled and reaching halfway to the knee, worn by Greek tragedians to increase their stature. Comedians wore socks for the opposite purpose. By association, buskin has come to mean tragedy. Milton used "the buskin'd stage" and "Jonson's learned sock" to characterize tragedy and comedy respectively.

Byronic Hero: A hero of the type characteristic of several poems and plays by Lord Byron (e.g., *Childe Harold* and *Don Juan*). The hero is portrayed as an egoistic rebel: proud, aloof, worldly and suffering from an unspeakable guilt. He is usually a passionate character, subject to fits of melancholy.

C

c. or **ca.**: Approximately, from the Latin word *circa*. The abbreviation is used in giving dates.

Cacempheton: (1) A word that sounds unpleasant. (2) A double entendre, such as those used by Juliet's nurse in Shakespeare's *Romeo and Juliet*. (See **Cacophony** and **Double Entendre**.)

Cacophony: A harsh, unpleasant combination of sounds or tones; the opposite of euphony. Though most often used in the criticism of poetry, the word is also used to indicate any disagreeable sound effect in other forms of writing.

Cadence: Measured, rhythmical movement in either prose or verse; the recurrence of emphasis or accent often accompanied by rising and falling modulations of the voice. Cadence is related to rhythm, but exists usually in larger and looser units of syllables than the formal, metrical movement of regular verses. (See **Free Verse**.)

Caesura (also Cesura): A pause or break in the metrical or rhythmical progress of a line of verse. Originally, in classical literature, the caesura divided a foot between two words. Usually, it was placed near the middle of a verse. Some poets, however, seek diversity of rhythmical effect by placing the caesura anywhere from near the beginning of a line to near the end. Examples of variously placed caesuras follow:

> Sleepst thou, Companion dear, ‖ what sleep can close
> Thy eye-lids? ‖ and remembrest what Decree
> Of yesterday, ‖ so late hath past the lips
> Of Heav'ns Almightie. ‖ Thou to me thy thoughts
> Wast wont, ...
>
> MILTON

Calendar: See **Almanac**.

Calligraphy: The art of beautiful handwriting. During the Middle Ages, the monks developed the art as they copied ancient manuscripts. Much literature was preserved through their skilful penmanship.

Calliope: See **Muses**.

Calvinism: The doctrines of reformer and theologian John Calvin (1509-1564). Calvinism stressed original sin and the necessity of divine grace for salvation. According to Calvinistic teachings, human nature was corrupted by Adam's fall, so that every human being is born with a totally depraved nature. Man can be saved only by God's grace, but each person is predestined for eternal salvation or condemnation.

Although neither Milton nor Bunyan was a fullfledged Calvinist, *Paradise Lost* was intended to justify the Calvinistic theology, and *The Pilgrim's Progress* reflects the effects upon human personality of the religion based upon Calvinism. Hawthorne's *The Scarlet Letter* is a protest against the effects of the Calvinistic system.

Canon: (1) A standard of judgment; a criterion. (2) The authorized or accepted list of books belonging in the Christian Bible. Apocryphal books are uncanonical. (See **Apocrypha**.)

The term is often extended to mean the accepted list of books of any author. *Macbeth* belongs in the canon of Shakespeare's work, while *Sir John Oldcastle*, although often credited to Shakespeare, is not canonical, because the evidence of Shakespeare's authorship is not convincing.

Cant: Insincere, specious language calculated to give the impression of piety and religious fervor. In critical writing, the term is also used to signify the special language and phraseology characteristic of a profession or art, such as *the pedagogue's cant*. In this sense, the term can indicate any technical or special vocabulary, as *thieves' cant* or *beggars' cant*. More loosely still, the word signifies any insincere, superficial display of language, planned to convey an impression of conviction, but devoid of genuine emotion or feeling; that is, language used chiefly for display or effect.

Canticle: A short hymn or song. The Biblical *Song of Solomon* is sometimes called the *Canticle of Canticles*.

Canto: A section or division of a long poem. Derived from the Latin *cantus* (song), the word originally signified a section of a narrative poem of such length as to be sung by a minstrel in one singing. Byron's *Childe Harold's Pilgrimage* is divided into cantos.

Canzone: A short lyrical poem, song or ballad, consisting of equal stanzas and an envoy of fewer lines than the stanza. The number of lines to the stanza ranges from seven to twenty, and the envoy from three to ten. Petrarch's *canzoni* usually consisted of five or six stanzas and the envoy.

Caricature: Descriptive writing that seizes upon certain individual qualities of a person and, through exaggeration or distortion, produces a burlesque, ridiculous effect. The term is more frequently associated with drawing (cartoons) than with writing. Like satire, caricature lends itself to the ridicule of political, religious and social foibles.

Carmen Figuratum: Meaning "a shaped poem," the verses of which are so arranged that they form a design on the page. When the design is an object, such as a cross or an altar, it is usually the theme of the poem. (See **Altar Poem.**)

Carol (Carole): In medieval times in France, a carole was a dance. Subsequently, the term was applied to the song that accompanied the dance. The leader sang the stanzas; the other dancers the refrain. In the twelfth and thirteenth centuries, the carole became very popular and spread through other European countries. Later, carol was used to mean any joyous song, then, a hymn of religious joy and, finally, to designate Christmas hymns in particular.

Caroline: Applied to that which belonged to or was typical of the age of Charles I of England (1625-1642), but more particularly to the spirit of the court of King Charles. Thus, Caroline literature might mean all the literature of the time, both Cavalier and Puritan, or it might be used more specifically to suggest that of the royalist group, such as the Cavalier Lyrists. (See **Cavalier Lyrists.**)

Carpe Diem: "Seize the day." The phrase was used by Horace and has come to be applied to literature, especially lyric poems, that exemplify the spirit of "Eat, drink and be merry, for tomorrow we may die." The theme was common in sixteenth- and seventeenth-century English love poetry, as in Robert Herrick's lines:

> Gather ye rosebuds while ye may,
> Old Time is still a-flying:
> And this same flower that smiles to-day,
> To-morrow will be dying.

Catachresis: The misuse of words; for example, confusing the usages of *implied* and *inferred*. The term can also apply to any strained or forced figure of speech. (See **Malapropism.**)

Catalexis (adj. — **Catalectic**): Incompleteness of the last foot at the end of a verse; omission of one or two syllables at the end of a line of poetry; the opposite of anacrusis. (See **Anacrusis** and **Truncation.**)

Acatalectic is used to designate particular lines where catalexis is *not* employed. In the following lines, written in dactylic dimeter, the second and fourth are catalectic because the second foot of each lacks the two unaccented syllables that would normally complete the dactyl.

The first and third lines, in which the unaccented syllables are *not* cut off, and which are therefore metrically complete, are acatalectic.

One more unfortunate,
Weary of breath,
Rashly importunate,
Gone to her death.

THOMAS HOOD

Catalogue: A long and detailed list. The catalogue is a characteristic part of an epic poem (e.g., Homer's catalogue of ships in the *Illiad* or Milton's catalogue of the fallen angels in *Paradise Lost*).

Catastasis: The complication immediately preceding the climax of a play; sometimes, the actual climax of a play. (See **Epitasis**.)

Catastrophe: The final stage in the falling action of a tragedy, the catastrophe ends the dramatic struggle and usually involves the death of the hero and others. By analogy, the term is sometimes used to designate a tragic ending in non-dramatic fiction. (See **Denouement** and **Dramatic Structure**.)

Catharsis: Aristotle described the effect of tragedy as a *katharsis* (literally, purging) of the spectator's emotions, "through pity and fear working a purification of these emotions." Scholars have offered many interpretations of what Aristotle meant. However, the term commonly denotes the purification of the emotions through the spectator's imaginative participation in the sufferings of the tragedy's characters, and the feeling of emotional relief and exaltation induced by tragic literature or art.

Cavalier Lyric: The sort of light-hearted poem characteristic of the Cavalier Lyrists, or a poem intended to illustrate the spirit or the times of the Cavaliers, such as Browning's *Boot, Saddle, to Horse and Away*.

Cavalier Lyrists: A group of court poets during the time of Charles I, especially Thomas Carew, Richard Lovelace and Sir John Suckling. The men were soldiers and courtiers first, poets incidentally. Their verse was light-hearted in spirit; graceful, melodious and polished in form; and sometimes licentious and sometimes cynical.

The themes usually dealt with were love, war, chivalry and loyalty to the king. Robert Herrick is sometimes classed with the Cavalier Lyrists, although he was a country parson, not a courtier.

Celtic Literature: Literature produced by a people speaking any one of the Celtic dialects. Linguistically, the Celts are divided into two main groups. The Brythonic Celts include the Ancient Britons, the Welsh, the Cornish (Cornwall) and the Bretons (Brittany). The Goidelic (Gaelic) Celts include the Irish, the Manx (Isle of Man) and the Scottish Gaels. At one time, the Celts, an important branch of the Indo-European family, dominated Central and Western Europe.

Celtic Renaissance: A general term for the movement in the late nineteenth and early twentieth centuries that aimed at the preservation of the Gaelic language, the reconstruction of early Celtic history and literature, and the stimulation of a new literature authentically Celtic (especially Irish) in spirit.

   In the nineteenth century, there was a growing interest in Celtic antiquities. The Gaelic Movement, stressing the use of the Gaelic language, began in the 1890s. The contemporaneous Anglo-Irish movement stimulated the production of a new literature in English (or Anglo-Irish) by Irish writers on Irish themes and in the Irish spirit. The movement was given impetus by such writers as W. B. Yeats, George W. Russell ("A.E."), George Moore, J. M. Synge and, later, James Stephens, Lord Dunsany and Padraic Colum. From the beginning, Lady Gregory was an enthusiastic participant.

   In 1899, the Irish Literary Theatre was founded in Dublin and became the Irish National Theatre Society in 1902. In 1904, the company moved to the Abbey Theatre in Dublin. It continued producing plays of nationalistic character until it burned down in 1951.

Celtic Revival: A term sometimes used for Gaelic Movement or for Irish Literary Movement, as well as for the eighteenth-century movement described below. (See **Gaelic Movement** and **Irish Literary Movement.**)

Celtic Revival (Eighteenth Century): A literary movement in the last half of the eighteenth century that stressed the use of the historical, literary and mythological traditions of the ancient Celts, particularly the Welsh. Through confusion, Norse mythology was included in Celtic.

   The movement stressed the primitive, the remote, the strange and mysterious. It supplied a new mythology for the overworked classical myths and figures. Specifically, it was characterized by an intense interest in the Druids and early Welsh bards.

Cento: Poetry made up of lines borrowed from established authors; for example, the hymns arranged by Metellus from the *Odes* of Horace.

cf.: Compare (an abbreviation of the Latin word *confer*).

Chain Verse: Verse in which the stanzas (occasionally lines) are linked by rhyme or various patterns of repetition. The villanelle is an example of chain verse. (See **Villanelle.**)

Chanson (also Canso): A song. Originally composed of two-line stanzas of equal length (couplets), each stanza ending in a refrain, the chanson is now more broadly interpreted to include almost any poem intended to be sung and written in a simple style.

Chanson de Geste: A "song of great deeds." The earliest example, *Le Chanson de Roland*, dates probably from about 1100. The early *chansons de geste* were written in ten-syllable lines, marked by assonance, and grouped in stanzas of varying length. Cycles developed, such as that of Charlemagne (*geste du roi*). The stories generally reflect chivalric ideals with little use of love as a theme. The form flourished for several centuries, and about eighty examples still exist. These epic tales supplied material for medieval romance, including English romances.

Chansonnier: A collection of troubadour poems. (See **Troubadour.**)

Chant: Loosely used to mean a song, the term more particularly signifies the intoning of words to a monotonous musical measure of few notes. Cadence is an important element and, usually, one note is used for a series of successive words or syllables. Repetition of a few varying musical phrases is a characteristic, and the intonation of the voice is important. Dirges are often chanted.

Chantey (Shanty): A sailors' song marked by strong rhythm. In the days of sailing ships, chanteys accompanied certain forms of hard labor (such as weighing anchor), performed by seamen working in a group. The leader of the singing was the "chantey man," who introduced a line or two, and was then joined in a refrain sung by the whole group.

Chant Royal: The tradition for this complex verse form demands a dignified, heroic subject that can best be expressed in rich diction and courtly formalities of speech. The chant royal consists of sixty lines, arranged in five stanzas of eleven verses each and an envoy of five verses. Ordinarily, the envoy starts with an invocation in the manner of the ballade. (See **Ballade.**)

The rhyme scheme usually followed is *ababccddede* for the stanza, and *ddede* for the envoy. The bold *e* indicates the recurrence of a complete line as a refrain at the end of each stanza and at the close of the envoy.

Chapbook: A small book or pamphlet such as was sold by peddlers or "chapmen" during the sixteenth and later centuries. Chapbooks dealt with a variety of topics and incidents: travel tales, murder cases, strange occurrences, witchcraft, biographies, religious legends and stories. They are of interest because they reflect contemporary attitudes.

Character: (1) A person in a novel, play, etc. (2) A type of composition, originated by Theophrastus and imitated in England and France during the seventeenth and eighteenth centuries. In this sense, a character is a brief descriptive sketch of a person who typifies some definite quality. The person is described not as an individual personality, but as an example of some vice, virtue or type, such as a busybody, a superstitious person, etc. Similar sketches of institutions, such as *the character of a coffee house*, were also called characters. (3) The qualities or features possessed by an individual. (4) In printing jargon, a letter, sign or mark appearing in type.

Characterization: The portrayal, in writing, of a person — his actions, manner of thought, personality, distinctive qualities and traits. The ability to create and depict fictional characters so that the reader perceives them as living beings is essential to the novelist or dramatist.

Early English novelists provided formal analyses of characters, listing the person's qualities and explaining his motives. In the more recent stream of consciousness novel (e.g., James Joyce's *Ulysses*), characterization is revealed by the author chronicling the person's thoughts as he passes through a series of experiences. Whatever the method, the convincing creation of characters is the basis of good fiction and drama. (See **Developing Characters.**)

Chartism: A political movement in England, just before the middle of the nineteenth century, that aimed at securing for the lower classes more social recognition and improved material conditions. The Chartists advocated universal suffrage, vote by ballot, annual parliaments and other social welfare programs.

Chaucerian Stanza: See **Rhyme Royal.**

Chiasmus: In verse or prose, a balancing pattern in which the second part of a line reverses and balances the words in the first part.

A wit with dunces, and a dunce with wits.

POPE

Love's fire heats water, water cools not love.

SHAKESPEARE

Chivalric Romance: Medieval romance reflecting the customs and ideals of chivalry. (See **Arthurian Legend, Chivalry, Courtly Love** and **Medieval Romance.**)

Chivalry: The medieval system of morals and manners pertaining to knighthood. Under the chivalric code, knights were bound to be faithful to God and king, true to their lady loves and ready to rescue maidens in distress or other victims of unjust tyrants, cruel giants or fiendish monsters.

Chaucer and Spenser have provided literary idealizations of the medieval knight, as did Tennyson in his *Idylls of the King.*

Choree: The same as trochee. (See **Trochee.**)

Choriamb: See **Aeolic.**

Choriambus: In meter, a foot in which two accented syllables flank two unaccented syllables: $-\ u\ u\ -$. (See **Foot** and **Meter.**)

Chorus: In ancient Greece, the groups of dancers and singers who participated in religious festivals and dramatic performances; the songs sung by the chorus.

At first, the choral songs made up the major part of the play, and the spoken monologue and dialogue were interpolated. Later, however, the chorus became subordinate, offering comments between the acts. In Elizabethan drama, the role of the chorus was often taken by a single actor, who recited the prologue and epilogue and gave inter-act comments that linked the acts and foreshadowed coming events. In Shakespeare's *King Henry V*, the chorus comments on the action, explains scene changes and asks the audience for a sympathetic attitude. Sometimes, within a play, one of the characters, like the fool in *King Lear*, is said to play a "choruslike" role when he comments on the action.

Chrestomathy: A collection of passages in prose or verse compiled as an aid to learning a language; loosely, an anthology. (See **Anthology.**)

Chronicle Play: A type of drama that flourished in the latter part of the reign of Queen Elizabeth I (1533-1603). The chronicle play drew its English historical materials from the sixteenth-century chronicles and stressed the nationalistic spirit of the times. (See **Chronicles.**)

The structure of the earlier chronicle plays was loose, and unity consisted mainly in the inclusion of the events of a single king's reign. The cast included a large number of characters. Much use was made of pageantry (coronations, funerals, etc.) and other spectacular elements, such as battles. The serious action was often relieved by comic scenes or subplots.

Chronicle plays had an important relationship to tragedy. Shakespeare's *Richard III* (ca. 1593) was an early example of a chronicle play developed into a tragedy of character, a tendency that culminated in such plays as *King Lear* (1606) and *Macbeth* (1606).

Chronicle: A certain form of historical writing. Chronicles differ from annals in their comprehensive or universal character and in their concern with world history.

The Anglo-Saxon Chronicle, begun under King Alfred late in the ninth century and carried on by various writers in succeeding centuries, has been called the first great book in English prose. A well-known Latin prose chronicle is Geoffrey of Monmouth's *The History of the Kings of Britain* (ca. 1136), which not only records legendary British history, but also romantic accounts of King Arthur.

Chronicles written in Elizabethan times — by Ralph Holinshed, Richard Grafton and John Stowe, among others — were important as sources for Shakespeare and other dramatists. (See **Chronicle Plays.**)

Chronique Scandaleuse: A type of writing portraying intrigues, love affairs and petty gossip, and usually associated with life at court. Usually, these writings give the impression of having been written by an eyewitness. The personal element is important, and scandal is the material upon which such chronicles thrive.

Ciceronians: Latin stylists. (See **Purist.**)

Cinquain: A stanza of five lines; a quintet.

Cipher: A method of transforming a text in order to conceal its meaning; a message in code.

Circumlocution: A roundabout way of speaking. For example, *the wife of your father's brother* is a circumlocution for *your aunt*. (See **Periphrasis.**)

Classic (noun): In the singular, a piece of literature that has achieved a recognized position in literary history for its superior qualities; an author of like standing. *Paradise Lost*, for example, is a classic in English literature. The plural is used in the same sense, as in the phrase *the study of English classics*. It is also used to designate collectively the literary productions of Greece and Rome.

Classic, Classical (adjectives): Used with meanings parallel to those given under classic (noun); of recognized excellence, or belonging to established tradition, such as *a classical piece of music*. Classical literature may mean Greek and Roman literature, or literature that has gained a lasting recognition or literature that exhibits the qualities of classicism. (See **Classicism**.)

Classical Tragedy: This term refers to the tragedies of the ancient Greeks and Romans (e.g., Sophocles' *Antigone*); to tragedies based on Greek or Roman subject material (e.g., Shakespeare's *Coriolanus*); and to modern tragedies modelled after Greek or Roman tragedy, or written under the influence of the critical doctrines of classicism. (See **Classicism**.)

Ben Jonson's tragedies, *Catiline* and *Sejanus His Fall*, are not only based on Roman themes, but are classical in their conscious effort to apply most of the rules of tragic composition derived from Aristotle and Horace.

In the Restoration period, John Dryden advocated classical rules and applied them to his *All for Love*, which contrasts with Shakespeare's romantic treatment of the same story in *Antony and Cleopatra*.

In the next century, Joseph Addison's *Cato* is an example of classical tragedy. (See **Classicism**, **Romantic Tragedy**, **Senecan Tragedy**, **Tragedy** and **Unities**.)

Classicism: As a critical term, a body of doctrine thought to be derived from (or to reflect) the qualities of ancient Greek and Roman culture, particularly literature, philosophy, art and criticism. Classicism is commonly opposed to romanticism and realism, although these qualities are not mutually exclusive. Ben Jonson, for example, advocated classicism as a critic and dramatist, yet his "classical" tragedies contain non-classical elements, such as comic relief and violation of one or more of the unities.

However, classicism does stand for certain definite ideas and attitudes, most of them drawn from the critical pronouncements of the Greeks and Romans, or developed through an imitation of ancient art and literature. These qualities include restraint, predominance of reason, unity of design and aim, clarity, simplicity, balance, moderation, respect for tradition and sense of form. (See **Classical Tragedy**, **Humanism**, **Neoclassicism**, **Realism** and **Romanticism**.)

Clausula: The final syllable or syllables of a line of verse.

Clerihew: A form of light verse quatrain, rhyming *aabb* and usually dealing with a person named in the initial rhyme. It was invented by Edmund Clerihew Bentley, who, while in school listening to a chemistry lecture, wrote:

Sir Humphrey Savy
Abominated gravy.
He lived in the odium
Of having discovered sodium.

(See **Light Verse** and **Quatrain**.)

Cliché: From the French word for a stereotype plate, a block for printing. Any expression used so often that its freshness and clarity are outworn is called a cliché, a stereotyped form. Some examples are: *bigger and better* and *sadder but wiser*.

Climax: The highest point of interest in narrative fiction. Also, in rhetoric, the term is used to indicate the arrangement of words, phrases, events or ideas in rising order of importance. Such an arrangement is climactic; the item of greatest importance, necessarily at or near the close, is called the climax.

In dramatic structure, the term commonly means the turning point of the action. In Shakespeare's *Macbeth*, for example, the appearance of Banquo's ghost at the emotionally climactic banquet scene — an event that shakes the spirit of the hitherto successful protagonist — may be regarded as the climax of the play.

Similarly, in fiction, the climax is often the turning point of the plot.

Clio: See **Muses**.

Cloak-and-Dagger: Literature having to do with spies and espionage, secret intrigue and adventure.

Cloak-and-Sword Romance: A play or novel characterized by much action and presenting gallant heroes in love with fair ladies. Settings and characters are often, though not necessarily, Spanish, Italian or French; the manners are courtly and gracious; and the plot is full of intrigue.

Closed Couplet: Two successive verses rhyming *aa* and containing a complete, independent statement. The couplet is closed in the sense that its meaning is complete within the two verses and does not depend on what precedes or follows for its grammatical structure or thought. Example:

One prospect lost, another still we gain;
And not a vanity is giv'n in vain;

POPE

Closet Drama: A play not ordinarily acted on the stage. Swinburne's *Atalanta in Calydon* is an example. Poetic dramas, such as Tennyson's *Becket* and Browning's *Strafford*, are often called closet dramas. Although their authors meant them to be acted, the works are actually more successful as literature than as acted drama. (See **Dramatic Poetry, Pastiche** and **Poetic Drama**.)

Cockney School: A derogatory title applied by *Blackwood's Magazine* to a group of nineteenth-century writers including Hazlitt, Leigh Hunt, Keats and Shelley, because of their alleged poor taste in such matters as diction and rhyme. Some offending rhymes were *name* and *time*, *vista* and *sister*, words that, the suggestion was, could rhyme only to a cockney ear. Cockney refers to a native or inhabitant of a section of London, England (strictly, within the sound of Bow Bells).

Coherence: A fundamental principle of composition demanding that the parts of any piece of writing be so arranged and bear such a relationship that the meaning of the whole is immediately clear. For coherence, words, phrases and clauses must be logically arranged within a sentence. In larger pieces of writing, sentences, paragraphs and chapters must be progressively ordered.

Coined Words: Words consciously and arbitrarily invented, as opposed to those that enter the language as a natural process of language development. Many words that were originally coined words (such as *television* and *astronaut*) have become accepted terms. Frowned upon as a literary practice, word coining is, nevertheless, constantly affecting the language. (See **Neologism**.)

Collaboration: The association of two or more people in a given piece of literary work. A famous instance of collaboration in the field of English literature is that of Francis Beaumont (1584-1616) and John Fletcher (1579-1625). Together, they wrote such plays as *Philaster* and *The Maid's Tragedy*.

Colloquialism: An expression used in conversation but not accepted as good usage in formal speech or writing. A colloquialism lies between the upper speech level of formal or literary language, and the lower level of slang. Eventually, a slang or a colloquial expression may come to be accepted as standard usage.

The word *flabbergast,* for example, entered the language as slang in the eighteenth century. It was probably a combination of *flabby* and *aghast*. Today, meaning "to amaze greatly," the word is generally acceptable in most instances.

Colloquy: A dialogue or conversation. Occasionally, the word is used in literary titles, as Erasmus' *Colloquies*. (See **Dialogue**.)

Colophon: A publisher's symbol or device formerly placed at the end of a book, but now more generally used on the title page or elsewhere near the beginning. The function of the colophon is to identify the publisher. Colophons at different times and with different publishers have incorporated one or more of these items: title and author of book, printer, date and place of manufacture.

Comedy: A form of drama that is intended to amuse and that ends happily. Comedy differs from farce and burlesque by having a more sustained plot, more weighty and subtle dialogue, more natural characters and less boisterous behavior. However, the borderline between comedy and other dramatic forms cannot be sharply defined, as there is much overlapping of technique, and different forms are frequently combined.

Since comedy strives to amuse, both wit and humor are utilized. The range of appeal is wide, varying from the crude effects of low comedy, to the subtle and idealistic reactions aroused by some high comedy.

English comedy developed from native dramatic forms growing out of the religious drama, the morality plays and interludes, and the performances of wandering entertainers, such as dancers and jugglers. In the Renaissance, the rediscovery of Latin comedy and the effort to apply the rules of classical criticism to drama significantly affected the course of English comedy. Foreign influences have also been important at times, such as the French influence on Restoration comedy or the Italian influence on Jacobean pastoral drama.

In medieval times, the word comedy was applied to non-dramatic literary compositions marked by a happy ending and by a less exalted style than was found in tragedy (e.g., Dante's *Divine Comedy*).

Comedy of Humours: A special type of realistic comedy developed in the closing years of the sixteenth century by Ben Jonson and George Chapman. Comic interest is derived largely from the exhibition of "humorous" characters; that is, persons whose conduct is controlled by some one characteristic or "humour." (See **Humours**.) Some single exaggerated trait of character gave each important figure in the action a definite bias of disposition and supplied the chief motive for his actions. Jonson's *Every Man in his Humour* (acted 1598) is an example.

The comedy of humours owes something to earlier vernacular comedy but more to a desire to imitate the classical comedy of Plautus and Terence. Satiric purpose and realistic method are emphasized in the comedies, which later led into more serious character studies, as in Jonson's *The Alchemist*.

The comedy of humours was closely related to the contemporary comedy of manners and exerted an important influence on the comedy of the Restoration period. (See **Comedy of Manners**.)

Comedy of Intrigue: See **Comedy of Situation**.

Comedy of Manners: The realistic, often satirical, comedy of the Restoration period, as written by Congreve and others. The term is also used for the revival, in modified form, of this comedy a hundred years later by Goldsmith and Sheridan, as well as for a revival late in the nineteenth century. In addition, the realistic comedy of Elizabethan and Jacobean times is sometimes called comedy of manners.

In the stricter sense of the term, the type is concerned with the manners and conventions of an artificial, highly sophisticated society. The characters are more likely to be types than individualized personalities. Plot, though often involving a clever handling of situation and intrigue, is less important than atmosphere and satire. The prose dialogue is witty and polished.

One distinguishing characteristic of the comedy of manners is a coarseness and immorality, partly because of the satirical purpose of this form of drama. (See **Comedy of Humours**, **High Comedy** and **Realistic Comedy**.)

Comedy of Situation: A comedy that depends for its interest chiefly upon ingenuity of plot, rather than upon character interest; a comedy of intrigue. Background is relatively unimportant. There is much reliance upon ridiculous and incongruous situations, a combination of mistakes, plots within plots, disguises, mistaken identity, unexpected meetings, etc. An example is Shakespeare's *The Comedy of Errors*.

The phrase comedy of situation is sometimes also used to refer merely to an incident, such as Falstaff's description of his fight with the robbers in Shakespeare's *King Henry IV*, Part I. (See **Farce Comedy**.)

Comic Opera: An operetta or comedy opera, stressing spectacle and music, but employing sung dialogue. An early example is Sheridan's *The Duenna* (1775). Among the best-known comic operas are those of Gilbert and Sullivan, e.g., *The Mikado* (1885). (See **Ballad Opera**.)

Comic Relief: A humorous episode or scene in a serious story or tragedy. The effect is to provide relief from tension and to heighten the serious elements of the rest of the drama.

The drunken porter scene in Shakespeare's *Macbeth* is a classic example of comic relief. (See **Dramatic Structure**.)

Commedia dell' Arte: Improvised comedy; a form of Italian low comedy dating from early times in which the actors, who usually performed conventional or stock parts, improvised their dialogue, though a plot or scenario was provided for them. A harlequin interrupted the action with low buffoonery at times. (See **Harlequin.**)

A parallel or later form of the commedia dell' arte was the masked comedy, in which conventional characters (usually masked) spoke in particular dialects.

Common Meter: A stanza form consisting of four lines, the first and third in iambic tetrameter (eight syllables, $\cup- \cup- \cup- \cup-$), and the second and fourth in iambic trimeter (six syllables, $\cup- \cup- \cup-$). The following is an example:

> He either fears his fate too much,
> Or his deserts are small,
> That dares not put it to the touch
> To gain or lose it all.

MARQUIS OF MONTROSE

Commonplace Book: A classified collection of quotations or arguments prepared for reference purposes. For example, a reader interested in moral philosophy might collect thoughts and quotations under such heads as truth, virtue or friendship. Commonplace books were utilized by authors of essays, theological arguments and other serious treatises. The term is also sometimes applied to private collections of favorite pieces of literature, such as the poetical miscellanies of Elizabethan times.

Compensation: In meter, a means of supplying omissions in a line; a form of substitution. Such omissions are usually unstressed syllables. The customary means of compensating for their absence is the pause, which has the effect of a rest in music.

Complaint: A plaintive poem, such as Chaucer's *A Complaint to His Lady* and the humorous *The Complaint of Chaucer to his Empty Purse*, written in the manner of the "complaints" of lovers to their unresponsive mistresses. In a complaint, which usually takes the form of a lyric monologue, the poet commonly explains his sad mood, describes the causes of it and discusses possible remedies, or appeals to some lady or divinity for help.

Complication: That part of a dramatic or narrative plot in which the entanglement of affairs caused by the conflict of opposing forces is developed. It is the tying of the knot to be untied in the resolution of the plot. (See **Dramatic Structure.**)

Conceit: Striking, strained or affected modes of expression. Conceits were common in Elizabethan love poetry and metaphysical verse.

John Lyly, for example, called love the "marrow of the mind," and Sidney forecasted his future by the "stars in Stella's face." (*Sonnet 26*) Metaphysical conceits are bolder and more ingenious. In one of Donne's poems, preachers are "God's conduits," and a philosopher is "Nature's secretary," while in another, the souls of two lovers are as "stiff twin compasses."

The conceits of the Elizabethan sonnets followed the vogue of the Italian and French imitators of Petrarch, while those of the next generation (the metaphysicals) were, in part, a development of the earlier style and, in part, a product of a new spirit. (See **Baroque**, **Gongorism**, **Marinism** and **Metaphysical Verse**.)

Concordance: An alphabetically organized index of words in a text or in the works of a major author. Thus, a concordance of the works of Shakespeare lists the words used in the plays, as well as where they may be found.

Concrete Terms: Words or phrases referring to things that exist in the material world, not merely as an idea or as a quality. For example, a *painting* is concrete, and its *beauty* is abstract.

In writing, the use of concrete terms adds vividness, clarity and interest. (See **Abstract Terms**.)

Concrete Universal: A critical term used to designate the idea that a work of art expresses the universal through the concrete and particular.

Confessional Literature: A type of autobiography, confessional literature involves the revelation by an author of events or feelings that are normally concealed. The Romantic tendency to explore the soul has made the confession a characteristically, though not exclusively, Romantic form.

Confidant (Confidante): A character in drama or fiction to whom a main character reveals his or her private thoughts, motives and intentions. In Shakespeare's *Hamlet*, for example, Horatio is Hamlet's confidant. (See **Raisonneur**.)

Conflict: The struggle that grows out of the interplay of the two opposing forces in a plot. Conflict provides the elements of interest and suspense in all forms of fiction. There are at least three major types of conflict: (1) those growing from the opposition of two physical forces and finding expression in a series of intense actions (as in many Dumas novels); (2) those springing from the play of one quality of character upon another quality of character in a second person (as the innate evil of Iago plays upon Othello's jealousy); and (3) those resulting from the internal struggle of one desire with another desire within the same character (as Hamlet's inability to bring himself to the point of action struggles with his desire to act).

Connotation: The implications inherent in words or phrases; what a word or phrase suggests, as distinguished from what it says specifically. For example, *portly*, *corpulent* and *obese* all *denote* (literal meaning) overweight, but *portly* also connotes *dignified*.

Consonance: (1) Harmony of sounds, the opposite of dissonance. (2) The repetition at the ends of lines or words with identical consonant sounds after different vowels. Examples are *yellow* and *shallow*; *click* and *flock*.

Conte: A French term referring to any short fictional tale of adventure.

Contrast: Used as a noun, contrast means difference. For example, *the contrast between novels and plays.* Used as a verb, to contrast is to compare two or more ideas, characters or objects so as to show their differences. Contrast can be a very effective literary device for emphasis and clarity.

Controlling Image: An image or metaphor that runs throughout and determines the form or nature of a literary work. (See **Imagery** and **Metaphor.**)

Conundrum: A form of riddle in which the answer involves a play on words. For example, *When is a boy not a boy? When he's a little pail.*

Convention: A literary convention is any device or style that has become, through habitual use, a recognized means of literary expression or an accepted element in technique. The use of alliterative verse by the Anglo-Saxons and of the heroic couplet in the time of Dryden and Pope are conventions in this sense. The personified virtues of the morality plays, the braggart soldier of the Elizabethan stage and the fainting heroine of sentimental fiction are examples of conventional stock characters.

Sometimes, conventions are so unrelated to customary human behavior that literature could not employ them if custom had not made them acceptable. The soliloquy in drama is an example of this type of convention. (See **Motif** and **Stock Characters.**)

Copyright: The exclusive legal right to publish or reproduce for sale works of literature, music, art or technology.

Coronach: A song of lamentation; a funeral dirge. A Gaelic word, meaning "wailing together," the coronach reflects a custom in the Scottish Highlands and in Ireland (where *keening* is the more commonly used term).

Corpus Christi Play: See **Mystery Play**.

Counterplayers: The characters in a drama who plot against the hero or heroine, e.g., Claudius, Polonius, Laertes and their associates, in *Hamlet. (See* **Antagonist.**)

Counterplot: A subplot. (See **Subplot**.)

Coup de Théâtre: An unexpected, usually unmotivated, surprising turn in a drama, which produces a sensational effect; by extension, anything designed solely for effect.

Couplet: Two lines of verse with similar end rhymes. Formally, the couplet is a two-line stanza form with both grammatical structure and idea complete within itself. The form has gone through numerous adaptations, the most famous of which is heroic verse. (See **Closed Couplet** and **Heroic Verse**.)

Court Comedy: The type of comedy written to be performed at the royal court. Elizabethan court comedy was developed to a high degree of effectiveness by John Lyly in such plays as *Endimion* and *Campaspe*. Characteristics of early court comedy included: artificial plot, little action, much use of mythology, pageantry, elaborate costuming and scenery, music (especially songs), lightness of tone, numerous characters often arranged in contrasting pairs, a style marked by wit, grace and verbal cleverness, prose dialogue and allegorical meanings embodied in the characters and action.

Court comedy in the seventeenth century was operatic in tone and spectacular in presentation. *Love's Labour's Lost* is a court comedy belonging to Shakespeare's early period.

Courtesy Book: A book dealing with the ideals and training of the courtly person. These books flourished during the late Renaissance.

Often in dialogue form, the courtesy book discussed such questions as the qualities of a gentleman or court lady, what constituted a gentleman, the etiquette of courtly love, the education of the future courtier or prince and the duties of a courtier as a state counsellor.

The courtesy book originated in Italy. A famous example was Castiglione's *Il Cortegiano* (The Courtier), (1528). The earliest English courtesy book is Sir Thomas Elyot's *Book of the Governour* (1531).

Courtly Love: A philosophy of love and a code of lovemaking that flourished in chivalric times, first in France and later in other countries, especially in England.

According to the courtly love convention, falling in love is accompanied by great emotional disturbances. The lover is bewildered, tortured by mental and physical pain, and exhibits symptoms such as pallor, trembling, loss of appetite, sleeplessness and sighing. His condition improves when he is accepted, and he is inspired by his love to great deeds. He and his lady pledge each other to secrecy, and they must remain faithful in spite of all obstacles. Courtly love abounds in medieval romance.

Courtly Makers: The court poets in the reign of Henry VIII who introduced the new poetry from Italy and France into England. Maker was the term used in the sixteenth century, in both England and Scotland, for poet.)

The courtly makers were credited by the Elizabethans for reforming or polishing the earlier English poetry. Their work exerted a powerful influence on Elizabethan poetry. Two of the most important poets of the group were Sir Thomas Wyatt and the Earl of Surrey. Sometimes the term courtly maker is applied to any court poet.

Courts of Love: Supposed tribunals for settling questions involving courtly love. (See **Courtly Love.**) The judge, a court lady or Venus herself would hear debate on such questions as: "Can a lover love two ladies at once?" Although it was once generally believed that such courts were actually held in chivalric times, modern scholarship tends to regard the courts of love as mere literary conventions.

Crisis: The part of the plot in fiction or drama that presents the critical stage in the dramatic action; the episode or incident wherein the situation in which the protagonist finds himself will either improve or deteriorate. Frequently, the crisis precedes the climax, yet it is related to the climax because the decision made by a character at the point of crisis largely determines the nature of the climax.

Critic: One who estimates and passes judgment on the value and quality of the work of others. Literary critics range from the journalistic reviewers who discuss three or four books a day, to the learned critics who study and make informed pronouncements on the merits and faults of literary works. (See **Criticism.**)

Criticism: The art of judging and defining the qualities and merits of a literary or artistic work. Each age has its critics, who, by setting standards and affecting tastes, influence the work produced by artists and writers.

In classical criticism, Aristotle, Longinus and Horace wrote treatises that are still debated by modern scholars. During the English Renaissance, Sidney's *The Defense of Poesie* was perhaps the most significant piece of criticism, although Bacon and Jonson also made important critical expressions. Later, Dryden, Pope, Johnson, and Coleridge defined standards and influenced English literature during their own and subsequent ages. Among modern Canadian men of letters, Northrop Frye is an internationally recognized critic.

Crown of Sonnets: Seven sonnets interlinked by having the last line of the first form the first line of the second, the last line of the second form the first line of the third, etc., with the last line of the last sonnet repeating the first line of the first. (See **Sonnet.**)

Cultural Primitivism: The belief that nature is preferable and fundamentally better than any aspect of man's culture.

Cursive: Typeface that resembles handwriting.

Cursus: The rhythm or patterned flow of prose.

Curtain Raiser: A one-act play or other entertainment that is performed at the beginning of a program.

Cycle: A collection of poems or romances centering around some outstanding event or character. Cyclic narratives are commonly accumulations of traditions given literary form by a succession of authors, rather than by a single writer. Examples include the Charlemagne epics and Arthurian romances, such as *The Cycle of Lancelot*.

Cyclic Drama: The great cycles of medieval religious drama. (See **Mystery Play.**)

Cynicism: Doubt of the generally accepted standards and of the innate goodness of human action. In literature, the term is used to characterize groups of writers or movements distinguished by dissatisfaction with contemporary conditions. The name comes from a school of Greek philosophers (the Cynics) led by Antisthenes. Samuel Butler's *The Way of All Flesh* and Somerset Maugham's *Of Human Bondage* have been called cynical novels.

D

Dactyl: A metrical unit or foot consisting of one accented syllable, followed by two unaccented syllables, as in the word *mān ni̯ kīn*. (See **Meter** and **Versification.**)

Dadaism: A nihilistic movement in literature and art started in Western Europe early in the twentieth century. The movement became popular in Paris after World War I but, by 1921, it was quickly being replaced by surrealism. (See **Surrealism.**) Dadaist literature was characterized by fantastic symbolic expression and nihilistic satire.

Dark Ages: A term commonly used to refer to the period of European history beginning with the fall of the Roman Empire (476 A.D.) and extending to the Italian Renaissance in the thirteenth century. Modern scholars object to the term, however, claiming that it misrepresents the period by implying that it was characterized by intellectual darkness. Most present-day writers, therefore, avoid the phrase.

Dark Comedy: See **Black Comedy.**

Debat: A medieval literary form in which two speakers dispute a topic; a debate.

Decadence: In literary history and criticism, denoting the decline or deterioration that commonly marks the end of a great period. In England, the drama of the period following Shakespeare was marked by such decadent qualities as a relaxing of critical standards, a lowered moral tone, sensationalism, a breaking down of types (with comedy and tragedy merging), a decreased seriousness of purpose and a loss of poetic appeal. The late years of the nineteenth century are sometimes called decadent because of the decline from Victorian standards. Individual writers of the period, such as Oscar Wilde, Arthur Symons and Aubrey Beardsley, are often called decadent.

Decadents: A group of late nineteenth- and early twentieth-century writers, principally in France but also in England and North America, who held that art was superior to nature and who, in life and in art, attacked the accepted moral, ethical and social standards of their time.

Decastich: A poem of 10 lines.

Decasyllabic Verse: Referring to verse of ten syllables.

Decorum: That which is proper to a character, subject or setting in a literary work. According to classical standards, the unity and harmony of a composition could be maintained by the observance of dramatic propriety. The style should be appropriate to the speaker, the occasion and the subject matter. Renaissance authors, therefore, were careful to have kings speak in a "high" style (majestic blank verse), old men in a "grave" style, clowns in prose and shepherds in a "rustic" style.

Dedication: An inscription to a patron, friend or relative at the beginning of a book.

Definition: A statement explaining the meaning or meanings of a term. Formal definitions consist of two elements: (1) the general class to which the term belongs, and (2) the specific ways in which the term differs from other objects within the same general class. For example: A *canoe* (term) is a boat (general class) pointed at both ends and propelled by paddling (ways in which it differs from other objects in the same class).

Deism: The creed of those believing in a God who rules the world by established laws, but not believing in the divinity of Christ or the inspiration of the Bible; "natural" religion, based on reason and a study of nature, as opposed to "revealed" religion.

The reputed father of the deists was Lord Herbert of Cherbury (1583-1648). The effects of deistic thinking upon literature were significant. The deism of Pope's *An Essay on Man* illustrates the effect on the classical school, while the doctrine of man's perfection in Shelley's poetry, and much of the Wordsworthian worship of nature are examples of deistic influences on the romantic school.

Denotation: The exact, literal meaning of a word. (Compare with **Connotation**.)

Denouement: In drama or fiction, the final unravelling of the plot; the solution of the mystery; the explanation or outcome. Denouement implies an ingenious untying of the knot of an intrigue, involving not only a satisfactory outcome of the main situation, but an explanation of all the secrets and misunderstandings connected with the plot complication. The final scene of Shakespeare's *Cymbeline* is an example of how clever and involved a dramatic denouement may be. (See also **Catastrophe**, **Dramatic Structure** and **Short Story**.)

Description: One of the four principal types of composition (see **Argumentation**, **Exposition** and **Narration**), description is used to portray a scene or setting. Descriptive writing is most effective when the details are carefully selected according to some purpose and to a definite point of view, when the images are concrete and clear, and when discreet use is made of words referring to color, sound and motion.

Detective Story: A novel or short story in which the plot is based on the solution, by a detective, of the mystery surrounding a crime that has been committed. (See **Mystery Story**.)

Deus ex Machina: The employment of some unexpected and improbable incident in a story or play in order to end a difficult situation. In the ancient Greek theater, when gods appeared in plays, they were lowered to the stage from the machine or stage structure above. The abrupt but timely appearance of a god who extricated the mortal characters of the drama from a situation so perplexing that the solution seemed impossible, was referred to in Latin as the *deux ex machina* (god from the machine). The term is now used to characterize any device whereby an author solves a difficult situation by a forced invention.

Developing Characters: When a character in a play or story changes during the progress of the action, he is said to be a developing character. He may deteriorate, like Shakespeare's Macbeth; he may develop strength as a result of conscious moral struggle, like Eliot's Adam Bede; or he may alter his philosophy and habits under the stress of changed social environment, like Howells' Silas Lapham. A character who is uninfluenced by the action is called a stationary or static character. Minor characters in drama and fiction are often static.

Tragedies and novels of character demand developing characters, while comedies and forms such as the mystery story, where interest depends chiefly on plot, have less need for them. (See **Characterization**.)

Diacope: The separation of a compound word, as *where by* or *never the less*.

Dialect: A variety of a spoken language peculiar to a geographical region or community. The chief cause of the development of dialects is geographic isolation or social barriers leading to lack of communication. Cockney is a dialect of the English language.

Dialectic: A method of logical discussion, inquiry and analysis used to ascertain the truth of an opinion or theory. Plato's Socratic dialogues are examples of dialectic through questions and answers.

In some forms of the dialectic process, a theory or thesis is presented and is then opposed by a contradictory theory (antithesis).

Ultimately, thesis and antithesis are united in a refined synthesis. (See **Synthesis.**)

Dialogue: Conversation between two or more people, either verbal or written. Most common in fiction, particularly in dramas, novels and short stories, dialogue is also used in general expository and philosophical writing (as in Plato's works). Among the literary and stylistic values of effective dialogue are these: (1) it advances the action; (2) it is consistent with the character of the speakers, their social positions and special interests, thus adding realism; (3) it gives the impression of naturalness; (4) it presents the interplay of ideas and personalities among the people conversing; (5) it varies in diction, rhythm, phrasing, sentence length, etc., according to the various speakers thus adding interest; (6) it serves, as used by some writers, to give relief from passages that are essentially serious or expository in nature.

Diary: A day-by-day chronicle of events; a journal; usually, a personal and more or less intimate record of events and thoughts kept by an individual. Probably the most famous diary in English is that of Samuel Pepys, which details events between January 1, 1660 and May 29, 1669.

More recently, the diary has become a conscious literary form, used particularly by travellers, statesmen, politicians, etc., to detail the important daily events in which they have been involved.

Diatribe: Written or verbal discourse characterized by bitter invective; an abusive argument; a harangue.

Diatyposis: Vivid presentation in literature by means of exciting language.

Dibrach: A metrical foot of two short syllables.

Dichoree: A metrical foot in which two trochees are treated as one unit ($-\cup-\cup$).

Diction: The use of words in verbal or written discourse. A simple list of words makes up a vocabulary; the accurate, careful use of these words makes good diction. Generally, good diction includes the following qualities: (1) the apt selection of the word for the particular meaning to be conveyed; (2) the use of legitimate words accepted as good usage (excluding all solecisms, barbarisms and improprieties); and (3) the use of clear-cut, specific words.

There are at least four grades of diction: *good usage* (which is literary and formal diction); *colloquial diction* (which is free and easy and suitable for discourse among intimates and acquaintances); *jour-*

nalistic diction (which is affected in greater or lesser degree by various newspapers) and *slang*.

Dictionary: A book containing the words, or a selection of the words, of a language, arranged alphabetically, with explanations of the meaning(s) and pronunciation(s) of each word. Frequently, illustrative quotations, synonyms and antonyms are also given. Sometimes a dictionary is restricted to a specific subject, such as a dictionary of law, medicine, art or literary terms. Two-language dictionaries give corresponding words in each language.

Probably the most important English dictionary is the Oxford *New English Dictionary*. It is especially useful because of the comprehensiveness of the illustrative examples given and the elaborate analyses of meanings and derivations.

Didacticism: That quality of writing that manifests the author's desire to instruct and improve the reader. Didacticism is evident, for example, in Bunyan's *The Pilgrim's Progress*.

Didactic Poetry: Verses designed essentially to teach a lesson.

Digest: (1) A publication devoted exclusively or primarily to abridgments of books or articles that have previously appeared elsewhere. For example, *Reader's Digest*. (2) The abridgment itself. (See **Abridge**.)

Digression: In a piece of writing, a departure or turning aside from the main theme or plot. Digression is often used in informal essays.

Dilettante: One who follows an art for the love of it, rather than as a serious profession. In literature, as with the other arts, the term has acquired a derogatory meaning. Usually, it is employed to indicate someone who reads and talks about books from hearsay or a careless reading, as opposed to the student who makes a careful and critical study of a writer, period, movement or book. Originally, dilettante meant an amateur; now it usually means one who dabbles.

Dime Novel: See **Penny Dreadful**.

Dimeter: A line of verse consisting of two feet. (See **Scansion**.)

Dionysian: Highly exuberant; frenzied; uninhibited; orgiastic. The word is derived from Dionysus, the Greek god of wine and fertility. The opposite of Dionysian is Apollonian. (See **Apollonian**.)

Dipody: In poetry, a pair of metrical feet treated as a single unit; a pair of similar feet in a verse.

Dirge: A wailing song sung at a funeral or in commemoration of death; a short lyric of lamentation. (See **Coronach, Elegy, Monody, Pastoral Elegy** and **Threnody**.)

Discord: A lack of harmony between persons and situations, or between the style and subject matter of a piece of literature.

Discovery: In a tragedy, the revelation of a fact previously unknown to a character, which results in the turning of the action.

Disguisings: See **Masque**.

Dissertation: A formal, involved exposition written to clarify some scholarly problem. Dissertation is sometimes used interchangeably with thesis. The usual practice, at least in university circles, is to reverse dissertation for the more elaborate essays and papers written in partial fulfilment of the requirements for the doctor's degree. The term thesis is used for smaller papers submitted for the bachelor's or master's degree. Both terms are commonly used outside academic circles to signify thoughtful discussions, in writing or speech, on almost any serious problem.

Dissonance: (1) The mingling of harsh or jarring sounds or rhythmical patterns; a synonym for cacophony. (See **Cacophony**.) (2) Inconsistency between one's beliefs or between one's beliefs and actions. (3) The mingling of closely related but not identical vowel sounds in one or more line of verse or music. (See **Assonance**.)

Distich: A couplet; any two consecutive rhyming lines; an epigram or maxim expressed in couplet form. For example:

> Hope springs eternal in the human breast;
> Man never is, but always to be blest.
>
> POPE

Disyllabic: Any word or metrical foot with two syllables.

Dithyramb: Literary expression characterized by wild, passionate language. The lyric power of the dithyramb relates it closely to verse, although its unordered sequence and development, as well as its seemingly improvised quality, often give it the form of prose. Dithyrambic verse, meant originally to be accompanied by music, was historically associated with Greek ceremonial worship of Bacchus or Pan. It was originally the choral element in Greek verse, developing later into Greek tragedy. In English, dithyrambic verse is related to the ode. An example is Dryden's *Alexander's Feast*.

Ditrochee (same as **Dicoreus**): A trochaic dipody that is considered as one compound foot. (See **Dipody**.)

Ditty: A song; a refrain. The term implies something familiar and is often applied to sailors' songs. It is also used, in the sense of theme, to refer to any short, apt saying or idea that runs through a composition.

Divine Afflatus, The: Poetic inspiration, particularly the exalted state immediately preceding creative composition, when the poet is said to be receiving his inspiration directly from a divine source.

Dizain: A French poem or stanza containing ten lines, each with eight or ten syllables.

Doctrinaire: (1) One whose attitude is controlled by a preconceived theory or group of theories and who is inclined to disregard other points of view. The doctrinaire's view is likely to be theoretical and narrow, as compared to practical and broad-minded. (2) Dogmatic; Stubbornly theoretical. Criticism like Samuel Johnson's may be termed doctrinaire because it is controlled by a definite code of critical doctrines.

Doggerel: Crude composition in verse; any poorly executed attempt at poetry. Characteristics of doggerel verse are monotony of rhyme and rhythm, cheap sentiment and trivial, trite subject matter. Some doggerel, however, is amusing and earns a place on one of the lower shelves of literature. Johnson's parody on Percy's *Hermit of Warkworth* is an example:

> As with my hat upon my head
> I walk'd along the Strand,
> I there did meet another man
> With his hat in his hand.

Domestic Tragedy: Tragedy based upon the lives of everyday, contemporary people. Running contrary to critical conceptions of tragedy as possible only when the principal characters are of high rank, domestic tragedy was slow to gain critical recognition. Thomas Heywood's *A Woman Killed with Kindness* (acted 1603) is an example of an Elizabethan domestic tragedy. A twentieth-century example is Arthur Miller's *Death of a Salesman*.

Doric: Simple; a term often applied to pastorals. In ancient Greece, the Doric dialect was considered to be lacking in refinement, and Doric architecture was marked by simplicity and strength, rather than by beauty of detail. Simple, idyllic pieces of literature such as Tennyson's *Dora* or Wordsworth's *Michael* are said to exhibit Doric qualities.

Double Dactyl: A metrical form composed of two dactyls ($-\cup\cup-\cup\cup$), as in *higgledy-piggledy*. In light verse, the form is sometimes used in a fixed pattern consisting of two stanzas, each containing four double-dactyl lines. The last lines of the stanzas rhyme.

Double Entendre: A play on words in which a word or phrase may be understood in two senses, one of which is frequently improper. The double entendre is a form of ambiguity. (See **Ambiguity**.)

Double Rhyme: See **Feminine Rhyme**.

Drama: In general, a work written to be performed by actors on a stage. Most dramatic works can be classified as tragedy or comedy.

Drama originated in ancient Greece, developing from religious ceremonies. The great classical writers of tragedy were Aeschylus, Sophocles and Euripides (in Greece) and the Roman philosopher, Seneca. Well-known comic writers of antiquity included the Greek, Aristophanes, and the Romans, Plautus and Menander.

Medieval drama developed from religious rituals commemorating the birth and resurrection of Christ. As it evolved, it took the form of mystery, miracle and morality plays.

In England during the Renaissance, a revived interest in classical drama united with the traditions developed from medieval techniques to produce the vigorous and varied Elizabethan drama.

The English theaters were closed in 1642 by the Puritans. However, during the Restoration, drama was revived under the auspices of the court. In the eighteenth century, neoclassical plays and the comedy of manners flourished.

Melodrama and spectacle predominated in most nineteenth-century drama until the end of the century, when shorter plays stressing ideas, problems or situations began to appear.

This trend toward a more faithful and accurate representation of life continued into the twentieth century. Further developments included expressionism and the introduction of the theater of the absurd.

Specific aspects of the drama are discussed in separate entries in this dictionary. (See, for example, **Comedy, Comedy of Manners, Elizabethan Drama, Expressionism, Little Theater Movement, Liturgical Drama, Medieval Drama, Melodrama, Theater of the Absurd, Tragedy** and the references included with these entries.)

Dramatic Irony: Often the words or acts of a character in a play carry a meaning unknown to himself but understood by the audience. The dramatic irony lies in the contrast between the meaning intended by the speaker and the added significance of which the audience is aware. Sometimes the term is extended to include any situation (such as mistaken identity) in which one or more of the characters are ignorant of facts known to the spectator. Occasionally, the term dramatic irony is applied to non-dramatic narrative.

Dramatic Monologue: A poetic soliloquy in which the speaker reveals his own character. Usually, a listener is present who does not speak but plays a part in the development of the poem. Browning frequently used dramatic monologues, as in *Andrea del Sarto*. Tennyson used the form in *Ulysses* and *Rizpah*.

Dramatic Poetry: Poetry employing dramatic form or some element of dramatic technique. The dramatic monologue is an example. The dramatic quality of the poem may result from the use of dialogue, monologue, vigorous diction, blank verse or the stressing of tense situational and emotional conflict. Not infrequently, the term dramatic poetry is extended to include compositions that, like Shakespeare's *The Tempest*, may more properly be classified as poetic drama or that like Browning's *Pippa Passes*, are more commonly called closet dramas. (See **Closet Drama** and **Poetic Drama**.)

Dramatic Structure: The structure of a traditional tragedy is based on the following elements:

The *introduction* creates the tone, gives the setting, introduces some of the characters and supplies other facts necessary for an understanding of the play. In *Hamlet*, the bleak midnight scene on the castle platform, with the appearance of the ghost, sets the keynote of the tragedy. The conversation of the watchers supplies antecedent facts, such as the quarrel between the dead king and the king of Norway.

The *rising action* or *complication* is set in motion (the ghost's revelation to Hamlet of the murder), and continues through successive stages of conflict between the hero and the counterplayers up to the climax or turning point (Hamlet's failure to kill Claudius at prayer).

The *falling action* stresses the activity of the forces opposing the hero. While some suspense must be maintained, the trend of the action must lead logically to the disaster with which the tragedy is to close. Relief scenes are often used in the falling action (the gravediggers in *Hamlet*).

The *catastrophe* marks the tragic failure, usually the death of the hero. It satisfies the spectator because it appears to be an inevitable result of the play's action and because it gives a final presentation of the nobility of the dying hero. A glimpse of restored order often follows the catastrophe, as when Hamlet gives his dying vote to Fortinbras as the new king.

Dramatis personae: The characters or actors in a play. Usually, a list of these characters is printed at the beginning of a play.

Dramaturge: A specialist in dramatic composition and theatrical presentation.

Dramaturgy: The composition of plays. The term is sometimes used to include the acting, as well as the writing, of drama.

Drame: A form of serious play between tragedy and comedy. Developed by the French in the eighteenth century, the drame was later introduced into England, where it is often called a drama.

Dream Allegory (or Vision): The dream was a conventional narrative frame that was widely used in the Middle Ages and is still popular today. The narrator falls asleep and, while sleeping, dreams the story that is being narrated. In a sense, *The Wizard of Oz* is an example of the dream allegory.

Droll: A short, comic piece, often coupled with dancing, performed most often at fairs during the Commonwealth (1649-1660) in England. Since the government had closed the theaters and forbidden full-length plays, the performances of drolls were among the few ways of evading the Puritan edicts.

As an adjective, droll means amusingly odd or humorously quaint.

Dumb Show: A pantomimic performance used as a part of a play. The term is applied particularly to the interludes of silent acting that appeared in Elizabethan drama. The dumb show provided a spectacular element and was often accompanied by music. It foreshadowed coming events in the action or provided comment like that of the chorus. Sometimes a dumb show appeared as prologue or between acts, and sometimes it was an integral part of the action. Examples appear in John Webster's *Duchess of Malfi* (1614) and Thomas Middleton's *The Changeling*. (See **Disguisings, Masque, Pageant** and **Pantomime.**)

Duodecimo: The page size of a book in which each leaf is one-twelfth of a printer's sheet of paper. (See **Folio, Octavo** and **Quarto.**)

Duologue: A conversation between two characters in a play or story; a dialogue between two people.

Dyslogism: A term that has a derogatory connotation, such as *old maid* for an unmarried woman.

Dysphemism: A term that emphasizes a defect or failing, as in *A dirty, slushy, sloppy day*. Dysphemism is the opposite of euphemism. (See **Euphemism.**)

E

Echo Verse: (1) A line and an "echo," which repeats the final syllables of the line with a change in meaning. (2) A poem made up of such lines.

Eclogue: In Greek, eclogue meant "selection" and was applied to various kinds of poems. From its application to Virgil's pastoral poems, however, eclogue came to mean a formal pastoral poem following the traditional technique derived from the idylls of Theocritus (third century B.C.).

Conventional eclogue types include: the singing match (two shepherds have a singing contest on a wager or for a prize, with a third shepherd acting as judge); the rustic dialogue (two countrymen engage in banter, perhaps over a mistress); the dirge or lament for a dead shepherd; the love song; and the eulogy. (See **Pastoral** and **Pastoral Elegy.**)

Edda: Either of two books, one in prose and one in poetry, written in Icelandic in the early thirteenth century. The prose Edda contains rules for writing poetry. The poetic Edda contains old Norse myths and legends.

Edition: All the copies of a book, newspaper, magazine, etc. printed at any time or times from the same set of type. If the original type is changed, the reprinted product is called a *second edition*. When the same edition is reprinted without any changes, it is called a *second impression* or *printing*, or it is said to be *reissued*.

In contrast, an *issue* is a special form of an edition in which, for the most part, the original material is used, but which differs by the addition of new material or in arrangement.

Edition is also used in such phrases as *a five-volume edition of*

Shakespeare (referring to the form of publication), and *Kittredge's edition of Shakespeare* (indicating that the material has been edited).

Editorial: A short essay, expository or argumentative in character, used in newspapers or magazines. The usual purpose of the editorial is to discuss current news events. The subjects may range from matters of purely local importance to provincial, national and international affairs.

Effect: Writers sometimes attempt to create, in a particular composition, a special impression (effect) in the reader's mind. Once the effect is chosen, everything in the story — incident, character, setting — must work to fulfil this controlling purpose. The works of Edgar Allan Poe are notable for effect.

e.g.: For example (from the Latin, *exempli gratia*).

Elaboration: A rhetorical method for developing a theme in such a way as to give the reader a complete impression. This may be done by repetition of the statement or idea, by a change of words and phrases or by supplying additional details. When used with restraint, elaboration results in clarity. Overelaboration, however, results in diffuseness and wordiness. In *Hamlet*, Polonius is given to overelaboration.

As an adjective, elaborate is also used as a critical term to characterize an ornate literary style. Oscar Wilde's style, for example, could be called elaborate.

Elegiac: (1) Of or suitable for an elegy. (See **Elegy**.) (2) Sad, mournful or melancholic. (3) In Greek and Latin verse, a dactylic hexameter couplet, the second line having only a long or accented syllable in the third and sixth feet. (See **Elegiac Stanza**.)

Elegiac Stanza: A stanza of four lines in iambic pentameter, usually rhyming *abab*. The stanza acquired its name because it was used by Gray in his *Elegy Written in a Country Churchyard* (1750). The following is an example from that poem:

> Full many a gem of purest ray serene
> The dark unfathom'd caves of ocean bear:
> Full many a flower is born to blush unseen,
> And waste its sweetness on the desert air.

Elegy: A lyric poem setting forth the poet's meditations upon death. It is characterized by conventional language expressing with dignity and decorum a formal grief. A classical form, common to both Latin and

Greek literature, an elegy originally signified almost any type of serious, subjective poetic meditation.

In classic writing, the elegy was more characterized by its form (a couplet in dactylic hexameter and pentameter) than by its subject matter.

Milton's *Lycidas* and Gray's *Elegy Written in a Country Churchyard* are well-known English elegies.

Elision: The omission of a part of a word for ease of pronunciation, for euphony or to secure a desired rhythmic effect. Usually, this is accomplished by the omission of a final vowel preceding an initial vowel, as *th'orient* for *the orient*. (See **Syncope**.)

Elizabethan Drama: A phrase commonly used for the entire body of Renaissance English drama produced in the century preceding the closing of the theaters in 1642. Sometimes it is used in a narrower sense to designate the drama of the later years of Elizabeth's reign and the few years following it. Modern English drama came into being in Elizabethan time, developing so brilliantly that the Elizabethan era is often considered as the golden age of English drama.

Elizabethan Literature: Usually, the English literature of the period from ca. 1550 to 1660, but sometimes used narrowly for the period during the reign of Elizabeth I (1558-1603). (See **Caroline, Jacobean** and **Renaissance**.)

Elizabethan Miscellany: See **Miscellany, Poetical**.

Elizabethan Theaters: See **Private Theaters** and **Public Theaters**.

Ellipsis: A figure of speech characterized by the omission of one or more words that, while essential to the grammatical structure of the sentence, are easily supplied by the reader. The effect of ellipsis is emphasis of statement. In the following quotation, the brackets indicate ellipsis:

> Where wigs [strive] with wigs, [where] with sword-knots sword-knots strive,
> [Where] Beaus banish beaus, and [where] coaches coaches drive.
>
> POPE

In writing or printing, *ellipses marks* (. . . or ***) indicate that some material has been omitted.

Emblem Book: A collection of emblems. An emblem consisted of a

65

motto expressing a moral idea and was accompanied by a picture and a short poem illustrating the idea. The poem was short; sonnets, epigrams, madrigals and various stanza forms were employed. The picture was symbolic. Emblems and emblem books, which owed their popularity partly to the newly developed art of engraving, were very popular in the fifteenth, sixteenth and seventeenth centuries. Several of Spenser's poems, such as *The Shepheardes Calender*, show the influence of emblems.

Emendation: A correction or improvement in any text or document.

Emotive Language: Language designed to evoke or express emotional reactions. The opposite of emotive language is referential language, which is designed to carry only denotative meanings. (See **Connotation** and **Denotation**.)

Empathy: The quality or process of entering fully, through imagination, into another's feelings or motives. Empathy is an important aspect of characterization. If the author can lead the reader to empathize with his characters, the reader will usually gain a better understanding and appreciation for the work as a whole.

Emphasis: A rhetorical principle dictating that important elements be given important positions and adequate development in a sentence, paragraph or composition. Usually, the most important positions are at the beginning and end. Emphasis may also be achieved: (1) by repeating important ideas; (2) by supplying specific details to develop important ideas; (3) by giving more space to the more important phases of the composition; (4) by contrasting one element with another; and (5) by selecting details so that subjects related to the main idea are included while irrelevant material is excluded.

Empiricism: In philosophy, the practice of drawing rules from experience. An empirical method is sometimes equivalent to an experimental method. In medicine, however, empiric can mean a charlatan. The term is sometimes borrowed by literary critics and used in a derogatory sense: an empiric judgment, in this sense, is an untrained one.

Encomium: An elaborate expression of praise; a eulogy. Originally, an encomium was a Greek song praising a hero.
Milton's *Hymn on the Morning of Christ's Nativity* is an example of encomiastic verse.

End Rhyme: See **Rhyme**.

End-stopped Line: A line of verse in which both the grammatical

66

structure and the sense reach completion at the end of the line; the absence of a run-on line. For example:

> All are but parts of one stupendous whole,
> Whose body Nature is, and God the soul.
>
> P<small>OPE</small>

English Language: The English language developed from the West Germanic dialects spoken by the Angles, Saxons and other Teutonic tribes who gradually invaded and occupied England in the fifth and sixth centuries. The word English reflects the fact that Anglo-Saxon literature first flourished in the north and was written in the Anglian dialects spoken in Northumbria and Mercia. Later, under King Alfred, the West Saxon region became the cultural center. The earlier Anglian literature was copied in the West Saxon dialect, now commonly called Old English, or Anglo-Saxon.

The changes that have made modern English look like a different language from Old English are the result of certain natural tendencies in language development, such as progressive simplification of the grammar, as well as the events in history, such as the Norman Conquest and the growth of London as a cultural center. The greatest change took place in the earlier part of the period known as Middle English (ca. 1100 to ca. 1500) or a little earlier.

Modern English (ca. 1500 on) has been marked by a significant expansion in vocabulary. The new words have been drawn from many sources, chiefly Latin and French. (See **Anglo-Saxon** and **Middle English**.)

Enjambment: A device used by poets to escape the monotonous rhythm of the regular couplet or of blank verse by running the sense and grammatical structure past the second line of a couplet. Enjambment occurs with the run-on line and is in contrast to the end-stopped line. The first and second lines below, carried over to the second and third for completion, are illustrations of enjambment:

> Or if Sion hill
> Delight thee more, and Siloa's brook, that flow'd
> Fast by the oracle of God.
>
> M<small>ILTON</small>

Enlightenment: A period covering most of the eighteenth century, which was regarded as a time characterized by a spirit of rationalism and scepticism in science and politics.

Enthymeme: A syllogism informally stated and omitting one of the two premises — either the major or the minor. The omitted premise is to be understood. Example: *Children should be seen and not heard. Be quiet, John.* The obvious minor premise — that John is a child — is left to the understanding of the reader. (See **Syllogism**.)

Entr'acte: The interval between two acts of a play; an entertainment, often musical, performed during this interval.

Envoy (Envoi): A conventionalized stanza appearing at the close of certain poems, particularly associated with the French ballade form. Usually addressed to a prince, a judge, a patron or other person of importance, the envoy repeats the refrain line used through the ballade. The stanza ordinarily consists of four lines and employs the *bcbc* rhyme scheme. (See **Ballade**.)

Epenthesis: The addition, in the middle of a word, of a letter, syllable or sound. Sometimes epenthesis is used for rhythm, as in the nursery rhyme, *Handy spandy, Jack-a-Dandy.* Sometimes it is the result of an error in pronunciation, as in *film* for film. Sometimes it occurs as a language develops, as in the addition of "b" to the Middle English word *momelen* to form the modern word *mumble.*

A similar addition at the beginning of a word (e.g., be*loved*) is called prosthesis; at the end of a word (e.g., *sweetie*) it is called paragoge.

Epic: A long narrative poem presenting heroic characters who take part in a series of adventures, usually over an extended period of time. The first epics took shape from the scattered works of various unknown poets. The classical epic, influenced by Virgil, developed certain devices which, to a varying extent, have been employed by later poets. Some of these characteristic devices were the invocation of the Muses, the statement of the epic purpose, descriptions of warfare and battles, and the use of the supernatural. In an epic, the speech of the characters is formal; epic catalogues and descriptions are given (often marked by considerable concrete detail), the epic simile is common and the story is presented in dignified and majestic language.

The Iliad and *The Odyssey* (attributed to Homer) and the Anglo-Saxon *Beowulf* are examples of folk epics. Some of the best-known art epics (those produced by a single writer) are Virgil's *Aeneid*, Dante's *The Divine Comedy*, Spenser's *The Faerie Queene* and Milton's *Paradise Lost.*

Epic Formula: The characteristic content, style and form of classical epics. (See **Epic**.)

Epic Simile: An elaborated comparison. An epic simile differs from an ordinary simile in that it is more involved, more ornate and is a conscious imitation of the Homeric manner. The secondary object or picture is developed into an independent aesthetic object, an image that, for the moment, excludes the primary object with which it is compared. The following from *Paradise Lost* is an example:

> Angel Forms, who lay entranced
> Thick as autumnal leaves that strow the brooks
> In Vallombrosa, where the Etrurian shades
> High over-arched embower; or scattered sedge
> Afloat, when with fierce winds Orion armed
> Hath vexed the Red-Sea coast, whose waves o'erthrew
> Busiris and him Memphian chivalry,
> While with perfidious hatred they pursued
> The sojourners of Goshen, who beheld
> From the safe shore their floating carcases
> And broken chariot-wheels.
>
> MILTON

Epicurean: Exhibiting a mood or spirit of surrender to the search for pleasure, especially such sensuous pleasures as eating and drinking. Epicurus, a Greek philosopher, advocated the doctrine that man's legitimate aim was the pursuit of pleasure. The sensuous connotation of pleasure developed later.

Epigram: A pointed, pithy saying. Epigrammatic style is concise, often antithetical, as *Man proposes; God disposes*.

Originally, in ancient Greece, an epigram meant an inscription, especially an epitaph. Greek epigrams were characterized by compression, clarity, balance and polish. The epigrams of the Roman poet, Martial, supplied models for Ben Jonson, whom critics acknowledged as the greatest writer of epigrams in the English Renaissance. Among later English poets, Walter Savage Landor (1775-1864) is perhaps the most accomplished writer of epigrams modelled on the Greek style.

Typically, an epigram is a short poem consisting of two parts: an introduction stating the occasion or setting the tone, and a conclusion that sharply and tersely (often with the effect of surprise) gives the main point. The first epigram in Jonson's collection is an example:

> To the Reader
> Pray thee take care, that tak'st my Book in hand,
> To read it well; that is, to understand.

Epigraph: (1) An inscription on a monument, building, statue or coin. (2) A motto or quotation appearing at the beginning of a written work or at the beginning of a section of the work.

Epilogue: A concluding statement; an appendix to a composition. Sometimes a peroration to a speech is called an epilogue, but more generally the term is applied to the final remarks of an actor addressed to the audience at the close of the play. Puck, in *A Midsummer Night's Dream*, recites an epilogue that is characteristic of Renaissance plays, in that it asks for the good will of the audience and courteous treatment by critics.

Epiphany: A term used in literary criticism for a moment of revelation or illumination that results in an altered perception. Usually, the sudden awareness is caused by a simple, casual event that takes on a new and intense meaning. James Joyce's Stephen Hero calls an epiphany "a sudden spiritual manifestation."

In the Christian Church, the Feast of the Epiphany (January 6, or Twelfth Night) celebrates the arrival of the Wise Men at the stable in Bethlehem after the birth of Jesus Christ.

Episode: An incident presented as one continuous action. Usually, the episode is accompanied by other episodes, woven together by the writer in order to create a story, drama or novel. More narrowly, the term is sometimes used to characterize an incident in a piece of fiction that simply illuminates character or creates background. In this case, the episode bears no definite relationship to the plot and does not advance the action.

Originally, in Greek drama, an episode referred to that part of a tragedy that was presented between two choruses. (See **Chorus.**)

Episodic Structure: A critical term applied to writing that consists of little more than a series of incidents. The episodes succeed each other with no particularly logical arrangement (except perhaps that of chronology) and without complication or a close interrelationship. Travel books usually have an episodic structure, as does the picaresque novel. (See **Picaresque Novel.**)

Epistle: Theoretically, an epistle is any letter, but usually the term is limited to formal compositions written by an individual or a group to a distant individual or group. The epistle differs from the common letter in that it is a conscious literary form, rather than a spontaneous, private composition. The most familiar use of the term is to characterize certain books of the New Testament. The term may also be used to indicate formal letters having to do with public matters and with philosophy, as well as with religious concerns.

Epistolary Novel: A novel in which the narrative is carried forward by letters written by one or more of the characters. The device was commonly used in the eighteenth century (e.g., Richardson's *Pamela* and Smollett's *Humphry Clinker*).

Epitaph: Inscription used to mark burial places; commemorative verses or lines appearing on tombs or written as if intended for such use. An epitaph usually includes the name of the deceased, the dates of birth and death, and some pious motto or invocation. Many prominent writers — notably Johnson, Milton and Pope — have left epitaphs written in tribute to the dead.

One of the most famous inscriptions is that marking Shakespeare's burial place:

> Good friend, for Jesus' sake forbeare
> To dig the dust enclosed here;
> Blest be the man that spares these stones,
> Cursed be he that moves my bones.

Epitasis: In a drama, the movement of the play towards the climax. A tragedy often consists of four parts: the protasis or introduction; the epitasis; the catastasis, where the action rises to a climax; and the catastrophe or denouement. (See **Freytag's Pyramid**.)

Epithalamium (Epithalamion): A bridal song; a song or poem written to celebrate a wedding. Many ancient poets (the Greeks, Pindar, Sappho and Theocritus, and the Roman, Catullus) cultivated the form. Spenser's *Epithalamion* (1595), written to celebrate his own marriage, is one of the finest of the English bridal songs.

Epithet: Strictly, an adjective or adjective phrase used to point out a characteristic of a person or thing, as Goldsmith's *noisy mansions* (for *schoolhouses*). Sometimes, however, the term is applied to a noun or noun phrase used for a similar purpose, as Shakespeare's "the trumpet of the dawn", (*the cock*). In literature, memorable epithets are often figurative, as Keats' "snarling trumpets" and Milton's "labouring clouds".

The Homeric epithet is often a compound adjective, as *all-seeing* Jove, *swift-footed* Achilles and *rosy-fingered* dawn.

Epitome: A summary or abridgment; a condensed statement of the content of a book; a representation in miniature of a subject. Thus, the Magna Carta has been called the epitome of the rights of Englishmen, and Ruskin referred to St. Mark's Church in Venice as an epitome of the changes in Venetian architecture during a period of nine centuries.

Epitrite: A metrical foot, consisting of one short syllable and three long syllables. The short syllable may be the first, second, third or fourth in the foot. An epitrite is also known as a paeon. Aristotle recommended the use of the paeonic pattern in prose.

Epode: One of the three stanza forms employed in the Pindaric ode. (See **Antistrophe**.)

Eponym: (1) A person from whom a nation, tribe, place, etc. derives or is reputed to derive its name. For example, *Romulus is the eponym of Rome.* (2) A person whose name is a synonym for something. For example, *Hitler is the eponym of dictator.*

Equivalence: A rule of classical versification whereby two short or unaccented syllables are equal to one long or accented syllable, so that one kind of metric foot can be substituted for another. For example, a spondee (−−) might be replaced by a dactyl (−υυ).

In English poetry, a similar substitution of three-syllable feet when the regular meter consists of two-syllable feet sometimes occurs. The first line of the following verses from Gray's *Elegy Written in a Country Churchyard* contains an example:

Nŏw fādes | thĕ glīm | mĕrĭng lānd | scăpe ōn | thĕ sīght, |
Ănd āll | thĕ aīr | ă sōl | ĕmn stīll | nĕss hōlds...

Equivocation: The use of a word or expression in two distinct meanings, with the intention to deceive.

Equivoque: A kind of pun in which the same word or phrase is so used that it has two different and incompatible meanings. (See **Pun**.)

Erato: See **Muses**.

Erotic Literature: Amorous writings. Literature is classed as erotic because of its subject matter, love, rather than the literary form employed. Erotic literature embraces the lyric, short story, novel and drama, even epigrams and elegies. These are characterized as erotic when their content emphasizes the physical aspects of love.

Erziehungsroman: Synonymous with bildungsroman. (See **Bildungsroman**.)

Esperanto: An artificial language constructed from roots common to the chief European languages and designed for universal use. Esperanto was devised by Dr. L. L. Zamenhof, a Russian, and introduced in 1887. The grammar can be mastered by most people after a few minutes of study; the spelling is phonetic; the language is euphonious and adaptable; and pronunciation is not difficult, since the accent always falls on the penult. Esperanto has grown in popularity: some four thousand books, including the Bible, have been translated into the language.

Essay: A discussion in prose of a certain topic. An essay may be classified as formal or informal, depending on its subject and style.

The formal essay is characterized by qualities of dignity, serious purpose and logical organization. Examples range from the brief, serious magazine article to scientific or philosophical treatises of book length. The chapters in Carlyle's *Heroes and Hero Worship* are a form of this type of essay, as are long, critical book reviews, such as those written by T. B. Macauley, George Eliot, Matthew Arnold and others.

The informal essay, sometimes called the "true" essay, includes moderately brief instructive essays, such as Bacon's; periodical essays, such as Addison's; and personal essays, such as Lamb's. Among the qualities that mark an essay as informal are: humor, graceful style, a personal element, unconventionality or novelty of theme, and freedom from stiffness and affectation.

In addition to those mentioned above, the following authors have written essays of distinction: Swift, Pope, Dr. Johnson, Goldsmith, Robert Louis Stevenson, Cardinal Newman and T. S. Eliot.

et al.: (1) And others (abbreviation of the Latin **et alii**). (2) And elsewhere (from the Latin **et alibi.**)

Etiquette Books (Renaissance): See **Courtesy Books.**

Etymology: The study of the origin and history of words.

Eulogy: Composition, oral or written, praising the character or life of a person.

Euphemism: A figure of speech in which an indirect statement is substituted for a direct one in an effort to avoid bluntness. Writers use euphemistic terms in an effort to mention a disagreeable idea in an agreeable manner. An example is *passed on* for *died*. (See **Dysphemism**.)

Euphony: A quality of good style that demands the selection of word combinations that sound pleasant to the ear. Harsh, grating, cacophonous sounds violate euphony.

Euphuism: An affected style of speech and writing that flourished in the late sixteenth century in England, especially in court circles. The name was derived from *Euphues* (1579) by John Lyly, who developed the style partly in an effort to refine English prose style and partly in an effort to attract the interest of feminine readers. Among the chief characteristics of euphuism are: balanced construction combined with alliteration; frequent inclusion of the rhetorical question; and extensive use of similes, illustrations and examples, especially those drawn from mythology.

Although the extravagance and artificiality of euphuism are often criticized, the style established the idea that prose (formerly heavy and Latinized) might be written with imagination and fancy. The emphasis on short clauses and sentences, and on balanced construction contributed clarity to prose style. These virtues remained after the extravagant artificiality was eliminated.

Euterpe: See **Muses**.

Exciting Force: In a drama, the force that starts the conflict of opposing interests and sets in motion the rising action of the play. In *Macbeth,* for example, the witches' prophecy stirs Macbeth to action with schemes for making himself king. (See **Dramatic Structure**.)

Excursus: In a written work, a digression providing detailed analysis of some point made in the text. Usually, an excursus is added as an appendix or note to the work.

Exegesis: An explanation or interpretation of any text. Usually, an exegesis is analytical and is meant to clarify a difficult passage.

Exemplum: A moralized tale. Medieval preachers made extensive use of tales, anecdotes and incidents, both historical and legendary, to point out morals or to illustrate doctrines. Collections of exempla, classified according to subject, were prepared for use in sermons.

The influence of exempla and example books on medieval literature was significant. Chaucer's *The Nun's Priest's Tale*, for example, uses exempla, and *The Pardoner's Tale* is itself an exemplum to show how avarice leads to an evil end.

Existentialism: A primarily twentieth-century philosophy that is concerned with the analysis of existence and of the way man finds himself existing in the world. Although the existentialists themselves differ markedly in doctrine and attitude, most are agreed that man is totally free and responsible to himself alone, and that reality is grounded in existence or the experience of existence. Jean Paul Sartre and Albert Camus are two well-known existentialist writers.

Exordium: The introductory part of a speech, treatise, etc. Classical rhetoricians established rules for the order of material presented in an oration: first, the introduction (exordium), followed by the statement, the argument and the conclusion. (See **Peroration.**)

Expletive: An interjection to add emphasis to a sentence; in verse, the use of a superfluous word for the sake of rhythm. Profanity is another form of expletive.

Exposition: One of the four chief types of composition (see also **Argumentation, Description** and **Narration**), exposition is used to explain the nature of an object or idea, and to make clear to the reader the subject under discussion. Some of the methods for achieving clarity in exposition are: analysis (dividing the object or idea into component parts), definition, classification, contrast and comparison with other objects, example and illustration. (For exposition as a part of drama, see **Dramatic Structure.**)

Expressionism: A literary manner that attempts to communicate the qualities inherent in an object or scene, rather than its physical appearance. Expressionist writers portray a highly personal vision, modifying or distorting an object or idea according to their own intellectual perceptions. Qualities obvious to the writer, but not necessarily to others, are emphasized. Some of the work of T. S. Eliot and James Joyce exemplify expressionism. (Compare with **Impressionism, Naturalism** and **Realism.**)

Extravaganza: A fantastic, extravagant or irregular composition. The term is most commonly applied to dramatic compositions such as those of J. R. Planché, the creator of the dramatic extravaganza. Often, the subject was a fairy tale. The elaborate presentation included dancing and music. An example is Planché's *Sleeping Beauty* (acted 1840). More recently, fantastic musical compositions have also been called extravaganzas.

Eye Rhyme: Words that appear to the eye as rhymes, but not to the ear. For example, *love* and *rove* are eye rhymes, as are *gone, done* and *bone.*

F

Fable: A brief tale, in either prose or verse, with a moral. Usually, but not always, the characters are animals. The subject matter is concerned with supernatural and unusual incidents, often drawn from folklore. Perhaps the best-known fables are those accredited to Aesop, a Greek slave living about 600 B.C. Almost equally popular are those of the seventeenth-century French writer, La Fontaine. Fable is also used to characterize any story that at one time was believed, but is now recognized as untrue.

Fabliau: A humorous tale popular in medieval French literature. The conventional form was eight-syllable verse. The fabliaux consisted of stories of various types and were marked by their humorous, sly satire on human beings. The themes, often risqué, were dealt with in such a way that made them readily understandable to the uneducated. Chaucer has left examples of fabliaux in English. (e.g., *The Miller's Tale*).

Fairy Tale: A story relating mysterious pranks and adventures of supernatural spirits who manifest themselves in the form of human beings. Fairy tales became popular toward the close of the seventeenth century; almost every nation has its own literature of this genre.

Falling Action: The resolution of the second half of a dramatic plot. Falling action follows the climax, exhibits the failing fortunes of the hero (in tragedy) and culminates in the catastrophe. (See **Dramatic Structure.**)

Falling Rhythm: The kind of rhythm that results when the stress in a line of verse falls on the first syllables of the metric feet. Dactyls and trochees are the basis of falling rhythm. (See **Dactyl, Rising Rhythm** and **Trochee.**) The following lines, based on trochees, are an example:

> Go and catch a falling star,
> Get with child a mandrake root . . .

DONNE

Familiar Essay: A personal, intimate type of informal essay. It deals lightly, often humorously, with personal experiences, opinions and prejudices, stressing especially the unusual or novel in attitude, and focussing on the varied aspects of everyday life. Goldsmith, Lamb and Stevenson were noted for their familiar essays.

Fancy: See **Imagination and Fancy.**

Fantastic Poets: A term applied by Milton to the school of metaphysical poets. (See **Metaphysical Verse**.)

Fantasy: Though sometimes used as an equivalent of *fancy*, and even of *imagination*, fantasy usually suggests a groundless or delusive invention. A fantastic plot, for example, may be interesting, amusing or clever, but not convincing. (See **Imagination and Fancy**.)

Farce: A dramatic piece intended to make the audience laugh, and relying less on plot and character than on exaggerated, improbable situations. The humor in farce arises from coarse wit or horseplay. Farce merges into comedy, however, and the same play (e.g., Shakespeare's *The Taming of the Shrew*) may be called a farce by some critics, a comedy by others.

The word developed from the Latin *farcire*, meaning "to stuff." Thus, an expansion in the church liturgy was called a *farse*. Later, in France, farce meant any sort of extemporaneous addition in a play, especially comic jokes. In the late seventeenth century, the term was used in England to mean any short, humorous play, as distinguished from regular five-act comedy.

Farce Comedy: A term applied to comedies that rely for their interest chiefly on farcical devices, but that contain some truly comic elements that elevate them above most farce. Shakespeare's *The Merry Wives of Windsor* is sometimes called a farce comedy. (See **Farce** and **Low Comedy**.)

Faust Theme: Johann Faust (1488-1541) was a German magician who reputedly sold his immortal soul to the Devil in exchange for knowledge, power and worldly goods. For hundreds of years this legend has continued to fascinate novelists, dramatists, poets and composers. In the sixteenth century, Christopher Marlowe used the Faust theme as the basis of his drama, *The Tragical History of Dr. Faustus*. Later, the German writer, Goethe, produced what is perhaps the best-known version of the theme, *Faust* (published 1775-1832). Two other German writers, Heine and Mann, and the British poet, Byron, are among other writers who have based works on the Faust legend.

Feature Article: A journalistic essay on some matter of timely interest. Distinct from a news story, which chronicles an event of the day, the feature article is both more human in interest and somewhat less hurried in preparation. By extension, the term is also used to signify any human-interest story.

Feminine Ending: An unstressed syllable at the end of a line of verse. A feminine ending commonly appears in iambic pentameter blank verse.

The following line from Shakespeare's *The Tempest* is an example:

And līke | thĕ bāse | lĕss fā | brĭc ōf | thĭs vī | sĭon . . .

Feminine Rhyme (Double Rhyme): A rhyme of two syllables, one stressed and one unstressed, as *waken* and *forsaken, audition* and *rendition.* For example:

Above the pines the moon was slowly *drifting,*
The river sang below;
The dim Sierras, far beyond, *uplifting*
Their minarets of snow.

BRET HARTE

Feudalism: The social and political structure that prevailed in Western Europe during much of the medieval period. In feudal theory, every landholder was the tenant of some greater landlord. Thus, the barons were the tenants of the king; the lesser lords, knights and churchmen were tenants of the barons; and the serfs and villeins were tenants of the lesser nobles. In practice, since the whole system was based on force, the relationships were more complicated. As rent, the various groups paid their immediate superiors "service," which might consist of property or military aid.

The ideas of chivalry grew out of feudalism, powerfully affecting the character of much medieval and even Renaissance literature, notably the romances and romantic epics. (See **Chivalry.**)

Fiction: Narrative writing drawn from the imagination or fancy of the author. The term is most frequently associated with novels and short stories, though drama and narrative poetry also include numerous examples of fiction. Fables, parables, fairy tales and folklore also have fictional qualities. (See **Drama, Fable, Novel** and **Short Story.**)

Figurative Language: Writing that embodies one or more of the various figures of speech. The most common figures of speech are: antithesis, apostrophe, climax, hyperbole, irony, metaphor, metonymy, personification, simile and synecdoche. (Each of these is defined in this dictionary.)

Figurative language is the result of the writer's deliberate departure from usual word usage to gain strength and freshness of expression. These lines from William Vaughan Moody are an illustration:

Lewd as the palsied lips of hags
The petals in the moon did shake.

The lines contain metaphor (*lewd lips*, *petals in the moon*) and simile (*lewd as the palsied lips of hags*.) (See **Imagery**.)

Filidh (pl. Fili): See **Poet Laureate**.

Final Suspense, Moment of: A dramatic term used to indicate the possibility of escape for the hero that appears just before the catastrophe of a tragedy. Thus, Macbeth's conviction that he cannot be hurt by "any man of woman born" keeps the reader or spectator in some suspense as to the apparently inevitable tragic ending. (See **Dramatic Structure**.)

Fin de Siècle: Translated from the French to mean "end of the century." A phrase often applied to the last ten years of the nineteenth century. The 1890s were a transitional period, during which writers and artists were abandoning old ideas and conventions and attempting to discover new techniques and artistic objectives. The phrase may also be applied to other end-of-age or end-of-century periods.

First-Person Narrative: A story told by a character who calls himself "I"; a narrative filtered through the consciousness of an individual character. Dickens' *David Copperfield* is narrated by David himself, and readers are aware of events only as they occur to, or are reported by, him. (See **Point of View**.)

Flashback: In a novel, play or motion picture, the interruption of the story's continuity to portray an episode or incident that occurred earlier.

Fleshly School of Poetry, The: From a critical essay published in the *Contemporary Review*, October, 1871. The article was signed Thomas Maitland, a pseudonym for Robert W. Buchanan. The following indicates the trend of Buchanan's criticism:

> The fleshly gentlemen have bound themselves by solemn league and covenant to extol fleshliness as the distinct and supreme end of poetic and pictorial art, to aver that poetic expression is greater than poetic thought, and by inference that the body is greater than the soul, and sound superior to sense; and that the poet, properly to develop his poetic faculty, must be an intellectual hermaphrodite . . .

The "fleshly gentlemen" were the poets Swinburne, Morris and

Rossetti. Rossetti replied to the denunciation by writing "The Stealthy School of Criticism," published in *The Athenaeum*, December, 1871.

Foil: Literally, a thin leaf of polished metal placed under a gem to give it added brilliance. By extension, a character whose behavior and qualities set off or enhance by contrast those of another figure. For example, Hotspur is a foil for Prince Hal in Shakespeare's *King Henry IV*; Fortinbras and Laertes are foils for Hamlet in Shakespeare's *Hamlet*.

Folio: (1) A printer's sheet of paper folded once to make two leaves or four pages. (2) An edition of Shakespeare's plays. The First Folio appeared in 1623. Others were published in 1632, 1663 and 1685.

Folk Drama: In the stricter sense, folk drama means the dramatic activities of the ordinary folk, particularly those dramatic events connected with festivals and religious rites. In England, such forms included the sword dance, the St. George play and the mummers' play. The medieval religious drama, though sophisticated in the sense of being based on Scriptural materials, has elements of folk drama, as do such twentieth-century plays as Marc Connelly's *The Green Pastures*.

Folk drama is also extended to include plays written by sophisticated playwrights, but reflecting the customs, language and attitudes of the folk. The plays of J. M. Synge, Lady Gregory and other authors of the Celtic Renaissance are examples.

Folk Epic: See **Epic**.

Folklore: Archaic myths, customs and traditions that have survived until the modern age. Folklore includes legends, stories, riddles, proverbs, nursery rhymes, charms, superstitions, popular ballads and customs dealing with birth, marriage and death.

Elements from folklore are an important part of literature. Some knowledge of the formulas and conventions of folklore is a useful background for understanding many works of fiction, poetry and drama.

Folk Song: A song that originated among the common people and has been transmitted, usually orally, from one generation to the next. Ballads, sea chanties and carols are forms of folk songs. (Each of these is defined in this dictionary.)

Songs that have become very well known are also sometimes categorized as folk songs. An example is *Over There*, from World War I.

Foot: In verse or prose, a measure or unit of rhythm consisting of a definite pattern. The four most common patterns are the iambus (u−), trochee (−u), anapest (uu−) and dactyl (−uu). Each of these is defined in this dictionary.

Foreshadowing: An indication of events that are to come. In fiction and drama, hints of forthcoming events prepare the reader or spectator for the eventual outcome of the action.

Foreword: An introduction to a book. A foreword is similar to a preface but usually is written by someone other than the author of the main work. (See **Preface**.)

Forgeries, Literary: See **Literary Forgeries**.

Form: The shape and structure of a work, as opposed to its content or substance. Identifying a written composition as poetry or prose is one step in the analysis of its form. Further analysis might identify the style in which it is written (formal, informal, etc.) and the category into which the work falls (the sonnet, essay, ode, novel, short story, etc.).

Formal Criticism: Criticism that examines a work of art in terms of the characteristics of the type or genre to which the work belongs. (See **Criticism**.)

Formal Essay: A serious, dignified and logically organized essay, written to inform or persuade. (See **Essay**.)

Format: The physical elements of a book, including the size, shape, binding, paper, print and general arrangement.

Four Senses of Interpretation: The levels frequently used in interpreting Scriptural and allegorical literature: the literal, the allegorical, the moral and the anagogical (that is, spiritual or mystical).

Fourteener: A verse form consisting of fourteen syllables arranged in iambic feet. The form is rarely used today.
    The second of the following lines, written by Henry Howard, Earl of Surrey (1517-1547), is a fourteener.

> Such wayward ways hath love, that most part in discord,
> Our wills do stand, whereby our hearts but seldom doth accord.

Frame Story: A story within a narrative setting or frame; a story within a story. Examples are *The Arabian Nights*, *The Decameron* and *The Canterbury Tales*.

Free Verse: Often called *vers libre* or polyrhythmic verse, free verse is distinguished by an irregular metrical pattern and the use of cadence, rather than uniform metrical feet. In conventional verse, the unit is the foot or the line; in free verse, the unit is the stanza or strophe.

Although many modern poets write in free verse, the form is not new to the nineteenth and twentieth centuries. The Biblical Psalms and the *Song of Solomon* are in free verse.

French Forms: Certain prescribed verse patterns that originated in France during the time of the troubadours. Among the French forms are: ballade, chant royal, pantoum, rondeau, rondel, roundel, sestina, triolet and villanelle. These terms are defined in this dictionary.

Freytag's Pyramid: Gustav Freytag (1816-1895), a German critic, analyzed the construction of the conventional five-act play as follows: introduction or exposition, arising from an inciting moment; complication or rising action; climax (at the peak of the pyramid); reversal or falling action; denouement; moment of last suspense. (See **Epitasis**.)

Fundamental Image: The central or controlling conception around which a description is written. When describing a complicated scene, a writer may select some important aspect or feature and shape the details of the description around it. This central unifying feature is the fundamental image.

Fustian: Referring to thick cotton cloth, the term has also come to mean bombastic or overly ornate language.

G

Gaelic Movement: The movement that began in the late nineteenth century and that was aimed at the preservation of the Gaelic language. The Gaelic Movement attempted to foster the production of a new native Irish literature in Gaelic. It was overshadowed by the Irish Literary Movement, however, which encouraged the use of English in creating a new Irish literature that used Irish materials. (See **Celtic Renaissance**.)

Gallicism: A word, phrase or idiom characteristic of the French language; a custom or turn of thought suggestive of the French people. The term is also applied to French words or phrases adopted and used by English-speaking people. Examples are *raison d'être* and *coup d'état*.

Gasconade: Since the natives of Gascony, France, were considered inveterate boasters, gasconade came to be used to mean bravado or boastful talk. Boastfully vain fiction may be called gasconade.

Gazette: (1) A newspaper. (2) An official government publication containing lists of promotions, appointments, etc. The first English newspaper, published in 1665, was the *Oxford Gazette*, which later became the *London Gazette*. The name is derived from an Italian coin, the *gazzetta*, the price for which the first Italian newspaper was sold.

Genre: A type or category into which literary works can be grouped according to form, technique or purpose. Comedy, epic, lyric, novel and tragedy are literary genres.

Genteel Comedy: A term employed by Addison to characterize such early eighteenth-century comedy as Cibber's *The Careless Husband*. This comedy was a continuation of the Restoration comedy of manners, adapted to the polite, genteel manners of the age of Queen Anne. Compared with Restoration comedy, the moral tone was higher, the motives of the characters more artificial, the wit less brilliant and the general atmosphere somewhat sentimental.

Georgian: Pertaining to the reigns of the four Georges (1714-1830). In this sense, the romantic poets from Wordsworth to Keats have been called Georgians. A group of minor poets, including Thomas Lovell Beddoes and Thomas Hood, are sometimes known as the second Georgian school. They are considered to represent a transition from the romantic to the Victorian poets. From 1911 to 1922, four anthologies of verse were published, entitled *Georgian Poetry*. Georgian here referred to the reign of George V, who came to the throne in

1910. W. W. Gibson, Rupert Brooke and John Masefield were among the poets included.

Georgic: A poem about rustic life. For example, the *Georgics* of Virgil.

Gest: An old word occasionally found in English, especially in literary titles from the medieval period, meaning a tale of war or adventure, as *The Gest Historiale of the Destruction of Troy* (fourteenth century.) The corresponding Latin word appears in a somewhat similar sense in the title of the collection of stories written about 1250, *The Gesta Romanorum* (the deeds of the Romans).

Gestalt: In literary criticism, a term used to denote the unified whole (or organic unity) of a literary work. Gestalt, from German, meaning "form," "figure" or "shape," is usually used in connection with psychology to refer to the total structure or pattern of various acts, experiences and perceptions.

Ghost Writer: One who does any kind of writing that is published under the name of another. Businessmen, artists, athletes — almost anyone who is in the public eye — often allow their names to be attached to articles and stories, relating to their special fields, written by journalists employed for the purpose.

Gift Book: A literary collection, published under a sentimental title, intended primarily for a souvenir gift or keepsake. Containing collections of work from different writers, gift books are aimed at the "refined" reader of elegant taste, rather than at those readers seeking intellectual excellence.

Gleeman: A musical entertainer among the Anglo-Saxons. Usually, gleemen were travelling professionals who recited poetry (especially stories) composed by others, though some gleemen were original poets. (See **Scop.**)

Gloss: An explanation, often as a marginal note. Greek manuscripts were glossed by Latin copyists, who gave a marginal or interlinear Latin word equivalent to the difficult Greek expression. Similar bilingual glosses were inserted in medieval manuscripts by scribes who used words in their vernacular to explain the Latin.

Later, the word came to have a broader use, as in the gloss to Spenser's *Shepheardes Calender* (1579), which undertakes to explain the author's purpose, to supply notes explaining difficult words and to make learned comments. Glosses, collected into lists, became glossaries.

"To gloss over" means to give a deceptive, consciously misleading explanation. For example, *In describing the crime, the thief tried to gloss over his part in it.* "To gloss over" can also mean to give a cursory look or glance. For example, *He was so busy that he only had time to gloss over his notes.*

Glossary: See **Gloss.**

Gnomic Verse (Gnomic): An aphorism, maxim or moral saying in verse form. Gnomic verses were written by the gnomic poets of ancient Greece (sixth century B.C.), who arranged wise sayings in a series of maxims. Later, gnomics formed a considerable portion of Old English literature (in the *Exeter Book* and *Beowulf*, for example). Francis Quarles' *Emblems* (1633) is a well-known collection of gnomics.

Goliardic Verse: Lilting Latin verse, usually satiric, composed by university students and wandering scholars in Germany, France and England in the twelfth and thirteenth centuries. Goliardic verse celebrated wine, women and song, and was marked by irreverent attacks on the church and clergy.

Gongorism: An affected elegance of style exhibited by the Spanish poet, Gongóra y Argote (1561-1627), and imitated by other writers. Gongorism is marked by bombast, complexity, puns, paradoxes, coined words, intricate metaphors and obscurity. Gongoristic elements are found in the works of the English metaphysical poets, especially Richard Crashaw.

Gothic: In architecture, a style marked by the pointed arch and vault, stained-glass windows, slender spires, flying buttresses, intricate traceries and a wealth of detail. The style flourished in Western Europe from the twelfth to the sixteenth centuries.

Eighteenth-century neoclassicists applied the term Gothic to literature, using it as a synonym for barbaric to indicate that which was not classical. The romanticists of the next generation, however, looked with favor upon the Gothic because it suggested the primitive, the wild and the free.

Gothic Romance: A form of novel in which magic, mystery and chivalry are the chief characteristics. Horrors abound, while ghosts, clanking chains and charnel houses impart an atmosphere of uncanny terror. One of the earliest Gothic romances was Horace Walpole's *Castle of Otranto* (1764). Anne Radcliffe's five romances, especially *The Mysteries of Udolpho*, added to the popularity of the form. The later novels of Scott, Charlotte Brontë and others, as well as the mystery and horror types of short stories exploited by Poe and his successors, contain materials and devices that can be traced to the Gothic novel.

Grand Guignol: Plays of a gruesome, sensational nature; the theater in which such plays are performed. Often, the subject of grand guignol is murder or some other act of violence. In the late eighteenth century, Guignol was the name of a French puppet and of the play (similar to the English *Punch and Judy*) in which he was the main character. Later, the Théâtre du Grand Guignol, in Paris, specialized in the presentation of sensational, melodramatic plays.

Graveyard School: The group of eighteenth-century poets who wrote long, gloomy poems on death and immortality. Graveyard poetry was related to early stages of the English romantic movement, reflecting the tendency to cultivate melancholy for its own sake. A forerunner of the school was Thomas Parnell, whose *A Night Piece on Death* (1721) anticipates some of the sentiment of Gray's *Elegy Written in a Country Churchyard* (1751), the most famous poem produced by the group.

Great Awakening, The: See **Awakening, the Great.**

Grub Street (also **Grubstreet** and **Grub-street**): Because struggling writers and literary hacks lived in Grub Street in London, the phrase Grub Street or Grubean has been used disparagingly since the seventeenth century to mean either the writers living there or the qualities that characterized such writers. Pope bitterly attacked Grub Street poets, and Dr. Johnson and Byron, among others, used the term to suggest literary trash.

H

Hadith: From the Arabic, a legend or tradition. More specifically, the term is used for the appendix to the Koran (the sacred book of the Moslems), which contains traditions relating to the prophet, Mohammed.

Hagiography (Hagiology): Literally, "holy writing"; literature dealing with the lives and legends of the saints; the study of saints.

Haiku (sometimes **Hokku):** A Japanese verse form consisting of seventeen syllables in three lines. There are five syllables in the first and third lines; seven in the second. Ezra Pound, Amy Lowell and Conrad Aiken are among the poets who have used the haiku form.

Hamartia: In tragedy, an error of judgment, made as the result of ignorance or human weakness, that contributes to the downfall of the hero. In the *Poetics*, Aristotle said that the ideal tragic hero is one whose misfortune is caused "not by vice and depravity, but by some error [hamartia]." (See **Tragedy**.)

Harangue: A speech, frequently addressed to a crowd, to urge a person or group of persons to action, or to influence attitudes by appealing to the emotions rather than to reason.

Harlequin: (1) In traditional Italian comedy and in pantomime, the lover of Columbine. He is usually masked, wears a costume of varied colors and carries a wooden sword. (2) A mischievous person; a buffoon.

Harlequinade: A play in which a harlequin or buffoon stars. (See **Commedia dell' Arte** and **Pantomime**.)

Harpies: In Greek mythology, winged monsters (half woman, half bird) whose cruelty makes them relentless pursuers and plunderers.

Hartford Wits: A group of Connecticut writers, many of whom were graduates of Yale University, active about the period of the American Revolution. The three most prominent members were Joel Barlow, Timothy Dwight and John Trumbull. These men, as well as being conservative in politics and philosophy, were conservative in their literary style, following Addison and Pope, the two literary leaders of their age.

Headless Line: A line of verse from which an unstressed syllable has been dropped at the beginning. (See **Catalexis** and **Truncation**.)

Head Rhyme: (1) Alliteration. (2) Rhyme at the beginning of lines of verse. (See **Alliteration** and **Rhyme**.)

Hebraism: The attitude toward life that subordinates all other ideals to those of conduct, obedience and ethical purpose. Hebraism is opposed to the Hellenistic conception of life, which subordinates everything to the intellectual. Throughout the centuries, literary discussions have centered on the two conflicting ideals.

Hedge Club: See **Transcendentalism.**

Hedonism: The doctrine that pleasure is the highest good in life and that happiness is a legitimate goal. Herrick's poem *To the Virgins, to make much of Time* expresses hedonistic philosophy.

Hellenism: See **Hebraism.**

Hemistich: A half-line of verse.

Hendecasyllable: A line of verse containing eleven syllables. The first and third lines of the following stanza from Browning's *The Statue and the Bust* are hendecasyllables.

> There's a palace in Florence, the world knows well,
> And a statue watches it from the square,
> And this story of both do our townsmen tell.

Hendiadys: A figure of speech in which one idea is expressed by two nouns and a conjunction. An example is Shakespeare's phrase, "the slings and arrows of outrageous fortune."

Heptameter: A line of verse consisting of seven feet.

Heptastich: A stanza of seven lines.

Heptasyllabic: A verse line with seven syllables.

Hero or Heroine: The central character in a work of fiction; the person of chief interest. In criticism, hero or heroine does not imply a person of moral superiority; it merely indicates the relationship of the character to the plot. The most important character structurally is the hero or heroine; he or she may be a rogue, an escaped convict or a morally depraved person.

Heroic Couplet: Iambic pentameter lines rhymed in pairs. A favorite meter of Chaucer (*The Legend of Good Women* is an example), this verse form did not come into its greatest popularity until the middle of the seventeenth century. Dryden made the form well known and accepted, using it in such plays as *Tyrannick Love* (1669) and *Aureng-Zebe* (1675). With Pope, the heroic couplet became so important that its influence dominated English verse for many years. An example of the heroic couplet occurs in these lines by Pope:

> But when to mischief mortals bend their will,
> How soon they find fit instruments of ill!

Heroic Drama: A type of tragedy and tragicomedy that developed in England during the Restoration period. Heroic drama was characterized by spectacle, violent emotional conflicts in the main characters, extravagant dialogue and exotic setting. Frequently, but not always, the plays were written in heroic couplets. The scenery was elaborate.

The influences that produced the heroic drama were the romantic plays of the Jacobeans, especially those of Beaumont and Fletcher, the development of opera in England and the French court romances that were brought to England by the court of Charles II. Dryden's heroic drama, *Conquest of Granada* (1670), typifies all that is best and worst in the type.

Heroic Quatrain (or Stanza): A stanza composed of two heroic couplets. (See **Heroic Couplet** and **Heroic Verse**.)

Heroic Verse: Poetry composed of iambic pentameter feet and rhymed in line-pairs. (See **Heroic Couplet**.)

Hexameter: A line of six metrical feet. As a classical verse form in Latin or Greek poetry, the term was restricted in a set pattern: six feet, of which the first four were dactyls or spondees, the fifth almost always a dactyl and the sixth a spondee or trochee. True hexameters are scarce in English poetry because of the rarity of actual spondees in the language. (See **Alexandrine**, **Dactyl**, **Feet**, **Spondee** and **Trochee**.)

Hexastich: A stanza containing six lines. (See **Sestet**, **Sestina**, **Sexain** and **Sonnet**.)

Hiatus: A pause or break between two vowel sounds not separated by a consonant. It is the opposite of elision, which involves the sliding over of one of the vowels. A hiatus occurs only when, in a break between two words, the final vowel of the first and the initial vowel of the second are each carefully enunciated. For example, *pre-eminent*. (Compare with **Elision**.)

In logic, hiatus signifies the omission of a logical step in the process of reasoning.

High Comedy: Pure or serious comedy, as contrasted with low comedy. High comedy appeals to the mind and arouses thoughtful laughter by exhibiting the inconsistencies and incongruities of human nature and the follies of social manners. The purpose is not consciously moralistic, though serious purpose is often implicit in the satire frequently present in high comedy. The true enjoyment of high comedy demands a certain intellectual effort and philosophic detachment on the part of the audience.

In neoclassical times, a criterion for high comedy was its appeal to and reflection of the "higher" social class and its observance of decorum, as illustrated in Congreve's plays. In a broader sense, the term is applied to some of Shakespeare's plays (e.g., *As You Like It*), and to G. B. Shaw's comedies. (See **Comedy, Comedy of Humours, Comedy of Manners, Low Comedy** and **Realistic Comedy**.)

Historical Fiction: See **Fiction** and **Historical Novel**.

Historical Novel: A novel in which the characters, setting and action are based on the records of a locality, a nation or a people. Although history has always been used in fiction, the historical novel, as such, did not appear until well into the eighteenth century. Among the well-known writers of historical novels are Sir Walter Scott, William Makepeace Thackeray and Charles Reade.

History Play: See **Chronicle Play**.

Hold: A rest or pause on a syllable to compensate for a previous omission in a line of verse.

Holograph: A document, such as the original manuscript of a literary work, wholly written by the author.

Holy Grail: The cup from which Christ is said to have drunk at the Last Supper and which was used to catch his blood at the Crucifixion. The Grail became the center of a tradition of Christian mysticism, and was linked with Arthurian romance as an object for which Arthur's knights searched. (See **Arthurian Legend**.)

Homeric Epithet: See **Epithet**.

Homeric Simile: A long extended simile such as characterizes Homer's *Iliad* and *Odyssey*, and is sometimes found in other works, especially epics. (See **Simile**.)

Homily: A sermon; a serious moral talk or written work.

Homograph: A word that has the same spelling as another, but a different meaning, origin and sound. An example is lead (the first place) and lead (the metal).

Homonym: A word that has the same pronunciation as another word, but a different meaning. Examples are *bear* and *bare*.

Homophone: A letter or syllable having the same sound as another. The letters *c* and *s* are homophones in the word *cyst*.

Horatian Ode: An ode, such as Keats' *Ode to a Nightingale*, in which each stanza follows the same metrical pattern. The name comes from the Roman poet, Horace.

Hornbook: A kind of primer used in the sixteenth, seventeenth and eighteenth centuries. On a sheet of vellum or paper were printed the alphabet, combinations of consonants and vowels commonly used in making up syllables, the Lord's Prayer and a list of Roman numerals. The sheet was mounted on wood and covered, for protection, by transparent horn.

In literature, *The Gull's Hornbook* by Thomas Dekker is an amusing and satirical primer of instructions for the young dandy of early seventeenth-century London.

Hovering Accent: This occurs when it is difficult to determine which of two consecutive syllables in a line of verse is to be stressed. Also called distributed stress, this may result from the poet's clumsiness, or it may be introduced intentionally to achieve certain effects.

Hubris: Pride; supreme overconfidence. In tragedy, the hero, because of an error of judgment (see **Hamartia**), becomes overly confident. Blinded by this confidence and pride (hubris), he plunges to disaster. Macbeth's soaring ambition and confidence in the prophecy that, "none of woman born can harm Macbeth," is an example of hubris.

Hudibrastic Verse: The octosyllabic couplet as adapted by Samuel Butler in his satiric poem, *Hudibras*. In this long poem (published between 1663 and 1678), Butler satirized the Puritans of England. Hudibras was marked by humor, elements of burlesque, a mock-heroic form and satiric epigram. The term is now used to characterize any verse written in this manner.

Huitain: A complete poem of eight lines.

Humanism: A philosophy that stresses the importance of human interests, rather than the supernatural or divine. More specifically, humanism involves the study of human culture — in particular, the life, thought, language and literature of ancient Greece and Rome.

In literary history, the term humanism designates the revival of classical culture that accompanied the Renaissance. The Renaissance humanists asserted the dignity of man and the importance of the worldly life, as opposed to medieval thinkers who looked on the present life as primarily a preparation for an eternal life after death.

Renaissance humanism developed during the fourteenth and fifteenth centuries in Italy. It spread to other Continental countries and finally to England. Unlike some Continental humanists, the English group retained their Christian faith, attempting to fuse the best of classical culture with Christianity. Much Renaissance literature, particularly the poetry of Spenser and Milton, illustrates this fusion.

A later phase of humanistic activity was literary criticism. In general, humanistic criticism upheld the classical values of dignity, grace, restraint and form.

Humanitarian Novel, The: See **Sociological Novel.**

Humor: See **Wit and Humor.**

Humours: According to Hippocratic theories of physiology, the four chief liquids ("humours") in the human body were blood, phlegm, yellow bile (choler) and black bile (melancholy). These liquids were closely allied with the four elements. Blood, like air, was hot and moist; yellow bile, like fire, was hot and dry; phlegm, like water, was cold and moist; black bile, like earth, was cold and dry. An individual's personal characteristics were explained by the state of his humours. The sanguine man was joyful and amorous; the phlegmatic man was dull and cowardly; the choleric man was impatient and obstinate; the melancholic man was thoughtful and sentimental. A disordered state of the humours produced more exaggerated characteristics.

In creating characters, Elizabethan writers drew on this theory of the humours. Humour came to mean disposition, then mood or characteristic peculiarity and, later, folly or affectation. (See **Comedy of Humours.**)

Hybrid: A word composed of parts from more than one language, e.g., *starvation* (English and Latin).

Hymeneal: A wedding song or poem (e.g., Spenser's *Epithalamion*). So called after Hymen, the ancient Greek god of marriage. Characteristic of the genre were joyous verses invoking the spirit of Hymen.

Hymn: A lyric poem or musical composition expressing religious emotion and usually intended to be sung by a chorus. Originally, the term referred to almost any song in praise of gods or famous men. The twelfth and thirteenth centuries saw the greatest development of Latin hymns (for example, *Dies Irae*). Among the well-known English hymn writers were Wesley, Cowper, Watts and Newman.

Hypellage: A figure of speech in which a descriptive adjective is transferred from the noun to which it naturally belongs to another noun. For example, hypellage occurs in the sentence, *Paul passed a sleepless night.* The night was not sleepless; Paul was.
Hypellage is also called transferred epithet.

Hyperbaton: The transposition of words from their usual order to achieve emphasis, as in *Crashed the waves against the shore.*

Hyperbole: A figure of speech based on exaggeration, as in *rivers of blood.* Hyperbole can be an effective device for securing attention, giving emphasis or creating a poetic effect.

Hypercatalectic: See **Hypermetric.**

Hypermetric: A line of verse that has an extra, unaccented syllable at the end. Such a line is also called hypercatalectic. The second of the following lines is hypermetric:

Yĕs, I'm | ĭn lōve, | Ĭ fēel | ĭt nōw,
And Cē | lĭa hās | ŭndōne | mĕ.

WILLIAM WHITEHEAD

(See **Feminine Ending.**)

Hypocorism: Use of a pet name or term of endearment, e.g., *Susie, sweetie pie.*

Hysteron Proteron: A figure of speech in which the element that should logically come at the end is put at the beginning. The term is also used to refer to the logical fallacy of assuming as a premise something that follows from what is to be proved.

I

Iambus (Iamb): A metrical foot consisting of an unaccented syllable (υ) and an accented syllable (−). Iambus is the most common metrical measure in English verse. This line from Marlowe is an illustration:

Cŏme līve | wĭth mē | ănd bē | mŭy lōve.

ibid. or **ib.:** In the same place, an abbreviation of the Latin word *ibidem.* The abbreviation is used in footnotes to refer to the book, article, periodical, etc. that has been mentioned in the preceding footnote.

Icon (or **Ikon**): A sacred picture or image of Christ, an angel or a saint.

Ictus: Accent; the stress given to certain syllables in poetry. In an iambic foot (υ −), the ictus (or accent) is on the second syllable. The unaccented syllable is called the thesis; the accented syllable is called the arsis. The ictus (accent) of an iambic foot falls on the second syllable, which is, therefore, the arsis. (See **Arsis.**)

Idiom: A use of words or a grammatical construction peculiar to a certain language. In English, for example, *carry out* literally means to bear something away (out of a room, perhaps). Idiomatically, it means to see that something is done, as in *carry out a command.*

Idyll: Primarily, a poem marked by pastoral, descriptive and narrative qualities. Whittier's *Maud Muller* is an example. The term is historically associated with the Greek poet, Theocritus (third century B.C.), who wrote short idylls about the simple, rustic life in Sicily.

Derived from the Greek, meaning "little picture," the term is also applied to longer descriptive poems, such as Tennyson's *Idylls of the King*, in which each idyll is a "little picture," describing an incident in the Arthurian legend.

In addition, a piece of prose with qualities of pastoral simplicity can be termed an idyll.

i.e.: That is (in Latin, *id est*).

Illusion: A false impression or belief; a false perception; an apparition or phantom.

Image: An image is a literal and concrete representation of a sensory experience or of an object that can be known by one or more of the senses. The image is one of the distinctive elements of the "language of art," the means by which experience is often communicated.

Images are used in literature and art to give meaning, not merely to decorate.

Imagery: The use of figurative language to enrich poetry or prose. Imagery conveys word pictures. Imagery evokes an imaginative, emotional response, as well as providing a vivid, specific description. Compare, for example, *What you are saying is unpleasant for me to hear*, with *"These words are razors to my wounded heart."* (Shakespeare, *Titus Adronicus*.) The first is fact, unimaginatively stated. The second expresses the same idea figuratively. (See **Figurative Language.**)

Imagination and Fancy: Until the early nineteenth century, the terms imagination and fancy were used almost synonymously. The romantic poets, however, thought of imagination as a unifying power that enabled the poet to see inner relationships, such as the identity of truth and beauty. In *Biographia Literaria*, Coleridge speculated that fancy and imagination were two distinct faculties. Imagination, he said, "struggles to idealize and to unify," while fancy is "a mode of memory emancipated from time and space." British critic, Leslie Stephen, stated (1879) that "fancy deals with the superficial resemblances, and imagination with the deeper truths that underlie them."

Imagists: A group of poets who became prominent in the United States about 1912-1914. Among the well-known imagists were Amy Lowell, Robert Frost, John Gould Fletcher, Carl Sandburg and "H.D." According to Amy Lowell (*Tendencies in Modern American Poetry*, 1917), the major objectives of the imagists were: (1) to use the language of common speech, but to employ always the exact word; (2) to avoid all clichés; (3) to create new rhythms as the expressions of a new mood; (4) to allow absolute freedom in the choice of subject; (5) to present an image (that is, to be concrete, firm and definite); (6) to strive always for concentration; and (7) to suggest, rather than to offer complete statements.

An example of imagist technique occurs in these lines by Amy Lowell:

The sight of a white church above thin trees in a city square
Amazes my eyes as though it were the Parthenon.

Imitation: In literary criticism, a term used to mean: (1) imitating the literary work of another writer; (2) representing or reproducing that which exists in life. Aristotle, at the beginning of his *Poetics*, said that all art is a form of imitation.

For many centuries, designing literary works based on classical models was an esteemed practice. However, with the romantic movement, this method of producing literature came to be regarded as inferior and, gradually, the term imitation yielded to such terms as a "realistic" or "naturalistic" portrayal of man and the universe. (See **Plagiarism**.)

Impression: See **Edition**.

Impressionism: In literature, a highly personal manner of writing in which characters and scenes are portrayed as they appear to the writer, rather than as they actually are. The term is borrowed from art. By the middle of the nineteenth century, the impressionist painters, including Manet, Monet, Cezanne, Renoir and Pissarro, rebelled against conventional conceptions of art. They held that it was more important to portray the impressions an object made on the artist than to reproduce it precisely as it appears. Literary impressionists present their material not as it appears to the realist, but as it is seen or felt by the writer. An example of impressionistic technique in literature is Virginia Woolf's *The Waves*. (See **Expressionism**.)

Imprint: (1) The name of the publisher, copyright, place and date of publication of a book, usually placed at the bottom or the back of the title page. (2) The printer's name on any printed matter.

Impropriety: See **Solecism**.

Incident: See **Episode**.

Incremental Repetition: A rhetorical device widely used in ballads. The repetition advances the story by successive changes of a single phrase or line.

Incremental repetition occurs in the first and second lines of these stanzas from *Sir Patrick Spens*:

O lang, lang may their ladies sit,
Wi thair fans into their hand,
Or eir they se Sir Patrick Spens
Cum sailing to the land.

O lang, lang may the ladies stand
Wi thair gold kems in their hair
Waiting for thair ain deir lords,
For they'll see thame na mair.

Incunabulum: A term applied to any book printed before 1500. From a historical and literary point of view, incunabula are interesting because they reflect the intellectual and literary interests of the late fifteenth century. Among famous incunabula are Caxton's edition of Chaucer's *The Canterbury Tales* and Malory's *Le Morte d'Arthur*.

Induction: An old word for introduction; in literary work, a preamble or prologue. In the sixteenth century, the term sometimes denoted a framework introduction. Shakespeare, in *The Taming of the Shrew*, provides an induction, in which a drunken tinker is persuaded that he is a lord for whose amusement a play is performed; the play is *The Taming of the Shrew*.

Industrial Revolution: During the last quarter of the eighteenth and the first quarter of the nineteenth century, England was transformed from a predominantly agricultural to an industrial nation. Invention, scientific discovery and changing economic, political and social ideals all contributed to and were influenced by the Industrial Revolution.

During the period, agriculture was all but abandoned, and home work gave way to factory work. Transportation facilities — roads, canals and railroads — increased. The invention of the spinning jenny, the power loom and the steam engine revolutionized English life and the sweatshop was born.

Contemporary writers showed deep concern for the effects of this revolution. Charles Dickens' novels focussed on the plight of the poor in London. Ruskin and Carlyle sought to point the way to reform. In his *Essays*, Arnold condemned England for measuring her greatness by her wealth and numbers. Social and political problems were seriously considered by writers such as John Stuart Mill, Jeremy Bentham, Robert Owen and Thomas Malthus. The changes brought about by the Industrial Revolution were reflected in the literature of the period.

Infinitive: See **Split Infinitive.**

Inflection: (1) A variation in the form of a word to indicate its grammatical function. The endings of inflected nouns may indicate number, gender and case; the endings of inflected verbs may indicate person, tense and mood. Unlike Latin and Greek, the English language has few inflections. Examples are pronouns such as *who* (nominative case) and *whom* (objective case), and comparisons such as *sweet* (positive degree), *sweeter* (comparative degree) and *sweetest* (superlative degree). (2) Change in the tone or pitch of the voice.

Informal Essay: As compared to the formal essay, the informal essay is less serious in purpose, easier in style and structure, more personal and written to please and entertain, rather than to instruct. Lamb's *A Dissertation on Roast Pig* is an example. (See **Essay.**)

Inkhornism (or **Inkhorn Term**): A bookish, pedantic or bombastic expression, usually borrowed from a foreign language. The term was coined by Thomas Wilson, in his *Arte of Rhetorique* (1553).

In Media Res: A Latin phrase meaning "in the middle of things," used to describe a piece of fiction that begins at a crucial point in the action. For some time, it was the conventional method of opening an epic. Milton's *Paradise Lost* is an example in English literature.

Inns of Court: The four voluntary, unchartered societies or legal guilds in London that have the privilege of admitting persons to the bar. The societies are named according to the buildings they have occupied since the fourteenth century: the Inner Temple, the Middle Temple, Lincoln's Inn and Gray's Inn. In late medieval times they were law schools. During the sixteenth and seventeenth centuries, they became cultural centers, as well as educational institutions.

Regular drama, masques and interludes were nurtured by the Inns. Shakespeare's *Comedy of Errors* was acted before the fellows of Gray's Inn during the Christmas season of 1594. Many English writers received their education, in whole or in part, in the Inns of Court. Chaucer may have belonged to one; Francis Bacon was admitted to law practice from Gray's Inn; and Thomas Shadwell and Nicholas Rowe were members of the Inner Temple. Dickens was living in one of the old buildings of Lincoln's Inn when he published *The Pickwick Papers*.

Innuendo: An oblique or indirect suggestion, often with a sinister or derogatory connotation. The device is frequently used in satire. The following lines from Swift's *Stella's Birthday* contain innuendo:

> Pursue your trade of scandal picking,
> Your innuendoes, when you tell us
> That Stella loves to talk with fellows.

Intentional Fallacy: In contemporary criticism, a term used to describe the error of judging the success and the meaning of a work of art by the author's expressed intention in producing it.

Intercalary Chapter: See **Interchapter.**

Interchapter: In literature, a chapter that provides the physical, social, political and historical background for the action of the story. Usually, interchapters, also called intercalary chapters, are fairly short, and often present the author's personal feelings on an important theme included in the work. For example, there are numerous interchapters in *The Grapes of Wrath*, by John Steinbeck.

Interior Monologue: A technique used in the stream of consciousness narrative in which a character's thoughts, impressions and associations are presented just as they flow through his mind. These inner thoughts may appear to be incoherent and unrelated. Molly Bloom's long interior monologue at the end of James Joyce's *Ulysses* is an example. (See **Stream of Consciousness Novel.**)

Interlude: A brief, witty play presented in the interval of a dramatic performance or entertainment. In England, interludes were particularly popular in the sixteenth century and made an important contribution to the development of realistic comedy.

Some interludes imitated French farce, while others were allegorical and moralistic. Among the best-known interludes were those of John Heywood, produced in the 1520s and 1530s. These include *The Four P's* and *The Merry Play of John John the Husband, Tyb his Wife*, and *Sir John the Priest*.

Internal Rhyme: See **Leonine Rhyme** and **Rhyme.**

Intonation: Cadence; variations in tone and sound produced by alternating accented syllables with unaccented syllables and by interrupting sound with pauses. The result is a rhythmic pattern of rising and falling verbal melody.

Intrigue Comedy: See **Comedy of Situation.**

Introduction: The opening sentences or paragraphs of a piece of writing; an essay printed at the beginning of a book to explain the author's chief ideas, purposes, hopes and disillusions regarding the book he has written. The term is also used for a more or less elementary book or essay, which prepares the reader for a more elaborate study, e.g., *An Introduction to Philosophy*.

Invective: Harsh, abusive language, used to denounce a person, cause or situation. Swift used invective in *Gulliver's Travels*, and qualities of invective are also found in Shakespeare's plays (e.g., *King Lear*, Act II, Scene 2; Act IV, Scene 1), Pope's *Epistle to Arbuthnot* and Dryden's *Absalom and Achitophel*.

Invention: Originality in thought, style, diction, imagery or plot. Renaissance and neoclassical critics used the term to mean the discovery of literary material as something to be imitated or represented. (In Latin rhetoric, invention means the "finding" of material.) Modern critics use the word to describe a quality of originality in thought and expression.

Inversion: Changing the normal word order in a sentence to gain emphasis or effect. For example, the usual word order for the following lines would be: *I saw a damsel with a dulcimer*. Coleridge writes:

> A damsel with a dulcimer
> In a vision once I saw.

Invocation: An address appealing to a deity or muse for aid. In classical literature and epics, the invocation, usually at the beginning of the work, was a literary convention. Milton, in *Paradise Lost*, follows the tradition, but instead of invoking the assistance of a muse of poetry, he addressed the

> Heavenly Muse, that, on the secret top
> Of Oreb, or of Sinai, didst inspire
> That shepherd who first taught the chosen seed
> In the beginning how the heavens and earth
> Rose out of Chaos:

Ionic: A classical foot of four syllables, in which the first two are long and the last two are short (the greater ionic), or the first two are short and the last two are long (the lesser ionic).

Ipse Dixit: Any dogmatic statement. Literally, the Latin means "he himself has said." The term is used, therefore, to characterize any edict or brief statement emphatically uttered.

Irish Literary Movement, Irish Literary Revival and **Irish Renaissance:** Variant terms for the movement that encouraged the production of Anglo-Irish Literature. (See **Celtic Renaissance**.)

Irony: A form of speech in which the actual intent is expressed in words that carry the opposite meaning. In Shakespeare's *Julius Caesar*, Antony's insistence, during his oration over the dead Caesar, that "Brutus is an honorable man" is an example of irony. Characteristically, irony uses words of praise to imply blame, and words of blame to imply praise. Oliver Goldsmith, Jane Austen and William Makepeace Thackeray frequently used irony. However, Jonathan Swift's *Modest Proposal for Preventing the Children of Poor People in Ireland from Being a Burden to their Parents* is perhaps the most sustained piece of ironic writing in English literature. (See **Dramatic Irony**.)

Issue: See **Edition.**

Italian Sonnet: See **Sonnet.**

Ivory Tower: A phrase suggesting the detachment and aloofness of the artist, philosopher, leader, etc. from the mundane preoccupations of the rest of mankind.

J

Jacobean: Derived from Jacobus (Latin for "James"), and meaning that which is characteristic of or took place during the reign of James I (1603-1625). Early Jacobean literature was a further development of Elizabethan literature. Shakespeare's later work, as well as most of Bacon's, Jonson's and Donne's was written in Jacobean times. Later Jacobean literature shows the new attitudes characteristic of Caroline literature. (See **Caroline.**)

Jargon: Confused, meaningless speech. Jargon can result from the mingling of several languages or dialects. Sometimes the term refers to nonsense or gibberish. Most frequently, however, the term is applied to the special language of a group or profession. Educators, computer specialists, lawyers and sociologists, among others, have their own jargon.

Jeremiad: Writing or speech with a tone of woeful complaint; a mournful lamentation. The term is derived from the Biblical *Lamentations of Jeremiah.*

Jestbook: A collection of humorous, witty or satirical anecdotes and jokes. Jestbooks were popular in England and Europe during and after the sixteenth century. The jests were usually short and characterized by ribaldry, satire and cynicism. The earliest English jestbook was *A Hundred Merry Tales* (ca. 1526). Another well-known jestbook was *The Gests of Skoggan* (ca. 1565), in which the jokes were clustered about one person. In the seventeenth and eighteenth centuries, similar jestbooks on Ben Jonson appeared.

Jester: A jest is a joke, and a jester is a person who mocks or makes fun of persons or situations. In the Middle Ages, jesters were often part of the court, and a king might have a favorite jester to amuse him.

Jesuits: Members of the Society of Jesus, a Roman Catholic religious order founded by Saint Ignatius Loyola in 1534. The Jesuits acted as a band of spiritual soldiers, living under strict military discipline and bound by vows of poverty, chastity and obedience. They became well-known as teachers and attempted to raise the educational, as well as the spiritual, standards of the clergy. They were also widely known as missionaries. Kingsley's *Westward Ho* (1885) is an unfavorable presentation of the Jesuits' political activities during the late sixteenth century. A favorable view of the Jesuits during that same period is presented in R. H. Benson's *Come Rack! Come Rope!* (1912). Jesuit poets include Robert Southwell (1561-1595), whose *Saint Peter's Complaint* and short poems, such as *The Burning Babe*, anticipate both the seriousness of Milton and the conceits used by Donne.

Jeu d'Esprit: A witty playing with words; a brief piece of writing marked by cleverness and humor. Oscar Wilde was skilled in this type of writing.

Jig: A non-literary, farcical dramatic performance during which the words were sung to the accompaniment of dancing. Jigs were popular on the Elizabethan stage and were often used as afterpieces. "He's for a jig, or a tale of bawdry," Hamlet says of Polonius in Shakespeare's *Hamlet*. (See **Droll**.)

Johnson's Circle: See **Literary Club**.

Jongleur: A French term for a professional musical entertainer of medieval times, similar to the Anglo-Saxon gleeman and the later minstrel. Though primarily one who sang or recited the lyrics, ballads and stories written by others, the *jongleur* sometimes made up his own composition and sometimes supplied non-musical forms of entertainment, such as juggling and tumbling. The transmission of literary forms and materials from nation to nation during the Middle Ages was due partly to the activities of the *jongleur* and the minstrel.

Journal: (1) A magazine or periodical. (2) A daily record of events and, often, of personal impressions of these events. Defoe's *A Journal of the Plague Year* (1722) is a fictional narrative in the form of a journal.

Juvenilia: Works done in one's youth. Byron's *Hours of Idleness* (1807), for example, was published when Byron was nineteen. The book was originally called *Juvenilia*.

K

Kabuki: A form of Japanese drama similar to an operetta. The kabuki plays are based on popular myths and legends and are usually presented on a revolving stage. Scenery, costumes and make-up are elaborate. The kabuki is a popular form of drama, as compared to the formal, stylized conventions of the Japanese Nō drama. (See **Nō Drama.**)

Kailyard School: A group of Scottish writers whose work dealt idealistically with ordinary people in Scottish villages. Dialect was an important element in their writing. The school was popular toward the end of the nineteenth century and included such writers as J. M. Barrie and "Ian Maclaren" (pen name of John Watson). Kailyard is also a Scottish term for a cabbage garden.

Katharsis: See **Catharsis.**

Kenning: A figurative phrase used in Old English and other Germanic languages as a synonym for a simple noun. Kennings are often picturesque metaphorical compounds. In *Beowulf*, for example, a ship is "the bent-necked wood," "the ringed prow"; the sea is "the swan-road" and "the whale-road"; the dragon is "the twilight-spoiler"; and the queen is "the peace-bringer among nations."

King's English, The: Correct English. One who speaks the King's English speaks the form of the language regarded as being the best and purest. The Queen's English is sometimes used with the same meaning.

Knickerbocker School: A group of writers who, during the first quarter of the nineteenth century, wrote in and about New York State. At that time, New York City was forging ahead of Boston as a center of activity and population in the United States. The name Knickerbocker was made famous by Washington Irving in his *Knickerbocker's History of New York* (1809). The group's association was one of geography and chance, rather than of common purpose. In addition to Washington Irving, well-known members of the school included James Fenimore Cooper and William Cullen Bryant.

Koran: The sacred book of the Moslems. According to Moslem beliefs, the text was revealed to Mohammed from time to time over a period of years. After many changes and much editing, an official transcription was prepared after the prophet's death (A.D. 632). As well as theology, the Koran presents moral teaching, liturgical directions and advice about religious conduct and ceremonials.

Künstlerroman: A novel that traces the story of an artist or the development of the artistic consciousness; from the German, meaning "artist story." Examples are Mann's *Death in Venice* and Joyce's *A Portrait of the Artist as a Young Man*. (See **Bildungsroman**.)

L

Lai: See **Lay**.

Lake School: A name used to characterize Coleridge, Wordsworth and Southey, who, at the beginning of the nineteenth century, were living in the Lake District in England. The *Edinburgh Review* used the term "lakers" in a derogatory way to describe the work of these poets. There was no "school" in the sense of the three poets working for common objectives, although Coleridge and Wordsworth shared certain convictions. In general, they advocated a return to the simple life of nature. (See **Romanticism**.)

Lament: An expression of grief or sorrow; a mourning song or ballad. *Deor's Lament*, an early Anglo-Saxon poem, for example, presents the plaintive regret of the scop (a court poet) after a rival has usurped his place in the esteem of a patron. The separate tragedies in such collections as the sixteenth-century *Mirror for Magistrates*, in which ghosts tell the stories of their fall from fortune during life, were also called laments. (See **Complaint**.)

Lampoon: A piece of writing that ridicules and satirizes a person, group or institution in a malicious or abusive way. *The National Lampoon*, a publication produced originally by students at Harvard University, is a modern example.

Latinism: A word, phrase or grammatical construction based on a Latin model. Often, Latinisms are somewhat more formal than words of Anglo-Saxon origin. *Liberate*, for example, is a Latinism; *free* is derived from an Old English word.

Laureate: See **Poet Laureate**.

Lay (Lai): A song or short narrative poem. The earliest existing French *lais* were composed in the twelfth century and were based on earlier verse tales sung by Breton minstrels. They were, therefore, called Breton *lais*. The prevailing verse form of the early French *lais* was the eight-syllable line and rhyming couplets. Later, French *lais* developed more complicated metrical forms.

The word lay was applied to English poems written during the fourteenth century in imitation of the Breton *lais*. Although a few of them were in couplets, the tail-rhyme stanza was more frequently used. (See **Tail-rhyme Stanza**.) English poets called almost any short narrative poem similar to the French *lai* a Breton *lay*. Some of the best known are the *Lay of Launfal*, *Sir Orfeo* and Chaucer's *The Franklin's Tale*.

Since the sixteenth century, lay has been used by English writers as synonymous with song. In the early nineteenth century, lay sometimes meant a short historical ballad, such as Scott's *Lay of the Last Minstrel* and Macaulay's *Lays of Ancient Rome*.

Leaf: A sheet of paper; each side of a leaf is called a page.

Legend: A narrative or tradition handed down from the past. A legend is distinguished from a myth in that the legend has more historical truth and less of a supernatural element. King Arthur, for example, is a legendary figure.

Saints' legends are narratives of the lives of the early church heroes. Chaucer's *Legend of Good Women* is an example.

Legend is also used for any brief explanatory comment accompanying paintings, maps, etc.

Legitimate Theater: Drama acted on the stage, as opposed to theatrical performances that include songs, dancing or musical accompaniment. The term is also used to distinguish plays from motion pictures.

The term arose because an early licensing act in England restricted dramatic performances to a few theaters. (See **Patent Theaters**.) The law could be evaded by the production of plays with music or musical interludes.

Leich: A lyric form very popular in Germany during the thirteenth century. It is distinguished by the number of unequal stanzas it employs.

Leitmotif: In literary criticism, a term used for a recurring theme within a book or a theme frequently used by a particular writer. The word is derived from the German *leitmotiv*, meaning "leading motive."

Leonine Rhyme: A form of internal rhyme in which the syllable at the end of a line of verse rhymes with the syllable preceding the caesura. The form is reputedly derived from the name of a writer of the Middle Ages, Leoninus, canon of St. Victor's in Paris, who wrote elegiac verses containing this kind of internal rhyme. An example of Leonine is italicized in the following line:

Ex rex Ed*vardus*, debacchans ut Leo*pardus*.

Tennyson used the form in *The Revenge*. Leonine rhyme is also called internal rhyme.

Letter Press: Used to distinguish the reading matter, or the text of a book, from the illustrative matter. This use of the term may have originated from the fact that, formerly in printing, the letter press printed directly from type instead of from the plates, woodcuts or blocks used for illustrations. The term is also employed to refer to the typography of a work or to printing in a general sense.

Letters: A general name sometimes given to literature. (See **Belles Lettres**.) More specifically, the classification refers to correspondence exchanged between acquaintances, friends or commercial firms. A sizable body of informal literature is preserved through collections of letters. The correspondence of Lord Byron, Jane and Thomas Carlyle, Lord Chesterfield, Charles Dickens, Charles Lamb, Virginia Woolf, to mention a few of the great letter writers, contribute significantly to literature. Letters, in this sense, are distinguished from epistles, in that letters are written to friends, whereas epistles are usually more formal documents prepared with the expectation that they will be read by some public. (See **Epistle**.)

Level Stress (Even Accent): This occurs when the stress falls evenly on two syllables in the same word, such as *daybreak*, or on two monosyllabic words that are closely linked, such as *snow storm*.

Lexicography: The art of making dictionaries or lexicons. The most ancient dictionary in existence is reputed to be a Greek lexicon, *Homeric Words*, prepared by the sophist, Apollonius, during the reign of Augustus (27 B.C. to A.D. 14). The technique of making lexicons and dictionaries evolved slowly from the explanation of difficult words by simpler ones in the same language, to the preparation of elaborate lists, alphabetically arranged, with derivations, pronunciation, spellings, illustrative quotations and meanings, either in the same or in other languages.

Lexicon: A dictionary. The term is now used primarily for dictionaries of such languages as Greek, Latin or Hebrew.

Libretto: The text or book, containing the story or plot of an opera or of any long musical composition. It is the diminutive form of the Italian *libro*, meaning "a book."

Light Opera: A form of opera that is less dignified and serious than grand opera. Usually sentiment, rather than passion, is stressed. An example is M. W. Balfe's *The Bohemian Girl* (1843).

Light Stress: In verse, a stress on a word not normally accented in speech.

Light Verse: Verse that is not serious or meditative in tone or intent. Light verse includes the Cavalier lyric, *vers de société*, the limerick, nonsense verse and parody. Each of these is discussed under a separate entry in this dictionary.

Limerick: A form of nonsense verse, usually consisting of five anapestic lines with the rhyme scheme *aabba*. The first, second and fifth lines have three feet; the third and fourth, two. Sometimes a limerick is written in four lines, in which case the third line contains an internal rhyme.

The origin of the limerick is obscure. One theory is that it is an old French verse form brought to Limerick, Ireland by the returning veterans of the Irish Brigade around 1700. Another theory is that this type of verse was sung at parties, where a group of people would extemporize on nonsense themes, following each stanza with the line "Will you come up to Limerick?"

The first recorded appearance of a limerick in print was in 1821, in Loane's *History of Sixteen Wonderful Old Women*. Limericks reached a peak of popularity when Edward Lear published his *Book of Nonsense* in 1846. The following, taken from Lear's book, illustrates the limerick form:

> There was an old Man of the Dee,
> Who was sadly annoyed by a Flea;
> When he said, "I will scratch it!"
> They gave him a hatchet,
> Which grieved that Old Man of the Dee.

Lingo: A term applied either humorously or in contempt to any strange speech or foreign language.

Linguistics: The study of language. *Descriptive linguistics* is concerned with classifying the characteristics of a language. *Comparative* or *historical linguistics* is concerned with the development of a language.

Among the major divisions in the field of linguistics are

etymology, the study of the history and origins of a word; *semantics*, the study of the meanings of words (see **Semantics**); *phonetics*, the study of speech sounds; *morphology*, the study of the forms or inflections of words; *syntax*, the study of the groupings of words into sentences or units of meaning.

Linked Rhyme: A form of rhyme found in early Welsh verse, formed by linking the final syllable in one line with the first syllable of the next.

Lipogram: A piece of writing in which a particular letter of the alphabet is deliberately not used. The work of the Spanish writer, Lope de Vega, for example, includes five novels, each lacking a different vowel.

Lira: A stanza form with five eleven-syllable and five seven-syllable lines that rhyme. The lira is most common in Spanish poetry.

Litany: A form of prayer consisting of a series of petitions. The form is sometimes adopted by writers, such as Rémy de Gourmont in *Litanies de la rose*.

Literal: Accurate to the letter; words used in their exact sense without embellishment. In the first sense, as in a *literal translation*, the word signifies accuracy and thoroughness in presenting the exact meaning of the original (the opposite of paraphrase). In the second sense, the term is used to distinguish language that is matter of fact and concrete from language that is marked by figures of speech. Literal language is the opposite of figurative language.

Literary Ballad: See **Art Ballad**.

Literary Club, The (Dr. Johnson's Circle): A club formed in London in 1764 at the suggestion of the painter, Sir Joshua Reynolds, and with the co-operation of Dr. Samuel Johnson. Among the seven other charter members were Edmund Burke and Oliver Goldsmith. Men admitted to membership during Johnson's lifetime included David Garrick (actor), Edward Gibbon (historian), Adam Smith (economist) and James Boswell (Johnson's biographer). At first, the members met at a weekly supper and, later, at a fortnightly dinner during parliament. At the meetings, there was much spirited discussion of books and writers. Johnson became a sort of literary dictator, and the club acquired a formidable power; complete editions of a book were sold in one day after its sanction.

Literary Forgery: The literary forger tries to make the world accept as the genuine writing of another something he has himself composed. Literary forgeries have been numerous in all countries and during all ages.

A forged diary of a supposed soldier in the Trojan War (Dares the Phrygian), actually composed by a Roman about the fourth century A.D., had the effect of turning the sympathy of Europeans from the Greeks to the Trojans and of supplying an account of the war that, for more than a thousand years, was accepted as more authentic than Homer's. In addition, the "diary" supplied the basis for what developed into the love story of *Troilus and Cressida*.

Centuries later, in Scotland, James Macpherson (1736-1796) composed *Fingal*, an epic he claimed had been written in the third century by Ossian, son of Fingal. Readers were sharply divided between those who accepted his "discovery" as genuine, and those who, like Dr. Johnson, denounced him as an imposter. The episode became known as the Ossianic Controversy.

Litote: A figure of speech in which an affirmative is expressed by stating a negative or the opposite of what one means. For example, *I'm sure you'd never do that*, meaning *I'm sure you would do that*. Sometimes a litote is used as the opposite of hyperbole, as in *It's just a simple supper*, when the meal served is rich and elaborate. (See **Irony** and **Understatement**.)

Litterateur: A literary man; one who occupies himself with the writing, criticism or appreciation of literature. The term is sometimes used to suggest a dilettante. (See **Dilettante**.)

Little Theater Movement: A term applied to a series of efforts in North America, the British Isles and Europe to encourage the writing and production of significant plays, as opposed to the more highly commercialized productions designed for box office success in major theaters. Little theaters have been important to the evolution of drama and theatrical art.

The movement was originated in Paris, in 1887, by André Antoine, to try out certain dramatic experiments. In England, little theaters began with the opening of the Independent Theatre (1891), under the management of Jacob Grein. Shaw, Jones, Pinero, Barrie, Galsworthy and Barker were, to some degree, influenced by the movement. In Ireland, the Little Theatre (1899) attempted to encourage new Irish writers and the use of Irish themes. J. M. Synge, Lady Gregory and W. B. Yeats were among those who wrote for the Abbey players. (See **Celtic Renaissance**.)

The movement began in the United States during 1906-1907, when three groups were organized in Chicago: The New Theatre, the Robertson Players and the Hull House Theatre. During the following decades, little theaters spread rapidly in North America, where they continue to flourish both in the United States and Canada.

Liturgical Drama: A term sometimes applied to an early phase of medieval religious drama, when plays were performed as a part or extension of a church service. In their original form, they were in Latin, and the lines were sung or chanted, rather than spoken. The mystery plays that eventually developed from the religious liturgy, or church service, are also sometimes referred to as liturgical drama. (See **Medieval Drama** and **Mystery Play**.)

Local Color, Literature of: Writing that focusses on the speech, dress, mannerisms, habits of thought and topography peculiar to a certain region. In local color writing, the locale and geographical setting are of primary importance. Robert Service's verse and much of the work of Farley Mowat are rich in local color.

loc. cit.: In the place previously cited (from the Latin, *loco citato*).

Locution: A manner of expression or phrasing; a peculiarity of idiom in speech or writing. The term frequently implies an indirect, round-about manner of expression, as the psychological locutions that often characterize the style of James Joyce.

Logaoedic: In Greek and Latin prosody, a meter composed of anapests and iambs, or of dactyls and trochees. The term is sometimes extended to refer to any mixed meter. (The above terms are explained elsewhere in this dictionary.)

Lollards: The followers of John Wycliffe, who inspired a popular religious reform movement in England in the late fourteenth century. In 1395, the Lollards presented a petition to parliament, demanding reform in the state church. Although the petition was not successful, its terms are important as early expressions of the attitude that culminated in the Reformation movement in the sixteenth century. It denounced the riches of the clergy, asked that war be declared un-Christian, and expressed disbelief in Catholic doctrines and practices such as transubstantiation (a changing of one substance into another, i.e., the changing of the substance of the bread and wine of the Eucharist into the substance of the body and blood of Christ) and pilgrimages. Lollardist attitudes were expressed in many of the pamphlets of the Reformation controversy.

Long Measure: A hymnal stanza in which all four lines are tetrameters.

Loose Sentence: A sentence consisting of an independent main clause followed by one or more dependent clauses. That is, the main idea is stated early in the sentence and additional details are given later. For example, *He studied poetry at the university and found it to be very interesting.*

The opposite of the loose sentence is the *periodic sentence*, in which the dependent clause(s) precede the main or independent clause. For example, *Among the interesting courses he took at the university was a course in poetry.*

Low Comedy: Comedy without serious purpose, intellectual appeal or subtlety. Typical features include quarrelling, fighting, noisy singing, boisterous conduct, clownishness, drunkenness, coarse joking and scolding. Shakespeare used low comedy for dramatic relief in such plays as *Macbeth* (the porter scene) and *The Merchant of Venice* (Launcelot Gobbo and old Gobbo). Low comedy is not recognized as a special type of play, as is the comedy of humours, for example, but is found either alone or combined with various kinds of comedy or tragedy. (See **Comedy, Farce** and **Vaudeville.**)

Lyric: A type of poetry marked by emotion, melody, imagination and a unified effect. In informal English usage, lyrics are the words of a song.

Originally, lyric poetry was sung to the accompaniment of a lyre. Today, the term encompasses poetry in which the poet expresses personal thoughts or feelings, as opposed to epic or dramatic poetry, which describe external circumstances and events.

In English literature, the history of the lyric goes back to the earliest epic, *Beowulf*, which contains passages with lyric qualities. The Anglo-Saxon poem, *Deor's Lament*, is essentially lyric in purpose. Before 1400, Chaucer had written a number of lyrics, many modelled on French forms.

In Elizabethan England, the lyric was further developed by such poets as Jonson and Herrick, as well as by Sidney, Spenser and Shakespeare. During the romantic movement at the end of the eighteenth century, Wordsworth, Blake, Coleridge, Shelley and Keats, among others, wrote powerful lyric poetry. Throughout the nineteenth century, such major poets as Tennyson, Browning and Swinburne also used the lyric extensively.

In contemporary literature, the lyric continues to be a widely used form of poetic expression.

Lyrical Drama: A term used for a dramatic poem in which the form of drama is used to express lyric themes (the author's own emotions or ideas of life), instead of relying on a story as the basis for the action. (See **Drama** and **Lyric.**)

111

M

Mabinogion: A collection of old Welsh tales translated (1838-1849) into English by Lady Charlotte Guest. The tales were from the *Red Book of Hergest*, a Welsh manuscript that was written in the thirteenth or fourteenth century and contained tales composed centuries earlier. *Mabinogion* is the plural of the Welsh word *mabinogi*, which means "tale of a hero."

Macaronic Verse: A type of humorous verse that mingles two or more languages. More specifically, the term is applied to poems incorporating modern words (given Latin or Greek endings) with Latin or Greek. The origin of macaronic verse is credited to a Benedictine monk, Teofile Folengo (1491-1544), who wrote a mock heroic epic called *Liber Macaronicus*. An example in English is the *Polemo-Middinia*, credited to William Drummond.

The following, by "E.C.B." is an example of the first two lines of a well-known nursery rhyme in macaronic verse:

Cane carmen sixpence, pera plena rye,
De multis atris avibus coctis in a pie.

Macron: A short, horizontal line placed over a vowel letter to identify a sound differing from that represented by the same letter without such a mark; an accent mark.

Madrigal: A short lyric usually dealing with love or pastoral topics, and suitable to be set to music. Usually, the madrigal consists of six to thirteen lines based on three rhymes. A six-line example is the following, from Shakespeare's *Measure for Measure*:

Take, O take those lips away,
That so sweetly were forsworn;
And those eyes, the break of day,
Lights that do mislead the morn:
But my kisses bring again, bring again;
Seals of love, but sealed in vain, sealed in vain.

Magazine: A publication appearing regularly and containing miscellaneous articles and/or stories by various writers. Usually, a magazine is planned to appeal to a particular audience, and the material included is selected to meet the interests and needs of that audience.

Magnum Opus: A great work, a masterpiece. Formerly, the term was used seriously, but today it often has a connotation of irony or sarcasm.

Malapropism: Incorrect use of a word, usually the result of using one word instead of another that is similar to it. The term is derived from a character in Sheridan's *The Rivals*, Mrs. Malaprop, who was constantly using expressions such as: "illiterate him, I say, quite from your memory," or "as headstrong as an allegory on the banks of the Nile."

Malediction: A curse; the opposite of benediction. The line in Shakespeare's epitaph, "Cursed be he that moves my bones" is an example.

Manifesto: A public declaration of motives or intentions; the announcement of a new movement or attitude. Perhaps the best-known manifesto is *The Communist Manifesto* (1848), written by Karl Marx and Friedrich Engels.

Mannerism: A highly individual element in a writer's style; a manner of writing that is distinctive or peculiar to an individual author. Often, the term is applied in a derogatory sense to writing that appears affected. However, writers as diverse as Milton and Hemingway have used mannerisms effectively.

Manners, Comedy of: See **Comedy of Manners.**

Manuscript, Medieval: A document or book written by hand during the Middle Ages. The medieval manuscript was the medium through which much classical and medieval literature was preserved.

The manuscripts were written and copied primarily in monasteries, first by ordinary monks and, later, by professional scribes. Usually, they wrote on parchment, although paper was used in the later Middle Ages. Frequently, the manuscripts were elaborately illuminated (colored and decorated). Despite losses by fire, war, robbery and neglect, thousands of medieval manuscripts are still in existence. Early printed books (see **Incunabulum**) were modelled on the medieval manuscripts.

Marginalia: Marginal notes; notes written in the margin by a reader as a commentary on the text.

Marinism: An affected poetic style practised by the Italian poet, G. B. Marini (or Marino) (1569-1625) and his followers. Marini expressed his poetic creed as follows:

> Astonishment's the poet's aim and aid:
> Who cannot startle best had stick to trade.

Exaggerated artificial imagery characterized Marinism. A typical Marini conceit is "blazing half-dimes of the celestial mint" (stars).

Marini influenced such English poets as Richard Crashaw and Thomas Carew.

Marivaudage: Writing characterized by psychological subtlety and stylistic elegance, in the manner of the eighteenth-century French playwright and novelist, Pierre de Marivaux.

Marprelate Controversy: In the 1580s, the Puritan opposition to the bishops of the established Church of England was expressed in outspoken pamphlets. Some of the authors of these Puritan tracts were severely punished. In 1585, the censorship of such publications was increased by a provision limiting printing rights to London and the two universities. In defiance of these regulations, the Puritans began issuing, in 1588, a series of violent attacks, printed privately and signed by the pen name, Martin Marprelate. The attacks were answered with corresponding violence by the conservatives. The authorship of the Marprelate pamphlets has never been definitely established but, whoever the author or authors were, they and their opponents wrote spirited prose satires.

Masculine Rhyme: See **Rhyme.**

Masked Comedy: See **Commedia dell' Arte.**

Masque: During medieval times in England, as well as in other European countries, certain games or spectacles were characterized by a procession of masked figures. In these "disguisings" or "mummings," a procession of masquers would go through the streets, enter each house, silently dance, play at dice with the citizens or with each other, and then leave. Adopted by the aristocracy, these games developed into elaborate and costly spectacles and, later, into the magnificent entertainments known as masques. The Epiphany spectacle of 1512, given by Henry VIII, is sometimes called the first English masque.

The major development of the masque came, however, in the latter part of the reign of Elizabeth I and in the reigns of James I and Charles I. In the first third of the seventeenth century, the masque reached its peak of popularity with such poets as Daniel, Beaumont, Middleton and Jonson. The greatest development was due to Jonson, poet laureate, and Inigo Jones, court architect and deviser of stage machinery.

Production of masques became increasingly elaborate. Expensive costumes, scenery and properties were used, and professional musicians, dancers and actors were employed. In the masque proper, which was the arrival and set dancing of masked figures, the actors were amateurs from courtly society — princes and princesses, even queens and kings.

Milton's *Comus* is one of the best-known masques. Spenser incorporates masquelike episodes in *The Faerie Queene*, and the influence of the masque is apparent in the betrothal masque in Shakespeare's *The Tempest*. *As You Like It* (also by Shakespeare) is masquelike in the lack of serious action, the prominence of music and the spectacular appearance of Hymen at the end. The era of the masque ended with the triumph of the Puritan Revolution (1642). (See **Antimasque.**)

Maxim: A short, concise statement, usually drawn from experience and offering some practical advice; an adage. For example, *A stitch in time saves nine*. (See **Aphorism** and **Proverb**.)

Measure: Though sometimes used as a synonym for meter or rhythm, the term more commonly means foot. (See **Foot, Meter** and **Rhythm**.)

Medieval Drama: A general term used to include all forms of drama in the Middle Ages, although the phrase is usually applied more specifically to religious drama and allied forms. The medieval religious drama grew out of the liturgical services of the Church. As early as the tenth century, tropes, or musical elaborations of church services, began to develop into drama. In the Easter Mass, the Latin lines telling the story of the resurrection were sung or spoken by priests, who impersonated Mary and the angels in the scene at the tomb of Christ.

Such dramatic tropes, developed around the Christmas and Easter services, became detached from the liturgical service, and medieval drama was born. Later, the performances were transferred from churches to the outdoors, Latin gave way to the native language everyone could understand and, eventually, the performances became secularized when the town authorities, utilizing the trade guilds as dramatic companies, took charge of the production of the plays. Cycles of Scriptural plays developed in which the whole plan of salvation was dramatically set forth. (See **Mystery Play**.)

About 1400, the morality play became popular and was an immediate precursor of Elizabethan drama. There was also a considerable body of folk drama in the late Middle Ages, performed on festival days — Robin Hood plays, sword-dance plays, mummings and disguisings.

Eventually, the cyclic drama and the morality plays became so secularized that the Church began to disapprove. The development of secular elements, especially the stressing of comic features, resulted in Elizabethan comedy. (See **Folk Drama, Liturgical Drama, Miracle Play, Mystery Play** and **Trope**.)

Medieval Manuscript: See **Manuscript, Medieval**.

Medieval Romance: Stories of adventure in which chivalry, gallantry and religious faith were the usual themes. The earliest medieval romances were in verse; later, they were written in prose.

The medieval romance first appears in Old French literature of the twelfth century. The works of Chrétien de Troyes are among the earliest and greatest of the French medieval romances.

In England, romances, most of them based on French originals, were being produced by the thirteenth century. Middle English romances may be grouped on the basis of their subject matter. The "Matter of England" includes stories based upon Germanic (including English) tradition. It includes *Richard Lionheart* (before 1300), *The Lay of Havelok the Dane* (ca. 1300) and *Athelstan* (ca. 1350). The "Matter of France" includes stories of Charlemagne and William of Orange, drawn from the French *chansons de geste*. Important romances of this group are *La Chanson de Roland* (late fourteenth century) and *Huon of Bordeaux* (fifteenth century). The "Matter of Antiquity" includes legends of Alexander the Great, Thebes and Troy (including Chaucer's *Troilus and Criseyde*). "The Matter of Britain" includes Arthurian literature and is represented by such classics as the fourteenth-century *Sir Gawain and the Green Knight* and Malory's fifteenth-century *Le Morte d'Arthur*. (See **Arthurian Legend, Courtly Love, Middle English** and **Romance**.)

Meiosis: Ironic understatement for emphasis or effect; the opposite of hyperbole. The following lines from A. E. Houseman's *A Shropshire Lad* provide an example of meiosis:

> Long for me the rick will wait,
> And long will wait the fold,
> And long will stand the empty plate,
> And dinner will be cold.

(See **Hyperbole**.)

Melodrama: A play based on a romantic plot and developed sensationally, with little regard for convincing motivation, and with a constant appeal to the emotions of the audience. Poetic justice is superficially secured, with the characters (who are either very good or very bad) being rewarded or punished according to their deeds. Although typically a melodrama has a happy ending, tragedies that use the same technique are sometimes referred to as melodramatic. Similarly, stories are sometimes termed melodramatic in character.

Originally, on the Greek stage, the entrance of an actor in a melodrama was accompanied by music, and in early nineteenth-century melodrama, music was an essential element. However, in later melodrama, music was not essential.

Melodrama flourished during the nineteenth century. Examples include Jerrold's *Maria Marten, or The Murder in the Red Barn*; Boucicault's *Ten Nights in a Bar Room*; Bradden's *Lady Audley's Secret*; and *East Lynne*, based on Wood's novel, *The Bells*. Melodrama is infrequently seen on the modern stage, but such plays as Hamilton's *Gas Light* and Christie's *The Mousetrap* have melodramatic qualities.

Melpomene: See **Muses.**

Memoir: A form of autobiography. Memoirs, however, typically emphasize events and personalities other than the writer's. Siegfried Sassoon wrote two autobiographical memoirs, *Memoirs of a Fox-Hunting Man* (1928) and *Memoirs of an Infantry Officer* (1930).

Examples of novels written in the form of memoirs are Defoe's *The Memoirs of a Cavalier* (1720) and Thackeray's *Memoirs of Barry Lyndon* (1844).

Menology: A liturgical calendar containing biographies of saints and martyrs, used especially in the Greek Orthodox Church. (See also **Hagiography.**)

Metaphor: A figure of speech based on a comparison that is implied rather than directly expressed. To say, *He was a lion in the fight* is to use metaphor, whereas to say, *He fought like a lion* is, since the comparison is directly expressed, to use simile. Many modern words stem from what was once a metaphor. *Transgression*, for example, means a misdemeanor, an error or mistake. Formerly, the word meant *to cross a line*. (See **Simile.**)

Metaphysical Verse: Sometimes used to describe philosophical poetry, verse dealing with the nature of being and reality, or the origin and structure of the universe. In this sense, Lucretius and Dante wrote metaphysical verse.

Ordinarily, however, the term designates the work of seventeenth-century poets such as Donne, Herbert, Vaughan, Crashaw and Cowley. The most noticeable qualities of this type of metaphysical poetry are the use of the conceit (an involved metaphor), obscurity of idea and extravagance of expression. The poetry is intellectual, analytical, psychological, often disillusioning and bold; it is absorbed in thoughts of death, physical love and religious devotion. The diction is simple, and the imagery is elaborate and ingenious. (See **Baroque** and **Conceit.**)

Meter: In verse, a rhythm established by a pattern of similar stressed and unstressed syllables. The most usual metric feet are the iambic

$(\cup-)$, trochaic $(-\cup)$, anapestic $(\cup\cup-)$ and dactylic $(-\cup\cup)$, with spondees $(--)$ and pyrrhics $(\cup\cup)$ occurring occasionally as variations. Each type is discussed in a separate entry in this dictionary.

The number of feet per line is indicated by the following terms: monometer (one); dimeter (two); trimeter (three); tetrameter (four); pentameter (five); hexameter (six); heptameter (seven); octameter (eight).

Metonymy: A figure of speech in which the name of one thing is substituted for that of another with which it is closely associated. For example *the crown* is used to mean the monarchy, *the stage* for the theatrical profession. (See **Antonomasia** and **Synecdoche**.)

Metrical Romance: A romantic tale in verse. The term is applied both to medieval verse romances (e.g., *Sir Gawain and the Green Knight*) and to the type of verse romances produced by Sir Walter Scott (e.g., *The Lady of the Lake* and *Marmion*) and Lord Byron (e.g., *Bride of Abydos* and *The Giaour*). The latter type has such romantic characteristics as the freedom of technique, sentimental qualities and remote settings. (See **Medieval Romance**.)

Middle Comedy: Athenian comedy that flourished during the last part of the fourth century B.C. It avoided the political satire of the Aristophanic old comedy and concentrated on love, intrigue and burlesques of mythological stories.

Middle English: The English spoken and written in the period following the Norman Conquest and preceding the Modern English period beginning at the Renaissance. The dates usually given are 1100 to 1500 although both are approximate. Middle English is also appliedto the literary period from 1066 to 1500. Often, the period is further divided into Early Middle English (1066-1350) and Late Middle English (1350-1500).

In the Early Middle English period, literature written in English had to vie for attention with the learned literature written in Latin and the courtly literature written in French. Little record remains of any literature written in English for more than a century following the Norman Conquest.

The earliest existing poems in English include, among others, *Poema Morale* (ca. 1170), *The Owl and the Nightingale* (ca. 1250), *Sir Tristrem* (thirteenth century), *Guy of Warwick*, *The Lay of Havelok the Dane* and *Richard the Lionheart* (fourteenth century). Many of these poems reflect a French influence in literary types and in verse form.

Late Middle English literature, stimulated in part by the substitution of English for French in courtly literature, includes ballads, cyclic religious drama and romances. Among the romances was *Sir Gawain and the Green Knight* (late fourteenth century), and poems included *The Pearl* and *Piers Plowman*. Geoffrey Chaucer, the first major English poet, wrote during the same century.

English prose of the period was used in romances, travel literature and the Wycliffe translation of the Bible. Sir Thomas Malory's *Le Morte d'Arthur* foreshadowed the later development of English prose.

Mid-Victorian: See **Victorian.**

Miles Gloriosus: The braggart soldier, a stock character in comedy. The *miles gloriosus* is cowardly, parasitical, boastful and subject to being victimized by practical jokers. The type appeared in Greek comedy, was featured by the Roman playwrights (e.g., Terence's *Thraso* and Plautus' *Miles Gloriosus*) and adopted by Renaissance dramatists. An early example is Ralph Roister Doister, central figure in the play of that name. Examples in Elizabethan drama are Captain Bobadil in Jonson's *Every Man in his Humour*, Quintiliano in Chapman's *May Day*, Shakespeare's Sir John Falstaff (*King Henry IV*, Parts I and II) and Ancient Pistol (*King Henry V*).

Mime: A play in which the actors use gestures and movements, not words; an actor who plays his part without speaking.

The mime developed during the fifth century B.C. in Italy as a form of comedy in which the events of everyday life were portrayed by dancing, imitative gestures and witty dialogue. It finally degenerated into sensual displays, which church disapproval drove from the public stage.

Mime continued to be performed, however, by wandering entertainers. In England, the exhibitions consisted generally of low forms of buffoonery. However, the mime aided the preservation of the comic spirit in drama. Its influence is apparent in the medieval mystery play, the Renaissance interlude and dumb show, and the modern pantomime.

Mimesis: The Greek word for "imitation," often used in criticism to indicate Aristotle's theory of imitation, as stated in his *Poetics*.

Minnesinger: A German word meaning "love singer"; a medieval, German lyric poet whose art was perhaps inspired by that of the French troubadour. (See **Troubadour.**) Minnesingers flourished during the twelfth and thirteenth centuries. Their poems, although reflecting the sentiments of courtly love, were generally more sincere in tone than those of the troubadours.

Minor Plot: See **Subplot.**

Minstrel: A musical entertainer or travelling poet of the later Middle Ages. During the late thirteenth and fourteenth centuries, minstrels played a prominent part in cultural life. Typically, the minstrel was a wandering entertainer, skilled with the harp and tabor, who sang songs, recited romances and carried news from town to town, castle to castle and country to country. He delighted all classes of society, from kings and knights to priests, burgesses and laborers. Love lyrics, ballads, legends and romances were composed and dispersed among the people by minstrels.

The *Lay of Havelok the Dane* is an example of the minstrel romance. However, minstrels declined in the fifteenth century and tended to disappear with the increase of literacy after the introduction of printing.

Miracle Play: Sometimes used in a broad sense to include the Scriptural cyclic drama (see **Mystery Play**), the term is usually restricted to its early sense of a non-Scriptural play based on the legend of some saint or on a miracle performed by a saint or sacred object. However common miracle plays in this stricter sense may have been in medieval England, few have been preserved. A play in English called *Dux Moraud* (thirteenth or fourteenth century), which exists in a fragmentary form, may have been a miracle play. Other existing English plays that are either miracle plays or plays of a similar character are the *Play of the Sacrament* (late fifteenth century), *The Conversion of St. Paul* and *Mary Magdalene* (ca. 1500).

A play in which the miracle was performed by the Virgin Mary is known as a virgin play.

Miscellany, Poetical: A collection of poems, usually by a variety of writers and from a variety of sources. In English literature, perhaps the best known is *Tottel's Miscellany*, a collection of poems by Wyatt, Surrey and others, published by Richard Tottell in 1557 as *Songs and Sonnets*.

Within the next fifty years, some twenty poetical miscellanies were published. Some miscellanies are specialized, such as the *Handful of Pleasant Delights* (1584), a collection of ballads. Some are collections of poetical quotations (e.g., *England's Parnassus*, 1600).

In addition to *Tottel's*, important miscellanies include *The Phoenix Nest* (1593) and *England's Helicon* (1600).

Mise en Scène: The stage setting of a play, including scenery, properties, etc.; hence, the surroundings of some event.

Modern drama relies more upon *mise en scène* for its effects than did earlier drama. The lack of scenery has been given as a partial explanation for the high literary quality of Elizabethan drama. The playwright was forced to rely upon language, rather than external properties, for his descriptive effects.

Mixed Figure: The mingling of two or more incongruous figures of speech. An example is: *The new measure took a firm foothold in the eye of the public.* Sometimes, however, mixed imagery can be deliberately used with effectiveness, as in Shakespeare's *Hamlet*, when Hamlet ponders whether it is wise "to take arms against a sea of troubles."

Mixed Metaphor: See **Mixed Figure.**

Mock Epic: A literary form that burlesques epic poetry by treating a trivial subject in a pompous manner. It mocks the characteristics of the classical epic, particularly the invocation to a deity, the formal statement of theme, the division into books and cantos, the grandiose speeches of the heroes, the descriptions of warriors, battles and games, the use of the epic or Homeric simile and the employment of supernatural machinery (gods directing or participating in the action). When the mock poem is much shorter than a true epic, it is sometimes called mock heroic, a term also applied to poems that mock romances rather than epics.

Swift's *The Battle of the Books* is an example of a satirical mock epic in prose. Pope's *The Rape of the Lock* is perhaps the finest mock heroic poem in English, satirizing in polished verse the trivialities of polite society in the eighteenth century.

Mock Heroic: See **Mock Epic.**

Monodrama: A short play in which there is only one performer. Cornelia Otis Skinner and Joyce Grenfell have made significant contributions to this form. Some poems are also categorized as monodrama, e.g., Browning's dramatic monologues. Samuel Beckett's *Krapp's Last Tape* is an example of a twentieth-century monodrama.

Monody: A dirge or lament in which a single mourner expresses grief; for example, Arnold's *Thyrsis, A Monody.* (See **Dirge, Elegy** and **Threnody.**)

Monograph: An article, essay or treatise written on one particular subject.

Monologue: An oral or written composition in which only one person speaks; any speech or narrative presented by one person; a soliloquy. Shakespeare's plays contain many monologues. Browning's *My Last*

Duchess and *Andrea del Sarto* are written in monologue form. (See **Dramatic Monologue.**)

Monometer: (1) A poem or stanza in which only one meter is used throughout. (Compare with **Polyrhythmic.**) (2) A line of verse containing one metrical foot (also known as monopody).

Monopody: A line of verse containing one metrical foot. Monopody is also known as monometer.

Monostich: (1) A line of verse. (2) A poem of one line.

Monosyllable: A word of one syllable. For example, *yes* is a monosyllable.

Montage: A film device used to establish an atmosphere or scene by a series of brief pictures or impressions following one another in rapid succession.

Mood: The tone or atmosphere (such as *pensive*, *fearful*, *serene*, *suspenseful*, etc.) prevailing in any work of drama, literature, art or music. (See **Tone.**)

Mora: In poetry, a unit of quantitative measure that equals the duration of a short syllable, represented in this dictionary as ʊ. The duration of a long syllable is two morae, represented in this dictionary by the symbol −.

Morality Play ("Morality"): A kind of poetic drama that developed in the late Middle Ages. The morality play was distinguished from the religious drama (such as the mystery play) by being a dramatized allegory in which the abstract virtues and vices (like Mercy, Conscience, Perseverance and Shame) appeared in personified form, usually with the good and the bad struggling for the soul of man. The best-known example is *Everyman* (ca. 1500).

Some of the later morality plays had political or didactic, rather than theological themes. By the sixteenth century some morality plays contained so much realistic material that they began to establish a tradition of English comedy. Figures such as the Vice and the Devil were especially well developed and influenced later comedy. Although morality themes were widely used in Renaissance drama of the sixteenth century, the morality plays lost their popularity in Elizabethan times.

Motif: In art, literature or music, a basic, recurring theme or idea; a conventional situation or incident employed in folklore, fiction or drama. For example, the *quest* is a basic motif in much literature, including *The Iliad*, Malory's *Le Morte d'Arthur* and Browning's poem, *Childe Roland to the Dark Tower Came.*

Motivation: The justification of the action of a character by the presentation of a convincing and impelling cause for that action. Motivated action is action justified by the particular human qualities of the character who performs it. For example, Shakespeare's Othello is a proud and jealous man; he smothers Desdemona when he thinks her unfaithful. Thus, Othello is said to have been motivated by pride and jealousy.

Movement: A critical term denoting action. A play is said to have movement when the dramatic action is rapid and strong; it is said to be lacking in movement if the action is weak or slow. The term is also used to indicate a new development in literary activity or interest, such as the *Oxford movement* and the *free-verse movement.*

MS. or **ms.:** Manuscript. The plural is MSS. or mss.

Muckrakers: A term applied to a group of American writers who, between 1902 and 1911, worked to expose the dishonest methods and unscrupulous motives operative in big business and government. The word is now applied, usually derisively, to anyone who works to expose the wrongdoings of any person, group or institution.

Mummery: A simple dramatic performance, usually presented by players masked or disguised; a farcical presentation; a sort of pantomime. (See **Masque.**)

Mummings: See **Masque.**

Muses: In Greek mythology, the nine daughters of Zeus and Mnemosyne who inspired and presided over song, literature and the liberal arts. In literature, their traditional significance is their inspiration and assistance to poets. During various periods of Greek history, the muses were given different names and attributes, but usually they were listed as follows: Calliope (epic poetry), Clio (history), Erato (lyrics and love poetry), Euterpe (music), Melpomene (tragedy), Polyhymnia (sacred poetry), Terpsichore (choral dance and song), Thalia (comedy) and Urania (astronomy).

Musical Comedy: Closely related, especially in its earlier forms, to burlesque and vaudeville, musical comedy developed in the early twentieth century in England and North America into one of the most popular of all dramatic forms. Although much use is made of music, both vocal and orchestral, the dialogue is spoken, not sung. The success of the form depends partly on the acting and dancing, partly on the songs and partly on spectacular staging. *Oklahoma* is an example of a successful musical comedy.

Mystery Play: A medieval religious play based on Biblical history; a Scriptural play. Mystery plays originated in the liturgy of the Church, developing from liturgical dramas into the great cyclic plays, performed outdoors and, eventually, on moveable stages. The most important forms of medieval drama in Western Europe, they flourished in England from the late Middle Ages until well into Renaissance times.

Three kinds of mystery plays developed: (1) Old Testament plays treating such events as the creation, the fall of man, the death of Abel, the sacrifice of Isaac, etc. and the prophet plays; (2) the New Testament plays dealing with the birth of Christ — the annunciation, the visit of the wise men, etc.; and (3) the death and resurrection plays — the entry to Jerusalem, the betrayal by Judas, the trial and crucifixion, the resurrection, Pentecost and, sometimes, the day of judgment.

Often, the mystery plays were known as Corpus Christi plays because they were performed on pageants (two-level scaffolds on wheels) in connection with Corpus Christi processions. Texts have been preserved for the York, the Chester, the Coventry and the Wakefield (or Towneley) cycles.

After the plays left the Church and became secularized, they were performed by trade guilds, sometimes on fixed stages or stations (the crowds moving from station to station) and sometimes on moveable pageants. (See **Liturgical Drama, Medieval Drama, Miracle Play** and **Pageant**.)

Mystery Story (or Novel): A short story or novel based on the posing and solving of a mystery. Frequently, the mystery involves a crime.

Critics generally agree that E. T. A. Hoffman in Germany and Edgar Allan Poe in the United States determined the form of the mystery story, though the main elements existed previously in the various Gothic romances of Horace Walpole, Ann Radcliffe and Charles Brockden Brown.

Structurally, the chief characteristic of the mystery story is the reversal of the sequence of events: the catastrophe (for instance, the murder) usually occurs at the beginning of the novel. The problem is to deduce, from the details presented, how, why and by whom the crime was committed.

Sir Arthur Conan Doyle is perhaps the chief master of the detective story form in English.

Mysticism: The belief in the possibility of the union of man's soul with some higher spirit or force, such as nature or a deity. The union is achieved through imagination or contemplation, and it involves the subordination of reason to intuition both as a means of contacting the higher force and as a source of knowledge.

English mystics and writers attempted to achieve this union in a variety of ways. Spenser, Shelley, Browning and Keats sought communion with a divine spirit through love or beauty; Vaughan and Wordsworth through nature; Donne, Carlyle and Tennyson through philosophy; and many others, including Crashaw, Herbert and Thompson through religion. All of these approaches were employed by Blake (1757-1827), perhaps the most well-known mystic of English literature.

Myth: An anonymous story, rooted in primitive folk beliefs, presenting supernatural episodes to explain natural events and phenomena. Myths attempt to interpret creation, divinity and religion; to explain the meaning of existence and death; to account for natural phenomena; and to chronicle the adventures of racial heroes. Myths have less historical background and more supernatural elements than legends. They are less concerned than fables with teaching morality, and they are the product of a racial or tribal group, rather than the creation of an individual. Every country and literature has its mythology.

Mythopoeic: A term applied to writers who create a mythic frame for their works. Most works of science fiction have a mythopoeic element. A good example of a mythopoeic writer is J. R. R. Tolkien.

N

Narration: In prose or poetry, the type of composition used to recount an event or series of events. (See also the other types of composition: **Argumentation, Description** and **Exposition.**) There are two forms of narration. In *simple narrative*, such as newspaper accounts, events are usually told in chronological order. A *narrative with plot* is often less chronological. Events are arranged according to a preconceived principle determined by the nature of the plot and the type of story.

The chief purpose of narration is to interest and entertain, although it may also be used to inform and instruct. Until Samuel Richardson and his novels, *Pamela* (1740) and *Clarissa Harlowe* (1747-1748), English fiction was almost entirely narrative. Since then, characterization has gained in importance. Among well-known narrative poems are Coleridge's *The Rime of the Ancient Mariner*, Arnold's *Sohrab and Rustum* and, more recently, Robert Frost's *Death of a Hired Man*.

Narrative Essay: An informal essay in narrative form — anecdote, incident or allegory. In a narrative essay, the story is a means of developing the author's idea, rather than being an end in itself. Addison's *Vision of Mirzah* is an example. (See **Essay.**)

Narrative Verse: A poem that tells a story. The ballad, the epic and the metrical romance (each defined separately in this dictionary) are types of narrative verse. The form is frequently used in English literature. Examples include Milton's *Paradise Lost* and the series of narrative poems that make up Chaucer's *The Canterbury Tales* and Tennyson's *Idylls of the King*.

Naturalism: A type of fictional writing that aims to reproduce life with absolute and objective fidelity. Naturalism is less selective and more all-inclusive than realism. (See **Realism.**) Naturalistic writing is scientific, detached and impersonal.

The beginning of naturalism is generally credited to the Goncourt brothers and to Emile Zola in France. Zola's *L'Assommoir* (1877) is the first example of naturalism in the novel. Among naturalists who wrote in English are George Moore, Theodore Dreiser and Eugene O'Neill.

Nature: (1) In the world, all things not made by man, especially natural phenomena such as mountains, oceans, flowers, birds, etc.; (2) the entire cosmic order; and (3) typical human tendencies or behavior.

Nature in the first sense — external nature — has supplied a large part of the substance of literature. In England, early Anglo-Saxon literature reflected both a love of nature and a skill in picturesque description (see **Kenning**), and a sense of mystery and awe in the presence of nature, as is evident in *Beowulf*.

Late medieval literature — Chaucer and the romances — often presented nature in idyllic, conventionalized forms. In the Renaissance, there was sometimes a genuine, subjective response to natural surroundings (e.g., some of Surrey's poems), but often the treatment was conventional, as in the pastorals and sonnets. Shakespeare demonstrated an unsurpassed faculty for drawing upon subjects from nature, to give appropriate settings and to impart an air of reality to dramatic situations and human moods.

The eighteenth century brought a conflict between the neoclassical and romantic attitudes toward external nature. The neoclassicists used nature as the basis for philosophical reflections and disliked its wilder aspects. The romantics, on the other hand, recognized nature as being able to reveal God to man and to minister to his spiritual needs. (Wordsworth's *Lines Composed a Few Miles above Tintern Abbey* is a good example.) Coleridge expressed romantic enthusiasm for the wild, disordered aspects of nature.

The poetry of other great romantic poets (Shelley, Keats and Byron) includes intimate, subjective presentation of nature in all its forms, from the delicate and mysterious to the grotesque and terrible. The attitude persisted in much Victorian poetry, notably in Tennyson's work.

The realistic, naturalistic and impressionistic movements of post-Victorian times have reacted against a sentimental use of nature as a subject or background for poetry. However, it still continues to provide a powerful and appealing imaginative impetus for modern poets. (See **Neoclassicism, Primitivism** and **Romanticism**.)

Nemesis: Divine retribution; a just punishment for evil deeds. In Greek mythology, Nemesis was the goddess of vengeance. The hero in dramatic tragedy, because of his pride (see **Hubris**), is overtaken by nemesis.

Neoclassicism: The classicism of the Restoration and eighteenth-century period (ca. 1660-1780), when writers reacted against the imaginative emotional appeal and the bold imagery and diction that were typical of Renaissance writing. This type of classicism is also called pseudoclassicism.

Neoclassical ideals included order, logic, restrained emotion, accuracy and "good taste." Details were to be subordinated to design; intellectual rather than emotional appeal was stressed. The literature of the period exalted form, polish, clarity and brilliance. It imitated the classics, cultivating literary forms and types such as the satire and ode. The classical critical requirements of universality and decorum were valued, and rhymed couplets were the prevalent verse form.

In Restoration literature, John Dryden is an outstanding exemplar of neoclassicism. However, the early eighteenth century (the Augustan Age), dominated by Pope, Swift and Addison, was the golden age of neoclassical literature. (See **Classicism**.)

Neologism: A word newly introduced into a language, especially as a means of enhancing literary style; the use of new words, or of old words in new senses.

The space age has brought neologisms such as *sputnik* and *astronaut*; changes in music have resulted in the introduction of words such as *disco* and *punk rock*; computer science has its own vocabulary for hardware and software. (See **Coined Words**.)

Neo-Platonism: See **Platonism**.

New Comedy: Greek comedy of the third and fourth centuries B.C. (See **Middle Comedy** and **Old Comedy**.)

New Criticism, The: In a strict sense, the term refers to the criticism written by John Crowe Ransom, Allen Tate, R. P. Blackmur, Robert Penn Warren and Cleanth Brooks, and it is derived from Ransom's book, *The New Criticism*, published in 1941.

Generally, the term is applied to the whole body of contemporary criticism that centers its attention on a work of art as an object in itself, finds in the work a special kind of language opposed to (or different from) the languages of science or philosophy, and submits the work, as a whole, to careful analysis. New criticism is really a cluster of attitudes toward literature rather than an organized critical system, the primary concern of which is to discover the intrinsic worth of literature.

New Humanism: A movement in writing and philosophy, primarily American, in the 1920s that reacted against the excesses of romantic individualism and realistic naturalism. Led by such authors as Irving Babbitt, Paul Elmer More and Norman Foerster, they advocated a stronger concern for human values. They insisted that man stood apart from nature and possessed free will. They advocated restraint, self-control and virtue. In both life and art, the nearest approach to their ideas of excellence had come, they felt, during the classical age of Greece. In general, the New Humanists were scholarly and conservative.

New Poetry, The: A term used at different times throughout English history to denote new poetic movements. For instance, the introduction of continental (especially Italian) forms by Wyatt and Surrey during the Renaissance produced a body of verse that was termed "the new poetry." (See **Courtly Makers**.)

More recently, the term has been applied to the changes in poetry that began in the United States soon after 1912. Conventional verse forms gave way to imagism and free verse, diction became more colloquial and an effort was made to find poetry in commonplace objects, rather than in poetic subjects. The poet, Carl Sandburg, found his inspiration in the stockyards and steel mills of Chicago. The poetry of Vachel Lindsay, Edgar Lee Masters and Max Eastman portrayed a blatant, noisy United States. Robert Frost used colloquial, direct language to give new significance to rural scenes.

The new poetry influenced modern poetry by bringing a new freedom of expression, subject and form.

Nine Worthies, The: Nine heroes of ancient legend and medieval chivalric romance. They are traditionally listed in three groups: Hector, Alexander the Great and Julius Caesar (pre-Christian pagans); Joshua, David and Judas Maccabeus (pre-Christian Jews); Arthur, Charlemagne and Godfrey of Boulogne (Christians). Shakespeare alludes to the Nine Worthies in *Love's Labour's Lost*.

Nobel Prize: A sum of money awarded annually to persons who are judged to have made the greatest contributions during the preceding year in various fields, including the physical sciences, chemistry, physiology, medicine, peace and literature. The awards are made at the bequest of Alfred Bernhard Nobel (1833-1896), a Swedish chemist and engineer, and the inventor of dynamite. The prizes were first awarded in 1901.

Nocturne: A poetic and often sentimental composition, expressing moods supposed to be especially appropriate to the evening or the night; a serenade; a song.

Nō (Noh) Drama: Lyric Japanese dramas written before the sixteenth century and intended for aristocratic audiences. The Nō form became crystallized early in the seventeenth century and has remained unchanged since that time. Usually, there are between two and six actors, most of them masked and formally costumed. All of these actors, even those playing female roles, are men. Lines are chanted to a musical accompaniment and a series of stylized dances are performed. Little scenery is used. Among the Western writers who have been interested in the Nō drama are Ezra Pound, who adapted some Nō plays, and Thornton Wilder, whose *Our Town* shows some Nō influences. (See **Kabuki**.)

Nom de Plume (Pen Name): A fictitious name adopted by a writer for professional use to disguise his true identity. Sidney Porter, for example, assumed the pen name, O. Henry. Mary Ann Evans, almost unknown by her real name, was famous as the English novelist, George Eliot.

Nonsense Verse: A variety of light verse marked by a strong rhythmic quality and a lack of logic or consecutive development of thought. Nonsense verse is often characterized by the use of coined nonsense words (e.g., *frabjous day*), a mingling of words from various languages (macaronic verse), tongue twisters and an arrangement of type to portray Christmas trees, pipes, men falling downstairs — anything that occurs to the fancy of the versifier. Limericks are a popular form of this verse. Edward Lear and Lewis Carroll are well known for their nonsense verse.

Norman Conquest: The conquest of England by the Normans following the victory of William I in 1066 at the Battle of Senlac (Hastings). The conquest directly and indirectly had a considerable influence on English literature. The substitution of French for English in the speech of the governing class permitted English, which was used only by the common people, to become grammatically simpler. Later, English vocabulary was enriched by the adoption of French words.

In addition, Norman churchmen stimulated literary activity in monastic centers, with a resulting increase in copying and composing of chronicles, legends, sermons and philosophical and scientific treatises.

Eventually, new literary types and techniques were adopted from the French. For a time, this new literature was written in French or Latin but, after 1200, English was used more extensively.

Novel: A long work of prose fiction containing characters and action portrayed in the form of a plot. The novel aims to present a picture of real life in the historical period and society in which it is set.

The novel may be regarded as the third stage in the evolution of fiction narrative, of which the epic was the first and the romance the second. Richardson's *Pamela, or Virtue Rewarded* (1740) is generally regarded as the first English novel.

Novels can be generally classified according to: (1) their purpose, or (2) their manner.

Almost all novels are written with one of three purposes: to entertain, to present a problem or thesis, or to portray a historical period.

Entertainment is the most common purpose, and this type of novel includes stories of adventure, picaresque novels, detective stories and stories of mystery and the supernatural. Novels that present a problem or thesis include character studies, the sociological novel and novels of religion, ethics and psychology. The third purpose, portraying a historical period, includes the type of fiction generally called the historical novel. None of these purposes excludes the other; one or more are combined in many works of fiction.

Novels are also classified according to their manner. On this basis, fiction is categorized as romantic, realistic, impressionistic, naturalistic, etc.

Novelette: A short novel. Usually, short stories contain six to ten thousand words, novelettes perhaps thirty to forty thousand and the novel anywhere from thirty thousand to two or three hundred thousand words.

Novella: A tale or short story. The term is particularly applied to the early tales of Italian and French writers, such as Boccaccio's *The Decameron* and Marguerite of Valois' *The Heptameron*. The later novel developed from this form, and many of them were used as source material by English writers.

Novel of Sensibility: See Sentimental Novel.

Novel of the Soil: Fiction presenting the life of a group of characters living in a remote rural section and struggling against the natural forces of their environment. An early forerunner of this type was E. W. Howe's *Story of a Country Town* (1883). Examples of the novel of the soil are Ellen Glasgow's *Barren Ground* (1925), John Steinbeck's *The Grapes of Wrath* (1939) and Patrick White's *The Tree of Man* (1956). Some of Thomas Hardy's works also exemplify this type of novel.

Nursery Rhyme: A little poem sung or recited to children. More than 800 nursery rhymes are believed to exist in the English language. Familiar examples include the following: *Humpty Dumpty*, *Old Mother Hubbard*, *Sing a Song of Sixpence*, *Jack and Jill*, *Simple Simon* and *Old King Cole*.

O

Obiter Dicta: Incidental remarks, as opposed to statements based on calculated, deliberate judgment. Legal in origin, the term sometimes has a literary association, as in assessing one author's *obiter dicta* as wiser than another's carefully considered expressions. English statesman and essayist, Augustine Birrell (1850-1933), published two series of informal essays, largely commentaries on literary topics, under the title, *Obiter Dicta*.

Objective Correlative: In literature, the presentation of a situation or series of events that immediately evokes a particular emotional response. According to T. S. Eliot, who used the term in an essay on *Hamlet* (1919), the writer should find and present the external facts that will immediately arouse a particular emotion in the reader or audience. Eliot's theory has provoked much critical discussion.

Objective Element in Literature: See **Subjective Element.**

Objectivity: The quality in a literary work of impersonality, of freedom from the expression of personal sentiments, attitudes or emotions by the author. (See **Subjective Element in Literature.**)

Obligatory Scene: An episode, usually highly emotional, the circumstances of which are so strongly anticipated by the audience that the dramatist is obliged to write it. For example, almost every western has at least one obligatory "shoot-out" scene in which the protagonist is forced to fight for his life and honor.

Occasional Verse: Poetry written to commemorate a social or historical event. The term includes *vers de société*, as well as writing of more serious and dignified purpose. Examples of occasional verse are Tennyson's *The Charge of the Light Brigade*, Hopkins' *The Wreck of the Deutschland* and Auden's *September 1, 1939*. (See **Vers de Société.**)

Octameter: A line of verse consisting of eight feet.

Octastich: A stanza of eight lines.

Octave (Octet): An eight-line stanza. The term is most frequently used to denote the first eight-verse division of the Italian sonnet as separate from the last six-verse division, the sestet. In strict sonnet form, the octave rhymes *abbaabba* and states a generalization later applied or resolved in the sestet. (See **Ottava Rima.**)

Octavo: A book in which the printer's sheets have been folded three times, producing eight leaves or sixteen pages. (See **Duodecimo, Folio** and **Quarto.**)

Octonarius: (1) A line of eight feet, common in Latin verse. (2) A stanza of eight lines.

Octosyllabic Verse: A verse made up of four metrical feet containing eight syllables. The octosyllabic couplet was common in medieval poetry.

Ode: A lyric poem expressing exalted or enthusiastic emotion. The ode is an elaborate lyric, expressed in language that is imaginative, dignified and sincere.

Originally a Greek form used in dramatic poetry, the ode was choral in quality and divided into strophe, antistrophe and epode. This was the form used by the Greek poet, Pindar (552-442 B.C.), who wrote odes celebrating public occasions. Horace (65-8 B.C.) wrote Latin odes that were more private and personal, and that consisted of a number of uniform stanzas.

Jonson's *Ode to Sir Lucius Cary and Sir H. Morrison* followed the Pindaric tradition, while Shelley's *Ode to the West Wind* was written in the Horatian manner.

Not all odes can be classified as Pindaric or Horatian (also called Aeolian). Irregular forms are more flexible, allowing freedom within the strophe and in the stanza pattern. Wordsworth's *Intimations of Immortality* is an example.

English literature is rich in a variety of odes, dating from Spenser's *Epithalamiom.*

Oedipus Theme: A Freudian term for the tendency of a child to be attached to the parent of the opposite sex and to reject the other parent. The term is derived from Sophocle's tragedy, *Oedipus Rex*, in which the king discovers that he has married his mother and killed his father. The theme is prevalent in much literature, such as Lawrence's *Sons and Lovers* (1913).

O. Henry Ending: A surprise ending to a story, such as that frequently used by the American writer, O. Henry (pen name of William Sydney Porter, 1862-1910). For example, in his story, *Gift of the Magi*, an impoverished young husband and wife have no money to buy Christmas presents for each other. The young husband secretly sells his watch and buys a pair of combs for his wife's beautiful long hair. At the same time, she has her hair cut and sells it to buy a chain for his watch.

Old Comedy: Greek comedy of the fifth century B.C. The old

133

comedy, which originated with the fertility festivals in honor of Dionysus, combines humor, lyric beauty and satire. (See **Middle Comedy** and **New Comedy**.)

Old English: The earliest phase of the English language (ca. 450-1066). In the earlier part of the period, many English poems were composed, reflecting the life of the pagan Germanic tribes on the Continent and in Britain. Those that have survived include the epic *Beowulf* (ca. 700) and such lyrics as *The Seafarer*, *Widsith* and *Deor's Lament*.

Early Christian literature included Caedmon's *Song*, Biblical paraphrases, religious narratives such as the *Crist*, *Elene*, *Andreas* and the allegorical *Phoenix* (a translation from Latin).

Literature first flourished in Northumbria but, in the reign of Alfred the Great (871-901), West Saxon became the literary dialect. Under Alfred, much Latin literature was translated into English prose, and the *Anglo-Saxon Chronicle* was revised and expanded.

A second prose revival took place under Aelfric and Wulfstan (tenth and eleventh centuries). Late examples of Anglo-Saxon verse are *The Battle of Maldon* and *The Battle of Brunanburh*. The Norman Conquest (1066) ended serious literary work in the English language for more than a century.

Old Wives' Tale: A foolish story with no basis in fact, such as might be told and passed on by gossipy old women. Usually, the story contains elements of superstitious belief. The myth that you can determine the sex of a fetus by interpreting the motion of a gold ring suspended over the mother's stomach is an example of an old wives' tale.

Omar Stanza: See **Rubaiyat Stanza**.

Omnibus: A volume of works, usually reprints, by one author or on related subjects. For example, a *Shakespeare omnibus* or a *science-fiction omnibus*.

Omniscient Point of View: A term used to describe the point of view in a work of fiction in which the author is capable of knowing, seeing and telling whatever he wishes in the story, and exercises this freedom at will. (See **Point of View**.)

One-act Play: A drama consisting of one act; the dramatic equivalent of the short story. Before 1890, one-act plays were used chiefly in vaudeville programs or as curtain raisers for the important play of the evening. However, with the Little Theater Movement, attention to the one-act play increased, and the form was adopted by such playwrights as J. M. Barrie, A. W. Pinero, A. Chekhov and G. B. Shaw. (See

Little Theater Movement.) Often, a group of two or three one-act plays are produced in a single theatrical presentation.

Onomatopoeia: The use of words in which the sense is suggested by the sound. *Hiss*, *buzz*, *gurgle* and *sizzle* are examples. A notable use of onomatopoeia occurs in these lines from Tennyson's *The Princess*:

> The moan of doves in immemorial elms,
> And murmuring of innumerable bees.

op. cit.: In the book, article, periodical, etc. that has been referred to previously (from the Latin *opere citato*).

Open Couplet: A couplet that requires the following line of the poem to complete the sense or meaning. For example:

> Strong is the lion — like a coal
> His eye-ball — like a basion's mole
> His chest against the foes.

CHRISTOPHER SMART (A Song To David)

Opera: Musical drama in which the dialogue is sung to the accompaniment of orchestra music.

Modern opera began in Italy about 1600, reaching England, where it was influenced by the masque, soon after 1700. During the Restoration period, operatic versions of Shakespeare's *The Tempest* and *Macbeth* were presented as dramatic operas, but the dialogue was spoken, not sung.

Early in the eighteenth century, operas were translated and sung by English singers. Later, bilingual operas appeared in which Italian singers sang part of the dialogue in Italian, while English singers sang the rest in English. The first completely Italian opera sung in Italian was *Almahide* (1710). The success of opera and various forms of burlesque opera at this time coincided with the decay of legitimate drama and the growing popularity of lyrical and spectacular elements on the English stage.

Opéra Bouffe: A French term for a very light form of comic opera, developed from vaudeville music and said to be the ancestor of the comic operas of Gilbert and Sullivan.

Operetta: See **Comic Opera.**

Opus: A literary work or musical composition. (Plural of opus is opuses or opera).

Oration: A formal speech intended to inspire listeners to some action. Carefully prepared and eloquently delivered, the oration carries its greatest power in the emotional appeal it makes. Although at one time a major cultural interest, the oration has lost its popular appeal and is now rarely heard.

Orthotone: A word, not usually stressed, that is given an accent in a poem to maintain the metrical rhythm. The *his* in the first of the following lines from the ballad, *The Twa Corbies*, is an orthotone:

> Ye'll sīt on̆ hīs whĭte hāuse-bāne,
> And I'll pīke out his bŏnny̆ blue een.

Ossianic Controversy: See **Literary Forgeries.**

Otiose: A style that is verbose and redundant. The term implies leisure and, in literary criticism, designates idle, inefficient writing, the use of language that is so much at leisure that it performs no useful function.

Ottava Rima: A stanza pattern consisting of eight iambic pentameter lines rhyming *abababcc*. The Italian poet, Boccaccio, is credited with originating the pattern, which was adopted by Tasso and Ariosto.

Some of the English poets who made important use of *ottava rima* are Spenser, Milton, Keats and Byron. The following illustration is from Byron's *Don Juan*:

> But words are things, and a small drop of ink
> Falling like dew, upon a thought, produces
> That which makes thousands, perhaps millions, think;
> 'Tis strange, the shortest letter which man uses
> Instead of speech, may form a lasting link
> Of ages; to what straits old Time reduces
> Frail man, when paper — even a rag like this,
> Survives himself, his tomb, and all that's his!

Oxford Movement: A movement to reform the English Church, launched at Oxford in 1833 by John Keble. It was also known as the Tractarian Movement and the Anglo-Catholic Revival. The leader was John Henry (later Cardinal) Newman, who wrote the first of the ninety papers (*Tracts for the Times*, 1833-1841) in which the group's ideas were advocated.

The reformers aimed primarily at restoring to the Church the dignity, purity and zeal of earlier times. Certain doctrines advocated by the group were regarded by some as being purely Roman Catholic and, after the publication of Newman's final tract, a storm of criticism arose. As a result, Newman lost his position at Oxford, became a layman and, finally (1845), joined the Roman Catholic Church. When Charles Kingsley attacked his sincerity, Newman replied with his *Apologia pro Vita Sua* (1864), a full statement of his spiritual and intellectual history.

Although some of Newman's followers also became Catholics, the Oxford Movement, led by E. B. Pusey, continued. In its later stages, it became less controversial and more practical, furthering the establishment of guilds, improvement of church music, revival of ritual and construction of church buildings.

Oxford Reformers: A group of humanist scholars whose association began at Oxford University in earlier Renaissance times. The group included John Colet, Sir Thomas More and the Dutch scholar, Erasmus. The group was interested in effecting reforms in church and state based on humanist ideas. They believed that moral training and moral reform should be accomplished through rational, rather than emotional, processes. Reason should dominate, and humanity should be improved through education. The church should be reformed from within by eliminating corrupt practices and by improving the standards, both moral and educational, of the clergy.

More recorded his dream of a perfect human society and government in his *Utopia* (1516); Colet founded with his own funds St. Paul's school for boys; Erasmus outlined his ideals of state in his *Institutes of a Perfect Prince*.

Oxymoron: Originally, "pointedly foolish"; a phrase bringing together two contradictory terms. Examples are: *wise fool*, *sad joy* and *the sound of silence*. Shakespeare's Hamlet uses oxymoron when he says, "I must be cruel only to be kind."

Oxytone: A word or line of verse in which the accent falls on the last syllable, as *erase*. Oxytone regularly occurs in anapestic or iambic verses.

P

Paean: A song of praise or joy. Originally, the term was restricted to odes sung by a Greek chorus in honor of Apollo. Later, it was broadened to include praise sung to other deities. Homer indicates that paeans were frequently sung on military occasions: before an attack, after a victory or when a fleet set sail. More recently, the term has come to mean any song of joy.

Paeon: See **Epitrite.**

Pageant: (1) A scaffold or stage on which dramas were performed in the Middle Ages. (2) Plays performed on such stages. (3) Modern dramatic spectacles designed to celebrate some historical event, often of local interest.

The medieval pageant, constructed on wheels for processional use, was designed for the production of a particular play and usually reflected this special purpose. The pageant for presenting a play on Noah, for example, would be constructed to represent the ark.

The modern pageant has developed from ancient tradition, including primitive religious festivals, Roman "triumphs," etc. Usually, it is an outdoor exhibition, designed to commemorate some important event. Recitations are given, and historically appropriate costumes are worn. Sometimes the pageant is processional, with a series of floats and uniformed marchers, and sometimes it is presented in an outdoor theater.

Palimpsest: A writing surface of vellum, papyrus or other material that has been used twice or more for manuscript purposes. Before the invention of paper, the scarcity of writing material made such substances very valuable. The vellum surfaces were often scraped or rubbed, or the papyrus surfaces washed. Frequently, the earlier script was not completely erased or, with age, showed through the new. In this way many documents of early periods have been preserved.

Palindrome: See **Anagram.**

Palinode: A poem or song that retracts or counterbalances something that has earlier been written. A well-known example in English literature is Chaucer's *Legend of Good Women*, written to counterbalance his portrayal of false women in *Troilus and Criseyde* and *Romance of the Rose*.

Pamphlet: (1) A booklet, usually in paper covers, that deals with topical issues. (2) Any small printed booklet.

Panegyric: A formal written or oral composition praising a person. In Roman literature, panegyrics were usually presented in praise of a living person. In Greek literature, they were more likely to be reserved for praise of the dead. Two famous panegyrics are those of Gorgias, *The Olympiacus*, and of Pliny the Younger, who, when he became consul, delivered a speech praising Trajan.

In modern usage, panegyric means extravagant praise, either written or spoken.

Pantheism: A philosophic-religious attitude that finds the spirit of God manifested in all things. Pantheism is an intuitive, transcendental belief in the unity of all. Objects are at once both God and the manifestation of God.

The word was first used in 1705 by the deist, John Toland, who called himself a pantheist (from *pan*, meaning "all" and *theos*, meaning "deity"). However, the pantheistic attitude pervaded the primitive thought of Egypt and India, was common in Greece long before the time of Christ, was taken up by the Neo-Platonists of the Middle Ages and has played an important part in Christian and Hebraic doctrine.

In literature, pantheism finds frequent expression as a faith in nature as a revelation of deity. Wordsworth in England and Emerson in the United States are two poets who have expressed the pantheistic conception. The following, from Wordsworth's *Lines Composed a Few Miles above Tintern Abbey*, is an example:

A sense sublime
Of something far more deeply interfused,
Whose dwelling is the light of setting suns,
And the round ocean and the living air
And the blue sky, and in the mind of man, —
A motion and a spirit, that impels
All thinking things, all objects of all thoughts,
And rolls through all things.

Pantomime: Silent acting; the form of dramatic activity in which silent motion, gesture, facial expression and costume are used to express emotional or narrative situations. The English dumb show was pantomime.

In English stage history, pantomime usually means the spectacular dramatic form that flourished from the early years of the eighteenth century. It included songs, dances, *commedia dell' arte* figures and a lavish setting.

Pantomime is also used for the theatrical entertainments produced in England especially during the Christmas season. These are usually based on fairy tales and feature songs, dancing and comedy.

Pantoum: A verse form of Malaysian origin. A pantoum may consist of an indefinite number of stanzas, but the second and fourth verses of one stanza must appear as the first and third lines of the following stanza. The stanzas are quatrains, and the rhyme scheme is *abab,abab*. Austin Dobson's *In Town* uses the pantoum; Victor Hugo also used it in *Les Orientales*.

Parabasis: The chief of the choral parts in ancient Greek comedy, sung by the chorus during an intermission in the action, and consisting of an address from the poet to the audience.

Parable: An allegorical story, usually containing a moral or lesson. Typically, the characters are human beings, rather than animals (as in a fable). Among the best-known parables are those in the New Testament, e.g., the parable of the prodigal son and the parable of the sower.

Paradigm: A pattern, model or example.

Paradox: A statement that seems contradictory or absurd and yet is true. Paradox is used to attract attention and provide emphasis. T. S. Eliot begins *East Coker* with a paradox: "In my beginning is my end," and closes the poem with another: "In my end is my beginning."

Paragoge: See **Epenthesis.**

Paragram: A play on words made by changing a letter or letters. In Shakespeare's *Julius Caesar*, Cassius uses a paragram when he says,

> Now it is *Rome* indeed and *room* enough,
> When there is in it but one man only.

Parallelism (also known as **Parallel Structure**): In writing, an arrangement of phrases, sentences and paragraphs so that elements of equal importance are equally developed and similarly phrased. The principle of parallelism is that co-ordinate ideas should have co-ordinate presentation.

Paraphrase: A restatement of an idea in such a way as to retain the meaning while changing the words and, frequently, the form. A paraphrase is usually an amplification of the original idea for the purpose of clarity, although the term is also used for any general restatement of an expression or passage. Thus, a paragraph in French could be paraphrased or loosely translated into English, or a poem could be paraphrased in prose. (Compare with **Abstract** and **Summary**.)

Pararhyme: Rhyme in which the vowel sounds are different and the consonant sounds before and after the vowels are the same. Examples are *braiding* and *breeding*; *fill*, *feel* and *fall*.

Parenthesis: (1) A qualifying or explanatory word, phrase or sentence inserted within brackets or commas in a passage. (2) Either or both of two curved lines used to set off an expression.

Parnassian School: A group of nineteenth-century French poets, including Paul Verlaine and Stéphane Mallarmé. The group took its name from its first anthology, *Le Parnasse Contemporain* (1866). The members of the group were impressionists. (See **Impressionism**.)

Parnassus: A mountain in Greece famed as the haunt of Apollo and the Muses. The word has also been used as a title for a collection or anthology of poems, e.g., *England's Parnassus* (1600).

Parody: A composition imitating or burlesquing the words, style, thought or form of another, usually serious, piece of work. A parody is intended to ridicule or to criticize the original work or its author. The parody is in literature what caricature and cartoon are in art. Fielding's *Joseph Andrews*, for example, is a parody of Richardson's *Pamela*. Stephen Leacock's *Nonsense Novels* and *Frenzied Fiction* contain parodies.

Paronomasia: An old term for a pun or play on words. (See **Pun**.)

Paronym: A word from the same root as another word, especially a word that has been adopted with only a slight change. An example is *paradoxon* (Greek); *paradoxe* (French); *paradox* (English).

Pasquinade: A piece of satirical writing displayed in a public place. The word is derived from Pasquino, the name of a Roman statue on which satirical Latin verses were placed.

passim: A Latin word meaning "in various places" and used in footnotes for referring to material that occurs in several places in the reference cited.

Pastiche: A literary patchwork; a parody or literary imitation. The French word is also used in art, where it is applied to a picture that captures something of a master's particular style, and in music to mean a medley or assembly of various pieces into a single work. Amy Lowell's *A Critical Fable* (1922) might be called a pastiche, since it is written in the manner of James Russell Lowell's *A Fable for Critics*.

Pastoral: A poem concerned with shepherds and rustic life. In classical literature, the pastoral was a conventional poetic form. Poets (Virgil is an example) wrote about friends and acquaintances as though they were poetic shepherds moving through rural scenes.

The form is artificial. Often, the shepherds of the pastoral speak in courtly language and appear in dress more appropriate to the drawing room than to the countryside.

Between 1550 and 1750, many conventionalized pastorals were written in England under the influence of the classical revival. In modern criticism, the term is often loosely used to mean any poem of rural people and setting. (Robert Frost, for example, has been termed a pastoral poet by some critics.) Since the classification is based on subject matter and manner, rather than on form, the term is used in association with other poetic types, as in pastoral lyrics, elegies, dramas or epics. Milton's *Lycidas*, Shelley's *Adonais* and Arnold's *Thyrsis* are examples of English pastorals. (See **Eclogue, Pastoral Drama** and **Pastoral Elegy**.)

Pastoral Drama: (See **Pastoral**.) The pastoral conventions are reflected not only in poetry and romance, but also in a form of drama. The pastoral drama developed in Italy during the sixteenth century. Tasso's *Aminta* and Guarini's *Il Pastor Fido* (1590) were models for English Renaissance pastoral plays written by Samuel Daniel, John Fletcher and Ben Jonson. Among the best known is Fletcher's *The Faithful Shepherdess* (acted 1608-1609).

Pastoral themes were also used in masques. Some of Shakespeare's romantic comedies, such as *As You Like It*, were affected by the pastoral influences and are sometimes called pastoral plays.

Pastoral Elegy: A poem employing conventional pastoral imagery, written in dignified, serious language and expressing grief at the loss of a friend or important person. The form is a combination of the pastoral eclogue and the elegy.

Milton's *Lycidas* is a pastoral elegy. The conventional divisions of the poem are: the invocation of a muse, an expression of grief, a procession of mourners, a digression and, finally, a consolation in which the poet submits to the inevitable and declares his conviction that, after all, everything has turned out for the best.

Other conventions include: appearance of the poet as a shepherd, flower symbolism, invective against death, reversal of the ordinary processes of nature as a result of death, bewilderment caused by grief, declaration of faith in some form of immortality and use of a refrain and of the rhetorical question.

The November eclogue of Spenser's *Shepheardes Calender* and Shelley's *Adonais* are examples of the pastoral elegy. (See **Eclogue, Elegy** and **Pastoral**.)

Pastoral Romance: A prose narrative, usually long and complicated in plot, in which the characters have pastoral names and pastoral conventions dominate. It often contains songs.

The Greek, *Daphnis and Chloe*, by Longus (third or fourth century) is classed as a pastoral romance. The form was reborn in the Renaissance with Boccaccio's *Ameto* (1342). Typical English examples are Sir Philip Sidney's *Arcadia* (1590) and Thomas Lodge's *Rosalynde* (1590), the source for Shakespeare's *As You Like It*. (See **Eclogue, Pastoral** and **Pastoral Drama**.)

Pastourelle: A medieval type of dialogue poem in which a shepherdess is wooed by a man of higher social rank. In the Latin *pastoralia*, a scholar does the courting; in the French and English equivalents, a poet. The body of the poem is the dialogue in which the case is argued. Sometimes the suit is successful, but often a father or brother happens along and ends the wooing.

The pastourelle seems to have influenced the pastoral dialogue lyrics of the Elizabethans and may have figured in the development of early romantic drama in England.

Patent Theaters: The theaters erected and used under a patent granted by Charles II. When the ban against theatrical performances in England was lifted in 1660, Sir William Davenant and Thomas Killigrew secured from the king a patent granting them the privilege of censoring plays, as well as the right to organize two companies and erect two theaters that would enable them to have a monopoly.

In 1661, Davenant's company (the Duke of York's Company) occupied a new theater in Lincoln's Inn Fields and, later, one at Dorset Garden. Killigrew's company (the King's Company) erected the Theatre Royal, the first of a succession of houses known, since 1663, as Drury Lane.

Despite strenuous efforts of rival managers to encroach upon the privileges of the patentees, the act remained in force until 1843, when it was repealed and the patents revoked. (See **Private Theaters**.)

Pathetic Fallacy: A phrase coined by Ruskin in 1856 to denote the tendency of writers to credit nature with the emotions of human beings.

Conventionally used in the pastoral elegy, the pathetic fallacy attributes human passions to inanimate objects. Ruskin gives an example and comments (*Modern Painters*, Vol. 3, Part IV, Chap. xii):

> They rowed her in across the rolling foam —
> The cruel, crawling foam.

"The foam is not cruel, neither does it crawl. That state of mind which attributes to it these characters of a living creature is one in which the reason is unhinged by grief. All violent feelings have the same effect. They produce in us a falseness in all our impressions of external things, which I would generally characterize as the 'pathetic fallacy.'"

Pathos: In literature and drama, the portrayal of an incident in such a way as to arouse feelings of pity, tenderness or sadness in the reader or spectator. The emotions evoked by pathos are less terrible and exalted than those aroused by tragedy. In Shakespeare's *Hamlet*, for example, the description of the death of Ophelia is marked by pathos. Excessive use of pathos can result in sentimentality or bathos. (See **Bathos** and **Sentimentalism**.)

Patois: The dialect spoken in any particularly geographical district.

Pause: In fiction, a resting point allowing the reader to think back on what has happened in the story and to prepare for the climax. The pause may contain a recapitulation or explanation of events, an indication that time has elapsed or a descriptive passage. In poetry, a pause is called a caesura. (See **Caesura**.) In drama, a pause is indicated by silence.

Pedantry: A display of learning for its own sake. The term is often applied to a style marked by a superfluity of quotations, foreign phrases, long words, classical allusions, scholarly terms, etc.

Pegasus: The winged horse of Greek mythology said to have sprung from Medusa's body at her death. Pegasus is associated with the inspiration of poetry because he is supposed, by one blow of his hoof, to have caused Hippocrene, the inspiring fountain of the Muses, to flow from Mount Helicon. Poets have sometimes invoked the aid of Pegasus as a symbol of poetic inspiration, instead of the Muses.

Penny Dreadful: A thrilling, sensational novel of violent action. Usually, the penny dreadful, so named for its price and content, was crudely written, cheaply printed and paper bound. However, the exciting tales of adventure, crime or mystery won wide popularity for this form of fiction in the nineteenth century. It was also called the dime novel.

144

Pentameter: A line of verse consisting of five feet.

Pentapody: A verse containing five metrical feet.

Pentastich: A stanza or poem made up of five lines. (See **Quintet**.)

Penult: The second-last syllable in a word.

Periodic Sentence: See **Loose Sentence.**

Peripety (Peripeteia): A sudden reversal of fortune occurring in the progress of a narrative or dramatic plot.

Periphrasis: An indirect, abstract, roundabout method of stating ideas. Writers sometimes use periphrasis for humorous effects. For example, the poet, William Shenstone (1714-1763), referred to pins as "the cure of rents and separations dire, and chasms enormous." (See **Circumlocution**.)

Peroration: The conclusion of an oration or discourse in which the speaker summarizes the discussion and attempts to reinforce his arguments by a pointed and rhetorical appeal to the emotions of his audience; a recapitulation of the major points of a speech.

Persiflage: Light, inconsequential chatter, written or spoken; a trifling, flippant manner of dealing with a theme or subject matter.

Persona: In literary criticism, the term applied to the narrator or speaker in a novel, short story or poem. For example, Socrates is the persona of Plato's dialogues.

Personification: (1) A figure of speech that endows animals, ideas, abstractions and inanimate objects with human form, character or feelings; the representation of imaginary creatures or things as having human personalities, intelligence and emotions. (2) An impersonation in drama of one character or person, real or fictitious, by another person.

Keats personifies the Grecian urn as the:

Sylvan historian, who canst thus express
A flowery tale more sweetly than our rhyme.

Earlier in the poem he uses personification when he refers to the urn as an "unravished bride of quietness" and a "foster-child of silence and slow time." (See **Anthropomorphic**.)

Persuasion: One form of argumentation, persuasion is an attempt to arouse the reader or listener to action. The most usual form of persuasion is the oration, and the most effective form combines an appeal to the intellect with an appeal to the emotions.

Petrarchan Sonnet: The Italian sonnet form that was used by Petrarch (1304-1374) and later adopted by English poets. (See **Sonnet**.)

Petrarchism: The style introduced by Petrarch (1304-1374) in his sonnets. It is a style marked by grammatical complexity, elaborate conceits and conventional diction.

Philippic: A bitter attack in words; a discourse filled with denunciations and accusations. The term comes from the twelve orations of Demosthenes in which he criticized Philip II of Macedon as an enemy of Greece.

Philistinism: The worship of material prosperity; the disregard of culture, beauty and spiritual things. The term was used by Matthew Arnold in his essay, *Sweetness and Light*, which appeared as the first chapter of *Culture and Anarchy* (1869). Arnold wrote:

> If it were not for this purging effect wrought upon our minds by culture, the whole world, the future as well as the present, would inevitably belong to the Philistines. The people who believe most that our greatness and welfare are proved by our being very rich, and who most give their lives and thoughts to becoming rich, are just the very people whom we call Philistines.

Philology: The scientific study of both language and literature; more specifically, the scientific study of language and linguistics.

Phoneme: A basic sound unit in a language. In English, *m* and *n* are separate phonemes; *f* and *ph* are the same. However, *c* and *k*, and *c* and *s* may be either separate or the same phonemes. In the word *circle*, for example, *c* has the same sound as *s* and as *k*.

Picaresque Novel, The: A chronicle, usually written in the first person, presenting the life story of a rogue of low social class who makes his living more through his wits than his industry. The structure is episodic as the *picaro* (rogue) undergoes a series of adventures that allow the author to satirize the various social classes. While the story may be romantic in nature, its plain language, faithful portrayal of detail and use of common incidents contribute realistic qualities.

From earliest times, the rogue has been a favorite character in story and verse. The Roman, Petronius, at the court of Nero, recognized the possibilities of the type in his *Satyricon*. In the Middle Ages, the fables continued the theme, although roguery was transferred from man to animals. In the sixteenth century, a Spanish picaresque novel, *La Vida de Lazarillo de Tormes y de sus fortunas y adversidades* was one of the most widely read books of the period. Cervantes adopted the form, and soon there were French imitators. Le Sage's *Gil Blas* (1715) was the most popular.

The English, as well, adopted the picaresque manner. The first important picaresque novel in English was Thomas Nash's *The Unfortunate Traveller: or, The Life of Jack Wilton*. With Daniel Defoe in the eighteenth century, the type gained importance. His *Moll Flanders* presents the life of a female *picaro*. Fielding's *Jonathan Wild* and Smollett's *Ferdinand, Count Fathom* were also picaresque novels.

Pindaric Ode: See **Ode.**

Pirated Edition: An unauthorized edition of a work.

Plagiarism: Literary theft. A writer who steals another writer's plot and uses it as new in a story of his own is a plagiarist. From flagrant theft of thought and language, plagiarism shades off into unconscious borrowing, borrowing of minor elements and mere imitation. In fact, the critical doctrine of imitation, as understood in the Renaissance period, often led to what would today be called plagiarism. Thus, Spenser, who freely borrowed material from other epics for *The Faerie Queene*, regarded this "imitation" as a virtue. (Compare with **Literary Forgeries**.)

Plaint: Verse expressing grief; a chant of lamentation; a lament; an expression of sorrow. (See **Complaint**).

Planh: In Provençal verse, a song of mourning for a deceased patron. The song traditionally contrasts the patron's virtues with the vices of those who survive.

Platonic Love: Spiritual love in which the beloved's beauty is considered a reflection of the beauty of the soul; non-physical love. So called after Plato (427-347 B.C.), a Greek philosopher who is said to have advocated this type of relationship. (See **Platonism**.)

Platonism: The idealistic philosophical doctrines of Plato. These doctrines have appealed strongly to certain English writers, particularly the poets of the Renaissance and romantic periods.

Unlike Aristotelian philosophy, which tends to be formal, scientific, logical and critical, and which occupies itself chiefly with the visible universe and mankind, Platonism is flexible, interested in the unseen world and concerned with man's possibilities and destinies.

Plato founded his Academy in 380 B.C. and, for a third of a century, he taught students (including Aristotle) attracted from near and far. Later leaders of the Academy and other followers, known as Neo-Platonists, modified and expanded Plato's teachings, so that it is difficult to distinguish the purely Platonic elements from those added by later Platonists.

Among the Neo-Platonists, two groups were of special importance: (1) the Alexandrian school. This group, especially Plotinus (third century), stressed the mystical elements and united them with ideas drawn from other sources. Their Neo-Platonism provided medieval Christian thinkers (including Boethius and St. Augustine) with many ideas. (2) the Neo-Platonists of the Italian Renaissance. Under the leadership of Marsilio Ficino (1433-1499), a highly complex and mystical theory developed, fusing Platonic philosophy and Christian doctrine. This particular kind of Neo-Platonism kindled the imagination of such Renaissance poets as Sidney and Spenser.

Representative English poems embodying Platonic ideas include Spenser's *Hymn in Honour of Beauty*, Shelley's *Hymn to Intellectual Beauty* and Wordsworth's *Ode on the Intimations of Immortality from Recollections of Early Childhood*.

Play: A dramatized story designed to be performed on a stage by actors. (See **Drama**.)

Pléiade: A term originally applied to an ancient group of seven authors (named after the constellation of the Pleiades) and to several later groups, including a group of critics and poets that flourished in France during the second half of the sixteenth century.

The leading figures were Ronsard, Du Bellay and (later) Desportes. The poetic manifesto of the group is Du Bellay's *Défense et Illustration de la Langue Française* (1549). It indicated an interest in developing a new vernacular literature, following the types cultivated by classical writers.

The group had an important influence on Elizabethan poets, especially Spenser. The Areopagus Club has been regarded as an English counterpart of the Pléiade, since Sidney and his group engaged in an effort to refine the English language and to create a new national literature based upon humanistic ideals. (See **Areopagus**.)

Pleonasm: The superfluous use of words. Pleonasm may consist: (1) of needless repetition; (2) of the addition of unnecessary words in an effort to express an idea completely; or (3) of a combination of the two. For example, in the sentence, *He walked the entire distance to the* *station on foot*, the last two words are pleonastic. (See **Redundant** and **Tautology**.)

Plot: The framework of a piece of drama or fiction; the planned series of interrelated incidents that make up the story being told. Typically, they are arranged in a logically ordered sequence to arouse interest and suspense and to lead to a climax and denouement that are artistically satisfying. There is constant interaction between the characters involved and the incidents portrayed. Thus, the characters affect the action of the plot, and the action affects the characters. However, not all drama and fiction have this conventional framework. For example, James Joyce's *Ulysses*, although purposefully developed, is not structured on a plot.

Poem: A composition in metrical form, characterized by qualities of imagination, emotion, significant meaning and appropriate language. A poem may be written in rhyme, blank verse or a combination of the two, but the expression is usually rhythmical and designed to give aesthetic or emotional pleasure. Poem may also apply to a written composition which, though not in verse, is characterized by imagination and poetic beauty in either the thought or the language. (See **Poetry**.)

Poetaster: One who writes inferior poetry; a minor versifier. The word is from the Latin *poeta* ("poet") and *-aster*, which denotes inferiority.

Poetical Miscellany: See **Miscellany, Poetical.**

Poetic Diction: Words chosen for their poetic quality. With time, styles in diction change, and words accepted by one age are dropped as new words are adopted. Most modern poets, for example, would avoid words once considered poetic, such as *ere*, *whilst*, *beauteous* and *e'en*. However, they might accept and use words another generation would not have considered appropriate for poetry, such as *brickyard* or *slut*.

Poetic Drama: Poetic plays written to be acted. T. S. Eliot's *Murder in the Cathedral* (1935) is an example. In the strict sense of the term, poetic drama is distinguished from dramatic poetry (such as Browning's *Andrea del Sarto*) and closet drama (such as Swinburne's *Atalanta in Calydon*). (See **Closet Drama** and **Dramatic Poetry**.)

Poetic Justice: An ideal situation in which good is rewarded and evil is punished.

Poetic Licence: The privilege, sometimes claimed by poets, of departing from normal order, diction, rhyme or pronunciation so that their verse will meet the requirements of their metrical pattern.

If the demands of prose are applied to poetry, most poetic expression will be classed as poetic licence. Prose, for instance, would state: *Kubla Khan decreed that a stately palace be built in Xanadu.* Coleridge, however, writes:

> In Xanadu did Kubla Khan
> A stately pleasure-dome decree.

The normal prose form is distorted but, as poetry, the lines are readily acceptable and effective.

Poetics: Theory concerning the nature of poetry; the principles and rules of poetic composition. The classic example is Aristotle's *Poetics*.

Poet Laureate: The official poet of a country; in England, a poet appointed by the king or queen to write poems celebrating court and national events.

Ancient kings and chieftains frequently maintained court poets, persons attached to the royal household to celebrate the virtues of the royal family and to sing the praises of military exploits. Court poets of this type included the *scop* among Anglo-Saxon peoples, the *skald* among the Scandinavian, the *filidh* among the Irish and the higher ranks of *bards* among the Welsh.

In a separate tradition, a student who was admitted to an academic degree in a medieval university was crowned with laurel. Later, poet laureate was used for a special degree conferred on someone by a university for skill in Latin grammar and versification.

In England, the official laureateship was established in the seventeenth century. The laureates have been: John Dryden (1668-1688), Thomas Shadwell (1689-1692), Nahum Tate (1692-1715), Nicholas Rowe (1715-1718), Laurence Eusden (1718-1730), Colley Cibber (1730-1757), William Whitehead (1757-1785), Thomas Warton (1785-1790), Henry James Pye (1790-1813), Robert Southey (1813-1843), William Wordsworth (1843-1850), Alfred, Lord Tennyson (1850-1892), Alfred Austin (1896-1913), Robert Bridges (1913-1930), John Masefield (1930-1968), Cecil Day Lewis (1968-1972) and John Betjeman (1973-   ).

Poetry: A composition that evokes emotion and imagination by the use of vivid, intense language, usually arranged in a pattern of words or lines with a regularly repeated accent or stress.

In content, poetry expresses thoughts that are significant and sincere. It is marked by the presence of power, beauty and dignity.

Because of these qualities, poetry is distinguished from doggerel and from light or occasional verse.

In form, the first characteristic of poetry is the presence of rhythm. Whatever the pattern of the lines, there is a regularity of rise and fall in accent that is more uniform than that of prose. Repeated rhymes and rhyme schemes frequently add to the musical effect of the verses.

A vital element in poetry is the use of concrete words and specific, evocative language. Because poetry is an intense form of expression, words are chosen for their connotations and associations. Poetic expression is rich in figures of speech and imagery. It appeals to the reader's imagination, re-creating and communicating the deep feelings the poet has experienced.

Conventionally, poetry is classified into three types: the epic, the dramatic and the lyric. These types are further classified according to set patterns (e.g., the sonnet, the ode, the elegy) and according to their mood or purpose (e.g., pastoral, satiric, didactic).

Point of View: The position and outlook of the narrator in relation to the scene being described or the story being told. A logical, consistent point of view is a unifying device.

The term is used in a special sense when applied to fiction writing. The writer may choose to tell the story from the point of view of someone who is involved in the action. Alternatively, he may write from the point of view of a witness to the story, as one before whom the events are unfolding. Or he may write with an omniscient point of view, as one who knows what is going on in the minds of the characters and who sees the motives for the action.

Polemic: A vigorous argument, controversy or dispute. Usually, religious, political or social concerns are involved. One of the most famous polemics in English literature is Milton's *Areopagitica* (1664).

Polyhymnia: See **Muses.**

Polyphonic Prose: Polyphonic means "many voiced," and polyphonic prose has many of the features, or "voices," of poetry, including rhythm, assonance, alliteration and rhyme. The American poet, Amy Lowell, developed the form and used it, for example, in *Can Grande's Castle* (1918).

Polyrhythmic: A term used to describe a poem in which more than one metrical pattern is used. (Compare with **Monometer.**)

Portmanteau Words: Words concocted by accident or for deliberate humorous effect by telescoping two words into one, as *squarson* for *squire* and *parson*. Lewis Carroll named this form of word coinage, which he used in *Through the Looking Glass*. In *Jabberwocky* (by the same author), for example, *slimy* and *lithe* are combined to produce *slithy*.

Posy (Posie): Sometimes used in the sense of "a collection of flowers" to indicate an anthology. The term also signifies a motto, usually in verse, inscribed on a ring.

Potboiler: A slang term for a book or an article written only for the income derived from it. It is writing that will "keep the pot boiling" and thus enable the author to eat until, presumably, he produces more significant work.

Poulter's Measure: A metrical pattern, now rarely used, for a couplet composed of a first line in iambic hexameter and a second line in iambic heptameter. The term is said to have originated from a custom of the London poulterers, who gave a customer twelve eggs in the first dozen purchased, and fourteen in the second dozen. Wyatt and Surrey, Sidney, Grimald and Brooke are some of the poets who have used the form.

A modified form of poulter's measure consists of a four-line stanza composed of iambic trimeter verses for the first, second and fourth lines, and an iambic tetrameter for the third. The opening lines of Arthur Brooke's *Romeus and Juliet* provide an example:

> There is beyond the Alps, a town of ancient fame,
> Whose bright renown yet shineth clear, Verona men it name;
> Built in a happy time, built on a fertile soil,
> Maintainéd by the heavenly fates, and by the townish toil.

Preamble: An introductory portion of a written document. In formal sets of resolutions, there is usually a preamble setting forth the occasion for the resolutions. The preamble is usually introduced by one or more statements beginning with "Whereas," and is followed by the resolutions, each of which is commonly introduced by the word, "Therefore."

Preciosity: A critical term sometimes applied to writing that is consciously affected or labored in style and overly refined in diction.

Précis: A brief summary of an article, book, speech, series of reports, etc. In a précis, the most important points made in the original are concisely presented in logical order and readable form.

Preface: A short introductory statement printed at the beginning of a book or article in which the author states his purpose in writing, acknowledges assistance received, points out difficulties and uncertainties in connection with the writing of the book, and informs the reader of facts pertinent to a reading of the text. Some writers, notably Dryden and Shaw, have written prefaces that are really extended essays.

Prelude: A short introductory poem prefixed to a long poem or to a section of a long poem. Lowell's *The Vision of Sir Launfal* contains preludes.

Pre-Raphaelitism: The Pre-Raphaelite movement, a phase of romanticism, originated with the establishment in 1848 of the Pre-Raphaelite brotherhood by Dante Gabriel Rossetti, Holman Hunt, John Everett Millais and other artists, as a protest against the conventional methods of painting then in use. The Pre-Raphaelites wanted to regain the spirit of simple devotion and imitation of nature that they found in Italian religious art before Raphael.

Several of the group were both artists and poets, and the effect of the movement became evident in English literature. Rossetti was the most influential. His *Blessed Damozel*, published in 1850, is a religious narrative with pictorial qualities.

In general, the characteristics of Pre-Raphaelite poetry are: pictorial elements, symbolism, sensuousness, tendency to metrical expression, attention to minute detail and an interest in the medieval and the supernatural. Certain critics, who saw sensuousness as the dominating characteristic of Pre-Raphaelite poetry, called the Pre-Raphaelites the "fleshly school." (See **Fleshly School**.)

The chief literary products of the movement were Rossetti's translation of Dante, his sonnets and his balladlike verse; Christina Rossetti's lyrics; and the poems of William Morris, such as *The Earthly Paradise* and *The Defense of Guinevere*.

Primary and Secondary Accent: Primary accent is the stress given to the principal syllable of a word, as in the *may* of *maybe*. Secondary accent is the stress given to the syllable less heavily emphasized than the principal one, as in the *be* of *maybe*.

Primitivism: The doctrine that primitive man, because he has remained closer to nature and has been less subject to the corrupt influences of society, is nobler and more nearly perfect than is civilized man. The idea flourished in eighteenth-century England and France, and was an important element in the creed of the "sentimentalists" of the romantic movement.

The movement received tremendous impetus from France by the writings of Rousseau, whose slogan "Return to Nature" was based upon his belief that man was potentially perfect and that his faults were due to the effects of society.

One of the primitivistic doctrines was that the best poetry is natural or instinctive, not cultivated. There was a feverish search for a perfect "untutored" poet. Gray's *The Bard* (1757) and James Beattie's *The Minstrel* (1771-1774) reflect this doctrine of primitive poetic genius. For a time, the forged Ossian poems of James Macpherson seemed to be the hoped-for discovery in Britain of the work of some primitive epic poet. (See **Literary Forgeries**.) When, finally, Robert Burns, the "singing plowman," appeared, he was received with extravagant enthusiasm.

Not all of England believed in primitivism. The movement was attacked by such conservatives as Dr. Johnson and Edmund Burke.

Private Theaters: The term seems to have been first used about 1596, when the Blackfriars Theatre was so described by its sponsors who were seeking privileges not granted to the public theaters. The name is misleading, since the private theaters, although they charged a higher admission fee than did their public rivals, were open to all classes. They did differ from the public theaters in that they were indoor institutions, artificially lighted, smaller and typically rectangular.

The Elizabethan private theaters were the Blackfriars, Paul's School, the Cockpit (or Phoenix) and Salisbury Court. The last two were also known as court theaters. Shakespeare's company in the early seventeenth century controlled both the Blackfriars, the chief private theater, and the Globe, the chief public theater.

Since the private theaters were indoor institutions of a somewhat aristocratic character, they became increasingly important in the seventeenth century, when the court was fostering elaborate exhibitions and encouraging drama with spectacular features. (See **Masque**.) It is from the private, rather than from the public theaters, that the elaborate playhouses of the Restoration and later times are directly descended. (See **Public Theaters**.)

Problem Novel: Prose fiction in which the primary concern is the working out, through characters and incidents, of a central problem. Problems introduced in this kind of fiction might involve choices between patriotic duty and personal concerns, between honorable poverty and dishonorable wealth or between the demands of a profession and the obligation to one's family.

The problem novel differs from the propaganda novel in that the latter is written for the deliberate purpose of extolling or criticizing the effects of a certain social or economic condition. The problem novel is a story *with* a purpose; the propaganda (or thesis) novel is written *for* a purpose. Hawthorne's *The Scarlet Letter* is an example of the problem novel, while Dickens' *Oliver Twist* might be called a propaganda novel.

Problem Play: A term used to describe serious drama in which the problems of human life are presented (e.g., Shakespeare's *King Lear*) and, in a more specialized sense, for the drama of ideas, exemplified by the plays of Ibsen, Shaw, Galsworthy and others.

Prochronism: A form of anachronism in which something is set into a period before its time. An example is Mark Twain's book, *A Connecticut Yankee in King Arthur's Court*. (See **Anachronism**.)

Proem: A brief introduction; a preface or preamble.

Prolegomenon: A preliminary observation; a foreword or preface. The heading of prolegomena (plural of prolegomenon) may be given to the introductory section of a book, containing observations on the subject of the work.

Prolepsis: An anticipating; an error in chronology, dating an event before the actual time of its occurrence; the treating of a future event as if it had already happened. Rhetorically, the term may be applied to a preliminary statement or summary that is to be followed by a detailed treatment. In argumentation, prolepsis is the device of anticipating and answering an opponent's argument before the opponent has an opportunity to introduce it.

Prolixity: In writing or speaking, tedious length and use of too many words so that the sense becomes obscured. (See **Circumlocution** and **Periphrasis**.)

Prologue: A preface or introduction usually associated with drama and especially popular in England in the plays of the Restoration and the eighteenth century. In ancient Greek plays, a speaker announced, before the beginning of the play, the facts that the audience needed to know in order to understand the play itself. In Latin drama, the same custom prevailed.

European dramatists in England and France followed the classical tradition from the time of the miracle and mystery plays. Prologues were often written by the author of a play and delivered by one of the chief actors. In the eighteenth century, however, established authors, such as Pope, Johnson and Garrick, frequently wrote prologues for the plays of their friends and acquaintances. Sometimes, as in the play within the play in *Hamlet*, the actor who spoke the prologue was called "the prologue."

The first part of Shakespeare's *King Henry IV* opens with an explanatory speech that serves the function of a prologue. Part two of the same play opens with a prologue called an induction. (See **Epilogue** and **Induction**.)

Propaganada Novel: See **Problem Novel**.

Proposition: (1) The part of a literary work, usually placed at the beginning, in which the author states the theme or intention of the work. A well-known example occurs at the beginning of Milton's *Paradise Lost*. (See also **Proem**.) (2) A form of speech in which an assertion or statement is made about a subject. A hypothetical proposition involves a theory (hypothesis) or condition assumed to be true.

Proscenium: In a modern theater, the part of the stage in front of the curtain. In the ancient theater, the proscenium extended from the orchestra to the background, and the term is not infrequently used, even today, as a synonym for the stage itself.

Prose: Spoken or written language that is not metrically versified, as distinguished from poetry or verse. While prose may be rhythmical, it is without the sustained metrical regularity of verse. Variety of expression is achieved through diction and sentence structure. Novels, essays, short stories and most modern drama are written in prose.

Prose Rhythm: The recurrence of accent and emphasis at regular or irregular intervals that gives prose a rising and falling movement. Unlike the rhythm of verse, prose rhythm never falls for long into a recognizable meter. Most good prose is marked by a constant flow of accent, always changing, yet always appropriate for the thought being expressed.

Prosody: The theory and principles of versification, particularly as they refer to rhythm and accent. (See **Versification**.)

Prosopopoeia: A term sometimes used for personification. (See **Personification**.)

Prosthesis. See **Epenthesis**.

Protagonist: From the Greek *protagonistes: protos*, meaning "first," and *agonistes*, meaning "actor." The chief character in a play or story. When the plot involves conflict, the chief opponent or rival of the protagonist is called the antagonist. If the main plot centers on the career of a hero who opposes and overcomes a villain, the hero would be called the protagonist, the villain the antagonist. If, however, the main plot interest is in the career of a villain, whose plans are defeated by the appearance of a successful hero, the villain would be called the protagonist and the hero the antagonist. In Shakespeare's *Hamlet*, Hamlet is the protagonist and King Claudius and Laertes are his antagonists. (See **Antagonist**.)

Protagonist is also used to mean a champion or chief advocate of a cause or movement, such as *a protagonist of women's rights*.

Protasis: In ancient drama, the first part of the play, in which the characters are introduced and the subject is proposed.

Prothalamion: A song or poem written to celebrate a marriage.

Prototype: An original or model for later forms; a first or primitive type. The periodical essays written by Addison and Steele were the prototype of the familiar essays later written by Lamb and Stevenson. Similarly, the Vice of the medieval morality plays is regarded as the prototype of the clown in Elizabethan drama.

Proverb: A sentence or phrase that briefly and succinctly expresses some truth or observation about life, and that has been preserved by oral tradition, although it may also be included in written language. Proverbs may appear in several forms: as a metaphor (*Still waters run deep*); as an antithesis (*Man proposes, God disposes*); as a play on words (*Forewarned is Forearmed*); or as an alliteration or parallel structure. Some are epigrammatic.

Proverbs pass freely from language to language and culture to culture. Those with a long literary history are often referred to as "learned proverbs." (See **Aphorism**.)

Provincialism: (1) Manners, habits or viewpoints peculiar to a specific province or region. (2) Narrow-mindedness. (3) A word, expression or pronunciation peculiar to a specific region.

Psalm: A lyrical composition of praise. Most frequently, the term is applied to the lyrics in the Biblical Book of Psalms ascribed to David.

Pseudoclassicism: See **Neoclassicism**.

Pseudonym: A fictitious name assumed by writers and others. (See **Nom de Plume**.)

Pseudo-Shakespearean Plays: The plays attributed to Shakespeare but not accepted as his by the best authorities. Because of Shakespeare's reputation, some non-Shakespearean plays, such as *Locrine*, were printed during Shakespeare's lifetime with his initials or name on the title page. Others, such as *The Birth of Merlin*, were similarly printed after Shakespeare's death. Another group, including *Mucedorus*, consists of plays labelled as Shakespeare's in the copies found in the library of Charles II. Many others have been assigned to Shakespeare by editors, booksellers or critics, chiefly on the basis of the literary or technical qualities of the plays.

Pseudo-statement: A term originated by I. A. Richards to distinguish between scientific and poetic truths. Richards defined statements as verifiable expressions of fact. Pseudo-statements, on the other hand — the kind made in poetry — are not necessarily verifiably true or even logically coherent.

Psychical Distance: See **Aesthetic Distance**.

Psychological Novel: Prose fiction that emphasizes internal rather than external action and is concerned primarily with the motives, emotions and thoughts of the characters involved. Usually, characterization is more important than plot.

The term was first applied in the middle of the nineteenth century to a group of novelists including Eliot and Meredith. Later, Thackeray, Dickens, Hardy and Conrad were classified as psychological novelists. In the twentieth century, with the advance of psychology as a science, the term has come to be used in a stricter sense. In this sense, Joyce's *Ulysses* and Virginia Woolf's *To the Lighthouse* are examples of psychological novels.

Public Theaters: The English playhouse developed in Elizabethan times as a result of the increased interest in drama. In earlier times, plays had been produced on pageants (see **Pageant**) and in rooms such as the halls of great houses, schools and the Inns of Court.

The demand for larger places resulted in the use of inn yards, which were square or rectangular courts enclosed by the inner porches or balconies of the inn. At one end, a temporary stage, connected with rooms of the inn, would be erected. The spectators might stand in the open court (groundlings) or be seated on the surrounding balconies.

To meet the need for a place for bear- or bull-baiting, spectacles and acrobatic performances, a ring or amphitheater developed. The plan of the first public theater evolved from the physical features of the inn yard (surrounding galleries, open central space, stage extending in this central space or pit), and the bear garden (circular form of building). The front stage was open to the sky, and the rear stage was covered by a ceiling. Above the ceiling was a room for the machinery needed for raising or lowering persons and objects to the stage. An inner stage at the rear was curtained and connected with a balcony above, also curtained.

The first public theater in London was the Theatre, built in 1576 by James Burbage in Shoreditch. In 1577, the Curtain followed. Some ten years later, Henslowe built the Rose on the Bankside and, in 1594, the Swan also appeared in this locality. In 1599, the Theatre was torn down and rebuilt on the Bankside as the Globe, the most important of the public theaters. The Globe was used and controlled by the company to which Shakespeare belonged. (For the distinction between public and private theaters, see **Private Theaters**.)

Puffery: The kind of literary criticism that overpraises a written work, "puffing" or "blowing it up" so that it will appear to have merits that are actually non-existent. Usually, the critic indulging in this kind of flattery hopes that his written work will be reviewed in a similar fashion. A classic example of this kind of critic is Mr. Puff in Sheridan's *The Critic* (1779).

The modern equivalent of puffery is sometimes found in the publisher's blurbs on book jackets, where the contents of the book are enthusiastically described and extravagantly praised. (See **Blurb**.)

Pun: A play on words based on the similarity of sound between two words with different meanings. An example is Thomas Hood's: "They went and told the sexton, and the sexton tolled the bell."

Purist: One who stresses, or overstresses, correctness in language, particularly in minor points of grammar, diction, pronunciation and rhetorical style. The term is frequently used as a reproach.

An example of purism is the insistence upon the use of subjunctive forms of the English verb in constructions where the subjunctive mood would be demanded by formal grammar based on the rules of Latin grammar. For example, a purist might write, *If it* be *a good idea, let us pursue it,* where *If it* is *a good idea, let us pursue it,* has become established as equally good English.

The purist, too, is likely to ignore the existence of different levels of speech and to insist upon the use of formal English on all occasions. However, it is sometimes difficult to draw the line between the purist and the person who strives to achieve accuracy and precision in language. The distinction is often a matter of degree or manner only.

The word is also applied to a person who feels that the purity of a language can be preserved only by the exclusion of foreign words and of words not used by the best stylists. Movements toward purism have included eighteenth-century efforts to standardize the English language through the establishment of a definite linguistic authority, Wordsworth's attempt to use in his poems only simple words drawn from actual speech, and later efforts to stress the Anglo-Saxon elements in the English vocabulary and to check the use of foreign words.

Puritanism: A religious-political movement that developed in England around the middle of the sixteenth century and later spread to North America. Although the movement ended politically with the return of Charles II to London in 1660, Puritanism was a continuing influence on the habits and thought of the people.

Puritanism also exercised an important influence on literature. In England, the years between 1625 and 1660 were called the Cavalier-Puritan Period and were dominated by John Bunyan and John Milton.

During the reign of Queen Elizabeth I, the term Puritan was applied to those who wished to "purify" the Church of England. In principle, the Puritans disapproved of certain established church practices. They objected, for example, to the wearing of the surplice, and they demanded the right to be seated while receiving communion. They advocated a reform of the church courts, the discarding of superstitious customs, serious observance of Sunday and various ecclesiastical reforms. Puritanism, which was an outgrowth of Calvinism, eventually was allied with Presbyterianism. The movement was built on the principles of simplicity and democracy.

The dissatisfaction of one group of Puritans led them to emigrate to America (1620) in order to set up a new society where the Puritan ideas of religion and government would be followed. Within ten years, there were twenty thousand English people in America, many of whom were educated, intelligent and cultured. The writings of the theologians, historians and poets of the period left a permanent imprint on American life.

Purple Patch: A passage of writing in which the author is obviously striving for an impressive or poetic effect. Purple patches, which stand out from the rest of the work, are marked by stylistic tricks and often ornate metaphor.

Putative Author: The alleged author of a work that has, in fact, been written by someone else.

Pyrrhic: A foot of two unaccented syllables ($\cup\cup$); the opposite of spondee ($--$). Frequently appearing in classical poetry, the pyrrhic is unusual in English versification and is not accepted as a foot at all by some prosodists, since it contains no accented syllable.

A "Pyrrhic victory" is a victory gained at too great a cost. The phrase is derived from the name of Pyrrhus, a Greek king (300-272 B.C.), who won a battle against the Romans, but suffered severe losses among his troops.

Q

Qasida: A type of formal ode, usually praising someone. The form has been used by Arabic, Persian, Turkish and Urdu poets. Tennyson imitated it when he wrote *Locksley Hall*.

Quadrivium: See **Seven Arts**.

Quantitative Verse: Greek and Roman system of versification that depends on the quantity of time required to utter a syllable, as opposed to the accentual verse, which depends on stress of syllables, used in English poetry and the poetry of the Germanic languages. (See **Quantity**.)

Quantity: The duration and intensity (stress) employed in pronouncing a syllable. The "quantity" of long or accented syllables is greater than that of short or unaccented syllables. In Greek and Latin poetry, one long syllable was, for purposes of meter, counted as the equal in quantity of two short syllables.

Although English versification is based on accent, rather than on quantity, quantity remains an element in verse style. For example, the one-syllable words *ton* and *town* are different in quantity, as are *ten* and *strange*. Even with a metrical system based on accent, all accented syllables are not of equal quantity, any more than are all unaccented syllables. (See **Accent** and **Stress**.)

Quart d'Heure: In the French theater, a brief one-act play, usually a curtain raiser.

Quartet: Four lines of verse, appearing as a stanza (see **Quatrain**) or as part of a longer poem. The English (Shakespearean) sonnet, for example, consists of three quartets followed by a rhymed couplet.

Quarto: (1) A book made from printers' sheets that have been folded twice to produce eight pages on four leaves. (2) The form in which early editions of Shakespeare's plays were printed. These are known as the First Quarto, Second Quarto, etc. (See **Duodecimo, Folio** and **Octavo**.)

Quatorzain: A poem or stanza of fourteen lines. The term is reserved for fourteen-line poems that do not otherwise conform to a sonnet pattern.

Quatrain: A stanza consisting of four verses. In its narrow meaning, the term is restricted to a complete poem consisting of only four lines.

In its broader sense, it includes any one of many four-verse stanza forms.

The possible rhyme schemes within the stanza vary from an unrhymed quatrain to almost any arrangement of one-rhyme, two-rhyme, or three-rhyme lines. Perhaps the most usual form is *abab*; other rhyme patterns are *aabb*, *abba*, *aaba* and *abcb*. A quatrain of the last pattern is this stanza written by Robert Burns:

> Ye flowery banks o' bonnie Doon
> How can ye blume sae fair?
> How can ye chant, ye little birds,
> And I sae fu' o' care?

Quibble: A pun or play on words; a verbal device for evading the point being discussed, as when debaters engage in quibbles over the interpretation of a question or term.

Quintain: See **Quintet**.

Quintet: A stanza with five lines. Usually, the rhyme scheme is *ababb*, and the line length varies.

Quip: A clever retort or jest; a witty saying, especially a pun or quibble.

q.v.: See. An abbreviation of the Latin phrase *quod vide* (meaning "see which"), q.v. is used to refer the reader to another book, article, periodical, etc. that is mentioned elsewhere in the work. The plural is qq.v.

R

Rabelaisian: Referring to or resembling the works of François Rabelais (1494-1553), a writer of exuberant satire and humor. The term is used to describe writing that is ribald, extravagant and satirically humorous.

Raisonneur: The French equivalent of the confidant in plays or novels. (See **Confidant**.)

Ratiocination: A process of reasoning; deducing consequences from premises.

As a literary or critical term, ratiocination signifies a type of writing in which some sort of enigma or problem is solved through reasoning. The term is particularly applied to fiction of the detective story type. Edgar Allan Poe wrote ratiocination tales, such as *The Murders in the Rue Morgue*, *The Gold Bug* and *The Purloined Letter*.

Rationalism: Systems of thought (philosophical, scientific and religious) that rely on the authority of reason rather than on sensory perceptions, revelation or traditional authority. In England, the rationalist attitude, especially during the eighteenth century, significantly affected religion and literature.

The early humanists (see **Oxford Reformers**) had inisted upon the control of reason, but their teachings had little impact upon prevailing religious thought until reinforced by the scientific thought of the seventeenth century. By the end of the century, theologians generally agreed that religious doctrines could be deduced by reason. The more conservative theologians insisted upon the importance of revelation, while the more radical deists (see **Deism**) rejected revelation.

The religion arising from rationalism stressed reason as a guide to good conduct. Three tenets were the basis of this religion: (1) there is an omnipotent God; (2) He demands virtuous living in obedience to His will; and (3) there is a future life when the good will be rewarded and the wicked will be punished. The stress on reason made rationalism an ally of neoclassicism, while the stress on the potential power and good in human nature led toward romanticism.

Rationalize: To find superficially rational explanations for a position or belief adopted through some intuitive process or prejudice. A writer rationalizes when he consciously seeks and cites reasons to justify a position prompted by his emotions, rather than his intellect.

Realism: In literature, a manner and method of picturing life as it really is, untouched by idealism or romanticism. As a manner of writing, realism relies on the use of specific details to interpret life faithfully and objectively. (See **Naturalism.**)

In contrast to romance, which is concerned with the bizarre and heroic, realism focusses on natural, everyday events. It is psychological in its approach to character, presenting the individual rather than the type. Often, fate plays a major role in the action.

Realism became prominent in the English novel with such writers as Daniel Defoe, Samuel Richardson, Henry Fielding, Tobias Smollett, Laurence Sterne, Jane Austen, Charlotte Brontë, Anthony Trollope and William Makepeace Thackeray. (Compare with **Expressionism, Impressionism, Naturalism** and **Romanticism.**)

Realistic Comedy: Any comedy employing the methods of realism, but particularly comedy developed by Jonson, Chapman, Middleton and other Elizabethan and Jacobean dramatists. Opposed to the romantic comedy, it reflects the reaction in the late 1590s against Elizabethan romanticism and extravagance, as well as an effort to produce English comedy in the manner of classical comedy.

This realistic comedy deals with London life, is strongly satirical and sometimes cynical in tone, is interested in both individuals and types of character, and centers upon an observation of contemporary life. The appeal is intellectual and the tone is coarse.

The comedy of humours was a special form, representing the first stage of the development of important realistic comedy. Jonson's *The Alchemist* and Middleton's *A Trick to Catch the Old One* are typical Jacobean realistic comedies. The Restoration comedy of manners owes something to this earlier form, and one Restoration dramatist (Shadwell) wrote comedy of the Jonsonian type.

Realistic Novel: See **Realism.**

Rebuttal: A term borrowed from debating procedure and signifying a reply to an argument, particularly a final summing up of answers to the arguments of the opposition.

Recessive Accent: An accent that falls on the first syllable of a word that is normally accented on the second syllable. The device of using recessive accent is common in poetry.

Recto and Verso: A right-hand page in a book is a recto; a left-hand page is a verso.

Redaction: A revision or editing of a manuscript; putting it into presentable form; preparing it for publication. Sometimes, too, the term implies a digest of a longer piece of work, or a new version of an older piece of writing. For example, Malory's *Le Morte d'Arthur* is a redaction of many of the Arthurian stories.

Reductio ad Absurdum: A "reduction to absurdity" to show the falsity of an argument or position. As a method of argument, this process carries a general statement to its extreme, but logical, conclusion. For example, one might state that the more sleep one has, the more healthy one is. By the logical reductio ad absurdum process, someone would point out that, on such a premise, he who has sleeping sickness and sleeps for days is really in the best of health.

Redundant: Writing characterized by the use of superfluous words. A redundant style of expression is marked by the unjustified repetition of unnecessary words. In *Hamlet*, Polonius is characterized as a doddering old man largely by the redundancies of his speech. For example:

> Madam, I swear I use no art at all.
> That he is mad, 'tis true; 'tis true 'tis pity;
> And pity 'tis 'tis true; a foolish figure;
> But farewell it, for I will use no art.
> Mad let us grant him, then; and now remains
> That we find out the cause of this effect,
> Or rather say, the cause of this defect,
> For this effect defective comes by cause;
> Thus it remains, and the remainder thus.

(See **Pleonasm** and **Tautology**.)

Reformation: The Christian religious movement in the sixteenth century that resulted in the formation of the various Protestant Churches. The attendant changes in life and thought colored and conditioned the work of Spenser, Milton, Bunyan and scores of other writers. The Protestant Reformation is also represented in English literature by the sermons and writings of William Tyndale, Thomas Cranmer and Hugh Latimer, as well as by the English Book of Common Prayer and the series of English Bibles that culminated in the King James version.

However, the English Reformation was essentially a popular movement and was accompanied by a flood of popular works: sermons and tracts that played their part in the development of English prose style; reprints of suppressed Lollard tracts of the pre-Reformation period; translations and imitations of German Protestant pieces; satirical verse; and the controversial plays of John Bale.

In Scotland, a mass of Reformation literature appeared, including Sir David Lyndsay's satirical morality play, *A Pleasant Satire of the Three Estates*, and the politico-religious prose of John Knox.

Reformed Comedy: See **Sentimental Comedy**.

Refrain: A group of words forming a phrase or sentence, and repeated at regular intervals in a poem, usually at the end of a stanza. Historically, the refrain probably developed from the old ballad in which the stanza was recited by a single speaker, while the whole group joined in the refrain.

Refrains are of various types. First, and most common is the use of the same line at the close of each stanza (as in most ballads). Another, less common form is that in which the refrain recurs somewhat erratically throughout the stanzas — sometimes in one place, sometimes in another. In other instances, a refrain may be used with a slight variation in wording at each recurrence. Still another variety of the refrain is the use of some rather meaningless phrase, which, by its mere repetition at the close of stanzas, seems to take on a different significance with each appearance. An example is Poe's ''Nevermore'' in *The Raven*.

Regional Literature: Writing that presents the habits, speech, manners, customs and historical background of the geographical area in which the story takes place. Thomas Hardy's novels about life in Wessex and Arnold Bennett's *Five Towns* series are examples of regional literature. Sometimes the term is applied to local color literature but, in the strict sense, the latter presents a more specific area than regional writing does. (See **Local Color Literature**.)

Relief Scene: A scene in a tragedy, usually as a part of the falling action, the purpose of which is to provide emotional relaxation for the audience.

Religious Drama: See **Medieval Drama**, **Miracle Play**, **Morality Play** and **Mystery Play**.

Relique: An old spelling of relic, meaning something that survives. A well-known use of the term in literature is in the title of Bishop Percy's printed collection of old ballads, *Reliques of Ancient Poetry* (1765).

Renaissance: The period, ranging from the fourteenth through the sixteenth centuries, that marked the transition from the medieval to the modern world in Western Europe. The Renaissance began in Italy, spreading through Northern Europe and England in the sixteenth century. Renaissance means ''rebirth'' and, during the Renaissance period, the classical culture of Greece and Rome was rediscovered. Renaissance man turned away from medieval ideas and ideals, finding inspiration in classical models and attitudes. A balanced development of mind and body was emphasized. The period was marked by a surge of creative activity in art and literature. (See **Elizabethan Drama, Humanism, Platonism** and **Reformation**.

Repartee: A quick, clever verbal response; conversation made up of brilliant witticisms. The term is borrowed from fencing terminology. Sydney Smith and Charles Lamb were well known for their command of repartee. An example of repartee is found in an Oxford account of the meeting of Beau Nash and John Wesley. When the two met on a narrow pavement, Nash was brusque. "I never make way for a fool," he said insolently. "Don't you? I always do," responded Wesley, stepping to one side.

Repetend: The repetition or partial repetition of a word, phrase or clause throughout a stanza or poem. Repetend differs from refrain in that the refrain usually appears at predetermined places within the poem, whereas the repetend appears irregularly and unexpectedly. A further difference is that the repetend only partially repeats, whereas the refrain usually repeats an entire line or combination of lines. Both Coleridge and Poe make frequent use of the repetend. In the following example from Poe's *Ulalume*, some of the repetends are italicized:

> The skies *they were* ashen *and* sober:
> *The leaves they were* crisped *and sere*—
> *The leaves they were* withering *and sere;*
> *It was* night in the lonesome October
> Of my most immemorial year;
> *It was* hard *by the* dim lake *of Auber*,
> *In the* misty mid region *of Weir*—
> *It was* down *by the* dank tarn *of Auber*,
> *In the* ghoul-haunted woodland *of Weir*.

Repetition: Reiteration of a word, phrase, sound or idea to secure emphasis. Employed deliberately, it adds force and clarity, and is frequently used effectively by orators. In poetry, repetition can be a unifying device. A notable example of effective repetition is in Poe's *The Bells*. (Compare with **Pleonasm** and **Tautology**.)

Requiem: The mass for the dead; a musical setting of the mass for the dead; a hymn or chant for the dead. The following lines, from Matthew Arnold's *Requiescat*, are an example of a requiem in verse:

> Strew on her roses, roses
> And never a spray of yew!
> In quiet she reposes;
> Ah, would that I did too!

Resolution: The events following the climax of a play or story; the term is used synonymously with falling action. (See **Climax** and **Falling Action**.)

Restoration: In English history, the re-establishment of the Stuarts to the monarchy with the return of King Charles II; the period between 1660 and 1702. For a discussion of the literature and drama of the period, see **Character, Classicism, Comedy of Manners, Essay, Heroic Plays, Neoclassicism** and **Satire**.

Restraint: A critical term applied to writing in which the emotional elements of a given situation are controlled and held in check. Often, the quality of restraint distinguishes great literature from the mediocre.

Revenge Tragedy: A form of drama made popular on the Elizabethan stage by Thomas Kyd, whose *Spanish Tragedy* (ca. 1592) is an early example of the type. The revenge tragedy imitated the plot and technique of the tragedies written by the Roman philosopher, Seneca (first century). The prevailing theme is the revenge of a father for a murdered son or vice versa, and the revenge is directed by the ghost of the murdered man.

Elements in revenge tragedies include the hesitation of the hero, real or pretended insanity, suicide, intrigue, a clever, scheming villain, philosophic soliloquies and the sensational use of horrors (murders on the stage, exhibition of dead bodies, etc.).

Examples of the type include Shakespeare's *Hamlet*, Marston's *Antonio's Revenge* and Tourneur's *Atheist's Tragedy*. (See **Senecan Tragedy** and **Tragedy of Blood**.)

Reversal: See **Peripety**.

Review: (1) A short article describing and discussing the merits and faults of a book, play, motion picture etc. (2) A magazine or journal containing articles on particular subjects, such as literature or art. The *Edinburgh Review*, founded in 1802, is a well-known example.

Revue: A light musical entertainment consisting of a variety of songs, dances, choruses and skits. There is no connected plot. Satiric comment on contemporary personalities and events is a characteristic element. Usually, the setting and scenery are elaborate.

Rhapsody: (1) In writing or speech, an extravagantly enthusiastic expression of emotion. (2) An epic poem, or part of an epic poem, suitable for a single, uninterrupted recitation. In ancient Greece, minstrels who recited epic poetry were known as rhapsodists.

Rhetoric: The body of principles and theory having to do with the presentation of facts and ideas in clear, convincing and attractive language.

The actual founder of rhetoric is said to be Corax of Syracuse, who, in the fifth century B.C., stipulated certain fundamental principles for public argument. He outlined five divisions for a speech: proem, narrative, argument, remarks and peroration or conclusion.

The traditional aim of rhetoric was to give effectiveness to public speech. According to Aristotle, rhetoric was a manner of effectively organizing material for the presentation of truth, for an appeal to the intellect through speech. It was distinct from poetry, a manner of composition presenting ideas emotionally and imaginatively.

In England during the Renaissance, such books as Sir Thomas Wilson's *The Arte of Rhetorique* (1553) did much to popularize the best practices of the early classical writers on the subject.

Because rhetorical devices are intentional, rhetoric sometimes has the connotation of the ostentatious or artificial. Among the rhetorical devices defined in this dictionary are: alliteration, allusion, antithesis, apostrophe, contrast, inversion and repetition.

Rhetorical Device: The deliberate use of words for effect. Rhetorical devices include alliteration, apostrophe, repetition and the rhetorical question. Each of these terms is defined in this dictionary.

Rhetorical Question: A question posed for its rhetorical effect and not intended to induce or require a reply. The rhetorical question is frequently used in persuasion and in oratory. Since the answer is obvious, it makes a deeper impression on the hearer than a direct statement would. Pope uses the rhetorical question repeatedly in the following lines:

> Was it for this you took such constant care
> The bodkin, comb, and essence to prepare?
> For this your locks in paper durance bound?
> For this with tort'ring irons wreath'd around?
> For this with fillets strain'd your tender head,
> And bravely bore the double loads of lead?
> Gods! shall the ravisher display your hair,
> While the fops envy, and the ladies stare?

Rhyme: Similarity or identity of sound in the accented syllables of two or more words. The similarity is based on the vowels of the accented syllables, which must, for a perfect rhyme, be preceded by different consonants. Thus, *cat* and *fat* are perfect rhymes, as are *hating* and *skating*, because the vowel sounds are identical and the preceding consonants *different*.

The types of rhyme are classified according to the position of the rhymed syllables in the line and according to the number of syllables in which the identical sounds occur.

Rhymes classified according to the position of the rhymed syllables include:

(1) *End rhyme*, the most common type, occurring at the end of the verse:

Tiger! Tiger! burning bright
In the forests of the night . . .

BLAKE

(2) *Internal rhyme*, occurring within a single line:

Say that health and wealth have missed me . . .

HUNT

One form of internal rhyme is *leonine rhyme*. (See **Leonine Rhyme.**)

(3) *Beginning rhyme*, which is rare, occurring at the beginning of the verses.

Mad from life's history,
Glad to death's mystery . . .

HOOD

Rhymes classified according to the number of syllables with similar sounds include:

(1) *Masculine rhyme*, where the correspondence of sound occurs in the final accented syllable, as in *cat* and *fat*.

(2) *Feminine rhyme*, where the sounds are identical in two consecutive syllables, as in *hating* and *skating*.

(3) *Triple rhyme*, where the sounds are identical in three consecutive syllables, as in *glorious* and *victorious*.

Rhyme Royal: A seven-line iambic pentameter stanza, rhyming *ababbcc*. The name is said to derive from its use by the Scottish king, James I. However, Chaucer and other predecessors of James had used rhyme royal, which is sometimes called the Chaucerian stanza. Chaucer's *Parlement of Foules*, *The Man of Law's Tale*, *The Clerk's Tale* and *Troilus and Criseyde* are written in rhyme royal.

Other poets who have used the form include Lydgate, Wyatt, Morris, Spenser, Shakespeare and Masefield.

The following stanza, from Shakespeare's *Rape of Lucrece*, is an example of rhyme royal:

When they had sworn to this advised doom,
They did conclude to bear dead Lucrece thence;
To show her bleeding body through Rome,
And so to publish Tarquin's foul offence:
Which being done with speedy diligence,
The Romans plausibly did give consent
To Tarquin's everlasting banishment.

Rhyme Scheme: The pattern, or sequence, in which the rhyme sounds occur in a stanza or poem. For the purpose of analysis, rhyme schemes are usually presented by assigning the same letter of the alphabet to each similar sound in the last word of a line. For example:

The time I've lost in wooing,	*a*
In watching and pursuing	*a*
The light that lies	*b*
In woman's eyes,	*b*
Has been my heart's undoing.	*a*
Tho' wisdom oft has sought me,	*c*
I scorned the lore she brought me,	*c*
My only books	*d*
Were woman's looks,	*d*
And folly's all they've taught me.	*c*

T<small>HOMAS</small> M<small>OORE</small>

Here *wooing, pursuing* and *undoing* all have the same rhyme and are given the symbol *a*; *lies* and *eyes* are alike and are assigned the symbol *b*; *sought me, brought me* and *taught me* are all alike and are given the symbol *c*; *books* and *looks* rhyme and are given the symbol *d*. The rhyme scheme of the stanza is *aabbaccddc*.

Rhythm: (1) A movement having a regular repetition of a beat, accent, stress, rise and fall, etc. For example, *the rhythm of prose, poetry, dancing, skating, swimming or of a particular piece of music.* (2) In poetry, the rhythmic forms succeed each other so regularly that the rhythm can be measured, and the poetry can be divided into metrical feet. In prose, the rise and fall of emphasis and accent are less regular. (See **Foot, Meter, Prose Rhythm** and **Quantity.**)

Rhythmical Pause: A pause that separates phrases when the speaker draws breath. Not counted as part of the metrical pattern, in the reading of verse with a strongly marked rhythm it tends to create a singsong effect.

Rhythmical Prose: See **Prose Rhythm.**

Riddle: A verbal puzzle, usually in the form of a question; a conundrum. For example: *What can go up the chimney down, but not down the chimney up*? (*An umbrella.*)

Riddles based on Latin prototypes were an important part of the informal literatures of Western Europe, including Anglo-Saxon. The riddles of Aldhelm (seventh century), though written in Latin, are English in tone, and *The Exeter Book* (eleventh century) contains nearly a hundred riddles in Old English.

Riding Rhyme: Heroic verse consisting of rhymed couplets, which were introduced into English verse by Chaucer, and constitute a major portion of *The Canterbury Tales*. For example:

> Whan that Aprille with his shoures soote
> The droghte of March hath perced to the roote,

Two theories regarding the source of the name exist: one, that it was related while riding a horse; the other, that the verse was made of such words as would allow no convenient caesura, and the verses ran until they ended. (See **Caesura**.)

Rime Couée: See **Tail-Rhyme Stanza**.

Rimur: Historic poems of Iceland, told in alliterative verse.

Rising Action: The part of a plot in which the complication of the action occurs. It begins with the exciting force, gains in interest and power as the opposing groups come into conflict and proceeds to the climax or turning point. (See **Dramatic Structure** and **Short Story**.)

Rising Rhythm: The kind of rhythm that results when the stress in a line of verse falls on the final syllables of the metric feet. Iambs and anapests are the basis of falling rhythm. (See **Anapest** and **Iambus**.)

The following lines, based on iambs, are an example:

> The Sun's | rim dips; | the stars | rush out: |
> At one | stride comes | the dark; |
> With far | heard whis | per, o'er | the sea, |
> Off shot | the spec | tre-bark.

COLERIDGE

Ritornello: A short, recurring passage in music or verse.

Rocking Rhythm: This occurs when the stressed syllable in a foot of verse falls between two unstressed syllables.

172

Rococo: A style of decoration developed in the first half of the eighteenth century, marked by elaborate ornamentation. In literature, a style of florid writing.

Rodomontade: Ostentatious bragging or blustering. Falstaff's description of his bold fight with the highwaymen in *Henry IV, Part One* is an example of rodomontade. The term is derived from Rodomonte, a boastful king in Ariosto's *Orlando Furioso*.

Roman à Clef: Literally, "a book with a key"; a literary work in which real persons are presented under thinly veiled disguises and can be easily distinguished.

This genre is usually used in connection with satire. For example, in Swift's *Gulliver's Travels*, many of the characters were clearly meant to represent contemporary politicians and clergymen.

Romance: In the Middle Ages, a fictitious story in prose or verse about knights, their ladies and their deeds. An example is *Sir Gawain and the Green Knight*.

The word romance was first applied to Old French, a language derived from Latin (*Roman*), to distinguish the language from Latin itself. That meaning has been extended to include any language that developed from Latin. Spanish and Italian, for example, are romance languages.

After the Middle Ages, the term came to be used for a story of adventure, such as Cervantes' *Don Quixote*. In modern usage, a love story or a tale of adventure is called a romance. (See **Arthurian Legend, Medieval Romance, Metrical Romance** and **Romantic Novel**.)

Romance of Chivalry: See **Chivalric Romance**.

Romanesque: A term sometimes applied to fanciful or fabulous writing. More rarely, romanesque is used to describe a written work that has some of the qualities of a romance.

Romantic Comedy: A comedy in which the primary theme is love, especially the type of comedy developed on the Elizabethan stage by such writers as Robert Greene and Shakespeare. Greene's *James the Fourth* (ca. 1591) is believed to have influenced Shakespeare's *Two Gentlemen of Verona*. Later romantic Shakespearean comedies were *The Merchant of Venice* and *As You Like It*.

Characteristics of the romantic comedy include: much out-of-door activity, an idealized heroine (who usually masks as a man), love subjected to great difficulties, reconciliations and a happy ending.

Romantic Criticism: A term sometimes used for the critical ideas that developed late in the eighteenth and early in the nineteenth century, as romanticism replaced the neoclassicism of the preceding period.

Coleridge and others devised new critical theories about Shakespeare, whom classicists had regarded as a "rude uncultivated genius," who succeeded in spite of his violation of classical rules for drama. Rather, Coleridge said, Shakespeare's work was successful because it followed the laws of its own organism, which were more authentic than formal, man-made rules. Shakespeare had "an implicit wisdom deeper even than our consciousness," and "in all points from the most important to the most minute, the judgment of Shakespeare is commensurate with his genius . . ."

Another aspect of romantic criticism was Wordsworth's theory that poetry should be based on simple themes drawn from humble life, and expressed in ordinary, rather than exalted, language.

In addition to Coleridge and Wordsworth, other romantic critics were Shelley, De Quincey, Lamb, Hazlitt and Hunt. (See **Romanticism**.)

Romantic Epic: A type of long narrative poem developed by Italian Renaissance poets (late fifteenth and sixteenth centuries) by combining the materials and some of the method of the medieval romance with the manner and technique of the classic epic. (See **Epic** and **Medieval Romance**.)

The literary critics of the time were divided in their attitudes toward the new type of epic. The conservatives strongly opposed it because it departed from classical standards. The form was generally popular with readers, however, and when Edmund Spenser came to write *The Faerie Queene*, he modelled it on the romantic epics of Ariosto (*Orlando Furioso*, 1516) and Tasso (*Jerusalem Delivered*, 1581). *The Faerie Queene*, epic in its patriotic purpose and in much of its technique, romantic in its chivalric atmosphere and Arthurian setting, became an outstanding example in English literature of a romantic epic.

Romanticism: A movement of the eighteenth and nineteenth centuries that marked the reaction in literature, philosophy, art, religion and politics against the neoclassicism and formal doctrines of the preceding period. One aspect is reflected in Victor Hugo's phrase "liberalism in literature," meaning especially the freeing of the artist and writer from the restraints and rules of the classicists, and also suggesting a spirit of individualism, which led to the encouragement of revolutionary political ideas.

In England, the romantic movement was marked by such qualities as sentimentalism, primitivism, love of nature, interest in the past (especially the medieval) and individualism. These qualities were expressed by the abandonment of the heroic couplet and the ode in favor of blank verse, the sonnet, the Spenserian stanza and many experimental verse forms. Conventional poetic imagery was replaced by fresh, bold expression. Other characteristics of romanticism in literature were: the idealization of rural life (Goldsmith); interest in human rights (Burns and Byron); sentimental melancholy (Gray); collection and imitation of popular ballads (Percy and Scott); and a renewed interest in Spenser, Shakespeare and Milton.

The romantic movement in English literature had its beginnings early in the eighteenth century (Shaftesbury, Thomson and Dyer). It became prominent in the middle of the century with the work of Gray, Richardson, Sterne, Walpole, Goldsmith and, somewhat later, Cowper, Burns and Blake. However, most major works of the romantic movement were produced early in the nineteenth century by Wordsworth, Coleridge, Scott, Southey, Byron, Shelley and Keats. (See **Classicism**, **Nature**, **Neoclassicism**, **Primitivism**, **Romantic Criticism** and **Sentimentalism**.)

Romantic Novel: A type of novel marked by strong interest in action and episodes based on love, adventure and combat. The romantic novel owes its origin to the early romances of medieval times. (See **Romance**.) Later, elements of the fabliau and the novella were added. (See **Fabliau** and **Novella**.)

In its modern meaning, a romance is a type of novel that is more concerned with action than with character, is more fictional than legendary and is read more as an escape from daily concerns than for the purpose of understanding the actualities of life.

Romantic Tragedy: Non-classical tragedy. The term is used for tragedy that does not conform to the traditions or aims of classical tragedy. It differs from the latter in its greater freedom of technique, wider scope of theme and treatment, and greater emphasis on character (rather than plot). Romantic tragedy is also looser in structure, has a greater variety of style and easily admits humorous, even grotesque, elements. Elizabethan tragedy is largely romantic. (See **Classical Tragedy** and **Tragedy**.)

Romany: The language of the gypsies. Romany is a corrupted form of the Indian branch of the Indo-Iranian languages, blended with words and phrases from various European languages, and spoken in many dialects. The term is also used to mean gypsy or to describe something pertaining to the gypsies.

Rondeau: A French verse pattern, generally used for light and fanciful expression. Characteristically, the rondeau pattern consists of fifteen lines, of which the ninth and fifteenth are short lines — a refrain. Only two rhymes (exclusive of the refrain) are allowed, and the rhyme scheme is: *aabba, aabC, aabbaC*. The *C*-rhyme represents the refrain, a group of words usually selected from the first half of the opening verse. The form is divided into three stanzas, with the refrain at the end of the second and third stanzas.

Rondel: A French verse form, a variant of the rondeau, to which it is historically related. The rondel usually consists of fourteen lines, with the rhyme scheme *ABbaabABbabbaAB*. (The capitalized rhymes here represent verses used as a refrain and repeated in their entirety.) In the rondel, as in the other French forms, repetition of rhyme words is not allowed. Sometimes only one line is used in the final refrain.

The rondel differs from the rondeau in two respects: the number of lines and the use of complete (rather than partial) lines for the refrain.

Rondelet: A short French verse form of five lines and two refrains in a single stanza. After the second and fifth lines, the first part of the opening line appears as a refrain. The rhyme scheme is, *abCabbC*, with *C* as the refrain.

Roundel: A variation of the French rondeau verse pattern, generally attributed to Swinburne, who wrote *A Century of Roundels* and gave the form its popularity. The roundel is characterized by an eleven-line form and the presence, in the fourth and ninth lines, of a refrain taken, as in the rondeau, from the first part of the opening line. The rhyme scheme (with *C* indicating the refrain) is: *abaCbababaC*.

Roundelay: A modification of the rondel, a French lyric verse form. The roundelay is a simple poem or song of about fourteen lines, in which part of one line frequently recurs as a refrain. The term is also used to mean the musical setting of a rondeau, sung or chanted as an accompaniment for a folk dance.

Rubaiyat Stanza: Named after *The Rubaiyat*, by Omar Khayyam, the Rubaiyat stanza is an iambic pentameter quatrain with a rhyme scheme *aaba*. (Also known as Omar stanza.)

Rune: A character in an alphabet developed during the second and third centuries by the Germanic tribes in Europe. The Runic characters were based on the letters of the Greek and Roman alphabets, simplified so that they were suitable for carving on wood, stone, drinking horns, weapons and ornaments. The Runic alphabet consisted of twenty-four letters.

Runes, inscribed in certain ways, were believed to have magical powers and were used for charms. Later, rune came to mean any secret means of written communication.

Runic writing was common in Anglo-Saxon England until it was replaced by the Latin alphabet used by Christian missionaries.

Old Finnish and Scandinavian poems are sometimes called runes.

Running Rhythm: A term invented by the English poet, Gerard Manley Hopkins (1844-1899), to describe the usual rhythm of English poetry. This type of rhythm is measured by metrical feet of two or three syllables, with occasional extra unaccented syllables. According to Hopkins, running rhythm is the opposite of sprung rhythm. (See **Sprung Rhythm.**)

Run-on Line: A verse without a grammatical stop at the end of the line.

When a poet uses run-on lines, the position of the caesura becomes important for internal pause then plays a greater part in the line's rhythm. (See **Caesura, End-stopped Line** and **Rhythm.**)

S

Saga: Originally, a medieval Icelandic or other Scandinavian story recording the legendary and historical accounts of heroic adventure, especially of members of important families. The earlier Icelandic sagas, like the early Irish epics and romances, were in prose. There were also mythological sagas.

Saga also came to be used for any historical legend developed by oral tradition until it was popularly accepted as true — a form between authentic history and intentional fiction.

Today, the term refers to any traditional tale of heroic achievement or extraordinary adventure. John Galsworthy used the term in the title of his series of novels, *The Forsyte Saga*.

Saint's Play: See **Miracle Play**.

Sapphic: A stanzaic pattern deriving its name from the Greek lyric poetess, Sappho (ca. 600 B.C.). The pattern consists of three verses of eleven syllables (−ᴜ | −− | −ᴜᴜ | −ᴜ | −ᴜ) and a fourth verse of five syllables (−ᴜᴜ | −ᴜ). English poets have attempted to use this pattern, but the demand for three spondees in each stanza frequently results in distortion. The following is an example from Swinburne:

Then to | me so | lying a | wake a | vision
Came with | out sleep | over the | seas and | touched me,
Softly | touched mine | eyelids and | lips; and | I too,
Full of the | vision, . . .

Sarcasm: A sneering or cutting remark; an ironical taunt. (See **Irony**.) Sarcasm is common in most forms of literature, especially rhetoric and humor.

Satanic School: A phrase used by Southey in the preface to his *Vision of Judgment* (1821) to designate the members of the literary group made up of Byron, Shelley, Hunt and their associates, whose irregular lives and radical ideas — defiantly expressed in their writings — suggested the term. These poets were frequently contrasted with the "pious" group of the Lake School — Wordsworth, Coleridge and Southey. By an extension of the term, writers who have attacked conventional moral standards have been referred to as belonging to the Satanic School of literature.

Satire: Verse or prose blending a critical attitude with humor and wit. The purpose of satire is to ridicule frailties in human customs and institutions and, by causing laughter, to inspire their reform.

Satire existed in the early classical literature of Greece and Rome, and persisted through the Middle Ages in the fabliau and beast epic.

In Spain, the picaresque novel developed a strong element of satire. In France, Molière and Le Sage satirized customs and manners, and Voltaire later established a reputation as an archsatirist of literature.

In England, from the time of Gascoigne (*Steel Glass*, 1576) and Lodge (*Fig for Momus*, 1595), writers such as Hall, Nash, Donne and Jonson condemned the vices and follies of their age in verse and prose. By the time of Charles I, however, interest in satire had declined, to be revived with the struggle between the Cavaliers and the Puritans. In Dryden's work, the heroic couplet, already the favorite form with most English satirists, developed into fine satire. The eighteenth century became a golden age of satire in poetry, drama, essays and criticism, written by such men as Dryden, Swift, Addison, Steele, Pope and Fielding. More recently in England, the satirical spirit has been evident in the work of such writers as Shaw, Bennett and Galsworthy.

Satiric Poetry: Verses treating their subject with irony or ridicule. (See **Satire.**) The term characterizes a method of treatment, rather than content or form. For example, Pope's *Dunciad* is a satiric epic; Stephen Crane's *War Is Kind* is a satiric lyric. Among the well-known masters of satire in English poetry are Dryden, Pope and Byron.

Saturday Club: A club of literary and scientific people in and around Cambridge and Boston, the members of which met chiefly for social intercourse and conversation. Some of the more famous members were Emerson, Longfellow, Agassiz, Pierce and Holmes.

Satyr Play: See **Tetralogy.**

Scald: See **Skald.**

Scansion: The division of verse into feet by indicating accents and counting syllables to determine the meter of a poem. Scansion is a study of the mechanical elements used by the poet to establish his rhythmical effects. A scansion of the following stanza from Keats' *The Eve of St. Agnes* shows the accents and divisions into feet:

> Ănd stīll | shĕ slēpt | ăn āz | ŭre-lĭd | dĕd slēep
> Ĭn blānch | ĕd līn | ĕn, smōoth | ănd lāv | ĕndered,
> Whīle hē | frŏm fōrth | thĕ clōs | ĕt brŏught | ă hēap
> Ŏf căn | dĭed āp | plĕ, quĭnce, | ănd plŭm, | ănd gōurd;
> Wĭth jēl | lĭes sōoth | ĕr thăn | thĕ crēam | y̆ cŭrd,
> Ănd lū | cĕnt sȳr | ŏps, tīnct | wĭth cĭn | nămōn;
> Mānnă | ănd dătes, | ĭn ār | gŏsy | trānsfĕrred

Fr̆om Fēz; | ănd spīc | ĕd dāin | tĭes, ēv | ĕry ōne
Frŏm sīlk | ĕn Sām | ăr cānd | tŏ cē | dărĕd Lēb | ă nōn.

The meter of the stanza is predominantly composed of an unaccented syllable followed by an accented syllable ($\cup-$), an iambus or iambic foot. (For other types of meter, see **Meter**.)

Most verses in the stanza contain five feet. Thus, the meter of *The Eve of St. Agnes* is iambic pentameter. (For verses of more or less than five feet, see **Meter**.)

There are two exceptions to the regular pattern of the stanza above. The first foot of the seventh verse consists of an accented syllable preceding an unaccented syllable (and is thus a trochee); the ninth verse consists of six iambic feet (and is thus a hexameter or an Alexandrine). The stanza, therefore, consists of eight iambic pentameter verses, with a ninth verse that is an Alexandrine. This pattern is called the Spenserian stanza. (See **Spenserian Stanza**.)

Scazon: The name of a meter in which the rhythm at the close of the line or period is imperfect. The term is also used to designate a catalectic trochaic tetrameter, where the syllable preceding the last one is long instead of the normal short syllable.

Scenario: A working synopsis of a story plot arranged according to the particular needs of motion picture production; an outline of any story, play, opera, etc.

Scene (of a drama): A part of an act (e.g., *Act I, Scene 2*); some particular incident or situation that occurs during the play (e.g., *the balcony scene in Romeo and Juliet*).

Scenes may vary in length and purpose. For example, a drama may include expository scenes, transitional scenes, development scenes, climactic scenes, relief scenes, etc.

Scholasticism: In the Middle Ages, a system of philosophical and theological teaching, based on an effort to reconcile Christian doctrine with the demands of reason, and relying on Aristotelian methods of logic. Scholasticism was characterized by a formal method of discussion and insisted on rigid, accurate reasoning.

The first era of scholasticism (twelfth century) marked a break from the freer reasoning of the early church fathers. The second era (thirteenth century) was dominated by the Aristotelian influence. Thomas Aquinas and Duns Scotus headed opposing groups known as Thomists and Scotists. Scholasticism declined during the third era (especially the fifteenth century) when, although its methods had been perfected, it became largely occupied with trivialities.

The decline of scholasticism, with its deductive method of reasoning, prepared the way for the inductive method, advocated by Francis Bacon, and was the beginning of the experimental scientific method.

Scholiast: One who wrote *scholia* or marginal comments explaining the grammar or meaning of passages in medieval manuscripts, particularly Greek and Latin texts.

School Drama: See **Academic Drama**.

Schoolmen: Medieval philosophers who followed the method of scholasticism in their debates. Francis Bacon called them "hair-splitters." (See **Scholasticism**.)

School of Sensibility: See **Sensibility**.

School of Spenser: A group of seventeenth-century poets who were influenced by the work of Edmund Spenser. Among them were Giles and Phineas Fletcher, William Browne, George Wither, William Drummond of Hawthornden, Sir John Davies and Sir William Alexander. Their work was characterized by sensuousness, melody, personifications, pictorial quality, interest in narrative, medievalism (especially in the use of allegory), archaisms, modified or genuine Spenserian stanza, pastoralism and moral seriousness. Since the poets of the school influenced Milton, they form a link between the two great Puritan poets of the English Renaissance, Spenser and Milton.

Schuttelreim: A form of nonsense poetry similar to a limerick or a clerihew. It is of German origin. (See **Clerihew** and **Limerick**.)

Science Fiction: A story based on real or imagined elements of scientific technology. Edgar Allan Poe is sometimes referred to as the first science-fiction writer. Later, Jules Verne and H. G. Wells wrote outstanding stories based on the possibilities of scientific advances. More recently, Arthur C. Clarke, Isaac Asimov, Ray Bradbury and Robert Heinlein are well-known for their contributions to science fiction.

Scop: In the Old English period, an Anglo-Saxon minstrel or professional poet who went from one court to another as an entertainer. The scop presented poems and songs, often of his own composition, in honor of the kings he visited or in celebration of battles and other important events, either contemporary or traditional.

In some instances, a scop was attached permanently to a royal household, somewhat like a poet laureate.

Screenplay: The script for a motion picture. Sometimes a screenplay is based on an existing piece of literature; sometimes it is an original work.

Scriptural Drama: See **Mystery Play**.

Semantics: (1) The study of the meanings of words, especially the development of, and changes in, meanings. (2) The study of the relationship between words and human behavior, i.e., of how behavior is influenced by words and vice versa.

Senecan Tragedy: The Latin tragedies attributed to the Stoic philosopher, Seneca (first century). Modelled largely on the Greek tragedies of Euripides they exerted an important influence on Renaissance playwrights. In general, the plays had the following characteristics: (1) conventional five-act division; (2) the use of a chorus (for comment), and such stock characters as a ghost, a cruel tyrant, the faithful male servant and the female confidante; (3) the presentation of much of the action through narrative reports recited by messengers; (4) the employment of sensational themes drawn from Greek mythology, involving unnatural crimes (adultery, incest, infanticide, etc.) and often motivated by revenge; (5) a highly rhetorical style, marked by hyperbole, detailed descriptions, exaggerated comparisons, epigrams and the sharp dialogue known as stichomythia; and (6) much use of introspection and soliloquy.

Renaissance humanism stimulated interest in the Senecan tragedies, and they were translated and imitated in early academic and court drama in Italy, France and England. Sackville and Norton's *Gorboduc* (acted 1562), called the first English tragedy, was an imitation of Seneca.

A more important group of plays began with those produced by Marlowe and Kyd for the popular stage. These plays, which combined native English tragic tradition with a modified Senecan technique, led to the typical Elizabethan tragedy. Kyd's *Spanish Tragedy*, for example, reflects such Senecan traits as sensationalism, bombastic rhetoric, the use of the chorus and the ghost. However, it departed from the Senecan method in that the murders and horrors took place on the stage, in response to popular Elizabethan taste and in defiance of Horace's dictum that good taste demanded leaving such matters for off-stage action. *Spanish Tragedy* inaugurated a long line of Elizabethan tragedies, including Shakespeare's *Hamlet*. (See **Revenge Tragedy** and **Tragedy of Blood**.)

Sense Element in Literature: See **Sensuous**.

Sensibility: A term used to indicate emotionalism as opposed to rationalism; a reliance upon the feelings, rather than reason and law, as guides to truth and conduct. Sensibility is connected with such eighteenth-century attitudes as primitivism, sentimentalism, naturalism and other aspects of romanticism. (See **Naturalism, Primitivism, Romanticism** and **Sentimentalism.**)

Sensuous: A critical term characterizing writing that plays on the various senses of the reader. For example, Keat's *The Eve of St. Agnes*, with images appealing to the senses of sight, touch, taste, smell and hearing, is a sensuous poem. The term should not be confused with "sensual," which usually denotes overemphasis on the passion of physical love.

Sentence: A rhetorical term formerly used in the sense of apothegm or maxim (Latin, *sententia*) and applied to quoted "wise sayings." In old writings, sentence sometimes means sense, gists or theme.

In modern usage, a sentence is a group of words having a subject and predicate, and expressing a complete thought. In law, it means the decision handed down by a judge on the punishment of a criminal, or the punishment itself. (See **Loose Sentence.**)

Sentimental Comedy: A kind of drama that appeared in the early years of the eighteenth century in reaction to what was regarded as the immorality of the Restoration comedy of manners. Indications of this reaction were expressed in Jeremy Collier's *Short View of the Immorality and Profaneness of the English Stage* (1698).

In the sentimental comedy, dramatic reality was sacrificed in an attempt to instruct through an appeal to the spectator's emotions. The characters were either so good or so bad that they became caricatures. Virtue always triumphed.

Richard Steele is generally regarded as the founder of sentimental comedy. His *The Funeral* (1701), *The Lying Lover* (1703) and *The Tender Husband* (1705) reflect the development of the form, and his *The Conscious Lovers* (1722) is an example of the fully developed type.

Further examples include Hugh Kelley's *False Delicacy* (1768) and Richard Cumberland's *The West Indian* (1771).

Sentimentalism: In literature: (1) an overindulgence in emotion, especially the conscious effort to induce emotion in order to analyze or enjoy it; the failure to restrain or evaluate emotion through the exercise of judgment; (2) an optimistic overemphasis on the goodness of humanity, partly a result of reaction against Calvinistic theology, which regarded human nature as depraved.

In the first sense, sentimentalism is found in melodrama, in the swooning heroines of sentimental fiction, in the melancholy verse of the Graveyard School, in political oratory and, more recently, in some movies. (See **Graveyard School** and **Melodrama**.)

In the second sense, it appears in sentimental comedy, sentimental fiction and primitivistic poetry. (See **Sentimental Comedy** and **Sentimental Novel**.)

Both types of sentimentality occurred frequently in the literature of the romantic movement. Writers reflecting eighteenth-century sentimentalism include Richard Steele (*The Conscious Lovers*), Joseph Warton (*The Enthusiast*), the poems of William Collins and Thomas Gray, Laurence Sterne (*A Sentimental Journey*), Oliver Goldsmith (*The Deserted Village*) and Henry Mackenzie (*The Man of Feeling*). (See **Primitivism** and **Sensibility**.)

Sentimentality: See **Sentimentalism**.

Sentimental Novel: The sentimentalism of the eighteenth century was reflected not only in drama forms such as the sentimental comedy and domestic tragedy, but in the early novels as well. Richardson's *Pamela, or Virtue Rewarded* (1740) was the beginning of the trend and, although the realistic novel was written in protest (e.g., Fielding's *Tom Jones*), the sentimental novel (also called novel of sensibility) continued to be popular for many years. Examples of the type are Goldsmith's *The Vicar of Wakefield* (1766) and Sterne's *Tristram Shandy* (1760-1767). An example of the extravagant sentimental novel is Henry Mackenzie's *Man of Feeling* (1771). (See **Novel** and **Sentimentalism**.)

Septenary: A seven-stress verse often employed in medieval and Renaissance poetry. (See **Fourteeners**.)

Septet: A stanza of seven lines, with varying rhymes and meter. (See **Rhyme Royal**.)

Septuagint: A Greek version of the Old Testament begun in the third century before Christ. It is still in use in the Greek Church, and is the version from which New Testament writers quote. Septuagint (from the Latin *septuaginta*, meaning "seventy") takes its name from an old but discredited story that it was prepared by seventy scholars in seventy days at the request of Ptolemy Philadelphus (284-247 B.C.).

Serenade: A sentimental composition, written as though intended to be sung outdoors at night under a lady's window. The last stanza of *The Bedouin Song* by Bayard Taylor, is an example.

Serpentine Verse: In poetry, a line or stanza beginning and ending with the same word.

Sestet: The second, six-verse division of a sonnet. The sestet follows the first, eight-verse division. (See **Octave**.) Usually, it makes specific the general statement presented in the octave, or describes the emotions aroused in the poet by the situation developed in the octave.

The most authentic rhyme scheme is *cdecde* (following the *abbaabba* of the octave). However, sonneteers have made so many rearrangements of the sonnet rhyme pattern that almost any sequence is acceptable.

Sestina: A complex French verse form, consisting of six six-line stanzas and a three-line envoy. The sestina is usually unrhymed, but there is a fixed pattern of end words in which the final words of each verse of the first stanza are used, in varying order, as the final words in the verses of subsequent stanzas.

Setting: The background against which the action of a story or play takes place. The elements that make up a setting are: (1) the geographical location in which the action occurs; the scenery (even the location of the windows and doors in a room); (2) the occupations and daily way of life of the characters; (3) the time or period in which the action takes place (the year, the season, etc.); and (4) the general environment of the characters (the religious, moral, social and emotional conditions).

Most fiction consists of four elements: setting, incident (or plot), characterization and effect. When setting dominates, or when fiction is written largely to present the manners and customs of a particular locality, the writing is often called a story of local color. (See **Local Color, Literature of**.)

Seven Arts, The: The seven subjects studied in medieval universities. The three studies pursued during the four-year course leading to the B.A. degree were known as the trivium. They were grammar (Latin), logic and rhetoric (especially public speaking). The four branches followed in the subsequent three-year course leading to the M.A. degree were arithmetic, music, geometry and astronomy. These were called the quadrivium.

Seven Deadly Sins: The seven cardinal sins, which, according to medieval theology, resulted in spiritual death and could be atoned for only by perfect penitence: pride, envy, wrath, sloth, avarice, gluttony and lust. The Italian poet, Dante (1265-1321), treated all seven as arising from imperfect love — pride, envy and wrath resulting from perverted love; avarice, gluttony and lust from excessive love; and sloth from defective love. Pride was the greatest sin because it led to treachery and disloyalty, as in the case of Satan.

Innumerable works on the seven deadly sins appeared in the Middle Ages, and thousands of sermons were based on them. The conception of the seven deadly sins also permeated the literature of medieval and Renaissance times. A few examples in English literature are Chaucer's *The Parson's Tale* in *The Canterbury Tales*, Langland's *Piers Plowman* and Spenser's *The Faerie Queene*.

The seven sins were matched by seven cardinal virtues: faith, hope, love, prudence, justice, fortitude and temperance.

Sextain: A stanza of six lines, known also as the sixain, sexain, sextet and sestet. (See **Sestet**.)

Shakespearean Plays, Pseudo-: See **Pseudo-Shakespearean Plays**.

Shakespearean Sonnet: See **Sonnet**.

Shavian: Referring to or characteristic of the works of the Irish dramatist and critic, George Bernard Shaw (1856-1950). Shaw's writing was frequently witty, provocative and satirical.

Short Couplet: A couplet in iambic or trochaic tetrameter.

Short Measure: A stanza widely used for hymns, consisting of four verses, rhyming either *abab* or *abcb*. It usually has the first and third lines in iambic tetrameter and the second and fourth lines in iambic trimeter.

Short Story: A brief piece of prose fiction, usually narrative in form, and made up of a series of incidents related to a central situation. While some modern stories of this type have no conventional plot, the structure of most short stories is based on five elements:

(1) The situation: a preliminary introduction giving the information necessary for an intelligent reading of the story. The situation may provide the setting of the story, present the main characters and/or plunge directly into the action.

(2) The generating circumstance: the episode or event that causes the rising action and starts the train of events. The generating circumstance is sometimes called the initial impulse or exciting force.

(3) The rising action: all the incidents that follow the generating circumstance and precede the climactic scene. The events are linked by the cause-and-effect principle, and all lead to the approaching climax.

(4) The climax: the scene of highest interest or greatest emotional intensity. At the climax, the action of the story reaches a balancing point, from which it will take one turn or another.

(5) The denouement: the resolution of the complication.

Sibilants (Sigmatism): The letters *s*, *z* and such related combinations of letters as *sh* and *zh*. Good writers usually try to avoid using too many sibilant sounds. However, they have been used effectively for certain effects in poetry. The sibilants in Poe's *Valley of Unrest*, for example, produce the effect of unease that the poet wants the reader to feel:

> Now each visitor shall confess
> The sad valley's restlessness.
> Nothing there is motionless —
> Nothing save the airs that brood
> Over the magic solitude.

Sigmatism: See **Sibilants**.

Signature: The printer's basic sheet of paper, which is folded to produce a folio, quarto, octavo, etc. The number or letter printed at the bottom of the first page of the printer's sheet, to facilitate the final arrangement of the book, is also called a folio. (See **Folio, Octavo** and **Quarto**.)

Simile: A figure of speech in which a similarity between two subjects is directly expressed. Most similes are introduced by *as* or *like*. For example: *He was as high as a kite*; *The shark's jaws gripped like a clamp*.

Sincerity: A term used in critical estimates of an author's style to express the degree to which honesty of thought is combined with honesty of style. The author who writes with sincerity avoids sentimentality and inappropriate literary ornamentation. He presents his interpretation of life honestly, without overelaboration or false emotional appeals. Hazlitt used the term when he wrote, "The beauty of Milton's sonnets is their sincerity."

Single Rhyme: A masculine or one-syllable rhyme, such as *grow* and *slow*. (See **Rhyme**.)

Sirventes: A type of Provençal lyric verse, written either to satirize political figures and personal enemies, or to give moral instruction. It has no fixed form.

Situation: A term used in the discussion of plot and referring to: (1) the conditions under which a story opens; the events that have occurred before the action of the story or drama proper begins; and (2) the circumstances of a particular incident within the story or drama.

In Shakespeare's *Hamlet*, for example, the situation in the first sense consists of the events that took place before the play opened: the murder of Hamlet's father, the remarriage of Hamlet's mother and the neglected condition of Denmark. In the second sense, Hamlet finds himself in a situation that requires him to make a decision when Laertes challenges him to a duel.

Skald (Scald): An ancient Scandinavian poet, especially of the Viking period, similar to the Anglo-Saxon scop. (See **Scop**.)

Skeltonic Verse (Skeltonics or **Skeltoniads):** A lively form of verse employed by the English poet, John Skelton (1460-1529). Skeltonic verse consists of short lines rhymed in groups of varying length, and is designed to give the effects of unconventionality and lack of dignity which Skelton felt to be a fitting vehicle for his "poetry of revolt." Something of its spirit and characteristics may be found in the following passage from *The Tunnynge of Elynoure Rummynge*:

> But to make up my tale,
> She brueth noppy ale,
> And maketh thereof sale
> To travellers, to tinkers,
> To sweaters, to swinkers,
> And all good ale-drinkers,
> That will nothing spare
> But dryncke till they stare
> And bring themselves bare,
> With now away the mare
> And let us slay Care,
> As wise as an hare.

Sketch: A brief composition, simply composed, and usually presenting a single scene, a single character or a single incident. Originally used in the sense of an artist's sketch as a preliminary to a more developed work, the term is now often applied to a finished product of simple proportions, as in a *character sketch*, *vaudeville sketch*, *descriptive sketch*, etc.

Slang: Vernacular speech, not accepted as literary, although much used in conversation and colloquial expression. Some authorities suggest that the term is derived from the Norwegian *sleng* in *slengja kjeften* — "to sling the jaw."

The aptness of slang is usually based on its humor, its exaggeration, its onomatopoeic effect or on a combination of these qualities. Frequently, slang develops as a short cut, an abbreviated form of expression. There are, as well, the special terms developed in professions or trades, in sports, in special localities and among groups sharing a common interest. (See **Colloquialism**.)

Slapstick: A form of low comedy marked by much physical action, clowning and pranks. Scenes in which one character throws a custard pie into another's face, or places a banana peel on stage so that another character will slip and fall, are typical of slapstick comedy.

Slice of Life: A work of drama or fiction that presents life factually, just as it is, without adornment. The term is often applied to the work of naturalistic and realistic writers. (See **Naturalism** and **Realism**.)

Sobriquet (or **Soubriquet**): From the French, meaning "nickname", especially one that has been used so often to refer to a person, place or thing that it has become easily recognizable. For example, *the city of light* is a sobriquet for Paris, and *the bard of Avon* for Shakespeare.

Society Verse: See **Occasional Verse** and **Vers de Société**.

Sociological Novel: Prose fiction deriving its major interest, background and theme from the conditions of the society in which the characters exist. The sociological novel (also called the thesis novel) is a form of the problem novel. Two examples, written almost a century apart, are Dickens' *Hard Times* (1854) and Alan Paton's *Cry, the Beloved Country* (1948). (See **Novel of the Soil** and **Problem Novel**.)

Sock: The low-heeled slipper conventionally worn by the comic actor on the ancient stage; by extension, comedy itself. (See **Buskin**.)

Socratic Irony: See **Socratic Method**.

Socratic Method: In argument or explanation, the use of the question-and-answer formula employed by Socrates in Plato's dialogues. Socrates would pretend to be ignorant of the subject under discussion, and would then proceed to develop his thesis by asking questions and persuading others to give answers consistent with his theory.

Socrates' pretence of ignorance, when he was regarded as the most knowledgeable of the group, was called, by his companions, his "irony." By extension, the method of assuming ignorance for the sake of taking advantage of an opponent in debate is known as Socratic irony. It has been suggested that Socratic irony originated in Socrates' sense of humor and his dislike of pretentiousness, rather than as a mere rhetorical trick.

Solecism: A violation of grammatical structure or idiom in speech and writing. *He don't* and *between you and I* are solecisms. The term is strictly used only for errors in grammar and idiom. It is distinguished from *impropriety*, which is used to indicate the false use of one part of speech for another (as *to suicide* for *to commit suicide*), and from *bar-*

barism, which indicates words coined from other words in good standing (as *preventative* is a barbarism for *preventive*).

Soliloquy: A speech of a character in a play or other composition delivered while the speaker is alone. The purpose of a soliloquy is to make the audience or reader aware of the character's thoughts or to give information concerning other participants in the action. A good example is Hamlet's famous soliloquy beginning, "To be, or not to be."

Solution: A term sometimes used in place of denouement to indicate the outcome of a piece of fiction. It presents a solution for the complication that has been developed in the plot. (See **Dramatic Structure** and **Short Story**.)

Song: A lyric poem either set to music or intended for singing. Song lyrics are usually short, simple, sensuous and emotional. Classification is impossible because so many types have been written on so many subjects. There are working songs, dance songs, love songs, war songs, play songs, drinking songs, songs for festivals, church gatherings, political meetings, and songs written for a host of other circumstances.

Elizabethan literature is rich in songs and song poems, such as Shakespeare's *Who is Sylvia?* and Jonson's *Drink to Me Only with Thine Eyes*.

Sonnet: A lyric poem of fourteen lines. The three characteristic types of sonnets in English literature are the Italian (Petrarchan), the English (Shakespearean) and the Spenserian.

The Italian form, also called the regular or classical sonnet, is divided into the octave (first eight lines) and the sestet (the last six lines). The rhyme scheme of the octave is: *abba, abba*; of the sestet, *cde, cde*, or *cd, cd, cd*.

The English sonnet characteristically has four divisions: three quatrains and a rhymed couplet. The rhyme scheme is: *abab, cdcd, efef, gg*. The concluding couplet is usually a comment on the preceding lines.

The Spenserian sonnet was developed by and named for Edmund Spenser (1552-1559). Like the English sonnet, it consists of three quatrains and a couplet. The rhyme scheme is: *abab, bcbc, cdcd, ee*.

Certain poets have written series of sonnets on a particular theme. Well-known sonnet sequences or cycles include those written by Sidney, Spenser, Shakespeare, Donne, Wordsworth, Rossetti and E. B. Browning.

Sonnet Sequence: See **Sonnet**.

190

Sotie: A type of farcical drama that was popular during the Middle Ages in France.

Spasmodic School: A phrase applied by W. E. Aytoun in 1854 to a group of English poets who wrote in the 1840s and 1850s. Their verse (influenced by Shelley and Byron) reflected discontent and unrest. Its style was marked by jerkiness and forced or strained emphasis. Members of the group included Sydney Dobell, Alexander Smith, P. J. Bailey, George Gilfillan and other minor writers. Tennyson's *Maud* is said to reflect spasmodic tendencies.

Spenserian Sonnet: See **Sonnet**.

Spenserian Stanza: A stanzaic pattern consisting of nine verses, the first eight in iambic pentameter, the ninth in iambic hexameter. The rhyme scheme is *ababbcbcc*. (See **Scansion**.) Edmund Spenser created the pattern for *The Faerie Queene*. The first stanza of Canto I is an example:

> A Gentle Knight was pricking on the plaine,
> Y-cladd in mightie armes and silver shielde,
> Wherein old dints of deepe wounds did remaine,
> The cruell markes of many a bloudy fielde;
> Yet armes till that time did he never wield;
> His angry steede did chide his forming bitt,
> As much disdayning to the curbe to yield;
> Full jolly knight he seemd, and faire did sitt,
> As one for knightly giusts and fierce encounters fitt.

Other poets who have used the Spenserian pattern include Burns, in *The Cotter's Saturday Night*, Shelley in *The Revolt of Islam* and in *Adonais*, Keats in *The Eve of St. Agnes* and Byron in *Childe Harold*.

Split Infinitive: An infinitive (a form of a verb, not limited by person and number) in which a modifying word or phrase comes between *to* and the verb, e.g., *to wisely judge*. Usually, split infinitives should be avoided, but sometimes it is impossible to place the modifier elsewhere in the sentence without producing awkwardness.

Spondee: A foot composed of two accented syllables ($--$). Spondees are rare in English verse, since most polysyllabic words have a primary accent. However, there are a few, for example, *childhood* and *bookcase*. Most spondees in poetry are composed of two monosyllabic words, as *all joy*. In Milton's line, "Silence, ye troubled waves, and thou deep, peace!" *deep, peace* is a perfect spondaic foot.

Spoof: A playful, lightly satirical piece of prose or verse that makes fun of a literary convention, a particular subject, a historical event or a literary or dramatic work. A twentieth-century example is *1066 and All That* (1931), a spoof of British history by W. C. Sellar and R. J. Yeatman. Unlike satire, the spoof is not usually bitter and is intended to amuse, rather than to arouse indignation. Often, it contains elements of parody and burlesque. The term is also used to mean a hoax, trick or deception.

Spoonerism: An expression in which the initial letters or sounds of two words are interchanged. The term is derived from the name of Reverend W. A. Spooner (1844-1930) of Oxford University in England, who habitually made this kind of transposition. A well-known example is *kinkering kongs* for *conquering kings*.

Sprung Rhythm: A term originated by the English poet, Gerard Manley Hopkins (1844-1899). The pattern of sprung rhythm is based on the number of accented syllables in each line; the number of unaccented syllables varies. Hopkins gave as an example the following nursery rhyme:

One, | two |
Buckle my | shoe.

Each line has two accented syllables, although the second line has four syllables.

Sprung rhythm was not Hopkins' invention. It was used in the Middle English poem, *Piers Plowman*, and in the chorus of Milton's *Samson Agonistes*. (See **Running Rhythm**.)

Stanza: A division of a poem, usually made according to a pattern. However, a poem is sometimes divided into stanzas according to thought, as well as form, in which case the stanza is a unit similar to a paragraph in prose. Strophe is another term used for stanza. Some common stanzaic forms are the couplet, ottava rima, quatrain, rhyme royal, Spenserian stanza and tercet. (Each of these is defined in this dictionary.)

Static Character: A character in a novel, short story or drama who changes little, if at all, during the story.

Stave: A stanza, particularly of a poem intended to be sung.

Stichomythia: A form of repartee developed in classical drama and often used by Elizabethan writers, especially in plays that imitated the

Senecan tragedies. Stichomythia is a kind of line-for-line verbal fencing match, in which the speakers in the dialogue retort sharply to each other in lines that echo the opponent's words and figures of speech. Antithesis is freely used. An example occurs in Shakespeare's *Hamlet* when Hamlet speaks with his mother in the scene during which Polonius is killed:

> Hamlet: Now, mother, what's the matter?
> Queen: Hamlet, thou hast thy father much offended.
> Hamlet: Mother, you have my father much offended.
> Queen: Come, come, you answer with an idle tongue.
> Hamlet: Go, go, you question with a wicked tongue.

A more sustained example is found in the interview between King Richard and Queen Elizabeth in Shakespeare's *King Richard III* (Act IV, Scene 4).

Stock Character: A conventional character type belonging by custom to certain forms of literature. For example, in a morality play, a boisterous character known as the Vice was expected to appear. The Elizabethan revenge tragedy commonly employed, among other stock characters, an intelligent, vengeance-seeking hero (e.g., Hamlet), the ghost of a murdered father or son, and a scheming murderer-villain (e.g., Claudius). In fairy tales, the cruel stepmother and the handsome prince are stock characters.

Storm and Stress: See **Sturm und Drang**.

Stream of Consciousness Novel: A variety of the psychological novel that is chiefly concerned with chronicling the mind and thoughts of the central character as that person undergoes a series of experiences. To the outside world, these experiences sometimes seem trivial, but to the central figure of the story, they are vitally important. The chief interest in this form of writing is in the consciousness — on the part of the central figure — of those external forces that affect him. The mind of the character becomes the stage on which most of the action occurs. Plot development lies not so much in activity as in the effect of the activity on the central character. The character's thoughts are set down in a long, rambling dialogue, called interior monologue.

The stream of consciousness novel is largely a twentieth-century development. Authors who have written this type of fiction include James Joyce, Dorothy Richardson, Virginia Woolf and Ernest Hemingway. James Joyce's *Ulysses* is perhaps the best example.

Stress: The emphasis given to a syllable or word in rhythmic writing. (See **Accent, Arsis, Ictus** and **Scansion**.)

Strophe: A stanza. In the Pindaric ode (see **Antistrophe**), the strophe is the first stanza and every subsequent third stanza (the fourth, the seventh, etc.)

Structure: The planned framework of a piece of literature. Usually, the term is applied to the general plan or outline of the work, the relation of the parts or elements to the whole. For example, the scheme of topics (as drawn up in a topical outline) determines the structure of a formal essay. In drama, the logical division of the action (see **Dramatic Structure**), as well as the division into acts and scenes, are matters of structure. In narrative, the plot itself is the key structural element. Groups of stories may be set in a larger structural plan (See **Framed Story**), as Chaucer did in *The Canterbury Tales*.

Sturm und Drang (Storm and Stress): The name given to a literary movement in Germany during the last quarter of the eighteenth century. In essence, it was a revolt against classical standards. The writers in the movement were more interested in character than in plot or in literary form. Their writings were intensely personal and portrayed emotional experiences, spiritual struggles and great passion.

The name of the movement was derived from the title of a drama, *Sturm und Drang* (1776), by Friedrich Maximilian von Klinger. However, the founder and pioneer of the movement was Johann Gottfried von Herder (1744-1803). Goethe's *Götz von Berlichingen* (1773) was probably the most significant single literary production of the group.

Style: In literary criticism, a characteristic manner of expression, combining the idea that is being expressed with the individuality (the particular "voice") of the author. Just as no two personalities are identical, no two styles are exactly alike. The best style is that in which the language is most appropriately suited to the thought that is being expressed.

A critical analysis of a writer's style may categorize a work as written in literary, journalistic or scientific style. The writing may be classified as abstract or concrete, formal or informal, sincere or artificial, dignified or comic, original or imitative. General qualities such as diction, sentence structure and variety, imagery, rhythm, coherence and emphasis are also elements of style.

In addition, a piece of literature can be categorized according to the period in which it was written (e.g., Augustan, Georgian) or according to its similarity to the writing of an individual author.

Subjective Element in Literature: A term applied in criticism to writing that expresses the inner convictions, beliefs or ideals of the author in an intensely personal manner. Subjective writing is the opposite of objective writing, which is impersonal, concrete and concerned principally with narrative, analysis or description of external appearances. Shakespeare's sonnets, for example, are characterized by subjective elements. In comparison, the novels of Henry James are objective.

Subplot: In fiction and drama, a subordinate or minor story. Usually, the secondary plot is directly related to the main plot, and contributes interest and complication to the total work. In Shakespeare's *Hamlet*, the Laertes-Hamlet subplot is subordinate to the Claudius-Hamlet major plot. In *The Merchant of Venice*, the love interest of the Jessica-Lorenzo story is subordinate to the Portia-Bassanio main plot.

Substitution: The use of a foot other than that normally required by the meter. The classical rule of equivalence makes two short syllables equal to one long one. In quantitative verse, therefore, dactyls, anapests, spondees, amphibrachs and tribachs may be substituted for one another. By the same rule, an iamb may be substituted for a trochee and vice versa. This form of substitution, like that of a dactyl for an anapest, results in a reversed or inverted foot. In accentual verse, such reversal is sometimes called inverted stress.

Summary: A brief statement or account of the substance or general idea, attitude or theme of a literary work. (Compare with **Abstract** and **Paraphrase**.)

Supernatural Element in Literature: Writing concerned with an attempt to explain or describe the mysteries of existence. In literature, the supernatural element is used in two ways: (1) in speculation about the influences on human existence of forces that are above or beyond what is natural; (2) in description of a strange, eerie or uncanny event or atmosphere that cannot be explained by logical analysis.

Wordsworth's *Ode on the Intimations of Immortality* is an example of the first type, as are books on religion or occult philosophy. Coleridge's *Christabel, The Arabian Nights* and mystery stories are examples of the second type. (See **Mysticism**.)

Surrealism: A method of writing that explores the interrelation of the conscious and subconscious mind. Surrealist writers are especially interested in dreams, hallucinations and automatic writing as revelations of the inner life of man. Imitating the non-logical operation of the human subconscious mind, the pattern of surrealistic writing is also non-logical.

Most of the best-known surrealistic writers have been French, including André Breton, Louis Aragon, Raymond Queneau and Julien Gracq. However, Thornton Wilder's play, *The Skin of Our Teeth*, shows surrealistic elements. Surrealism has had a strong influence on the theater of the absurd and the antinovel, both of which are defined in this dictionary.

Suspense: In a literary work, an expected uncertainty concerning the outcome of the plot. To hold the reader's interest and heighten the suspense, the writer of a detective story, for example, may resort to sudden disappearances of key characters or the introduction of clues that implicate apparently innocent people, always keeping the final solution just out of sight.

"Sweetness and Light": A phrase made popular by Matthew Arnold, who used it as the title for the first chapter of *Culture and Anarchy* (1869). Arnold borrowed the term from Swift's *The Battle of the Books* (1697), in which the fable of the spider and the bee was used to illustrate his argument for the superiority of ancient over modern writers. Swift contrasts the "dirt and poison" produced by the spiders (modern writers) with the bees' contributions that "fill our hives with honey and wax, thus furnishing mankind with the two noblest of things, which are sweetness and light." Arnold equates these two "noblest of things" with beauty and intelligence, the most important contributions of the artist.

Syllabic Verse: Verse that is measured by the number of syllables in each line, rather than by stress or quantity. (See **Quantitative Verse**.)

Syllabus: An outline or abstract containing the major points included in a book, a course of lectures, an argument or a program of study.

Syllepsis: (1) A grammatical construction in which a single word modifies or governs two or more other words, although, properly, it can be applied to (or agrees with) only one. An example is: *Neither the boys nor the girl has arrived.* (2) A construction in which a single governing or modifying word is applied to more than one word and has a different meaning with each of them. An example of this type of syllepsis is: *On Saturday, I caught three fish and a cold.* Another name for syllepsis is zeugma.

Syllogism: A formula for presenting an argument logically. The syllogism consists of three divisions: a major premise, a minor premise and conclusion. For example:

Major premise: All public libraries should serve the people.
Minor premise: This is a public library.
Conclusion: Therefore, this library should serve the people.

Symbol: A symbol is something that exists in its own right and yet stands for or suggests something else. For example, a *flag* is a piece of colored cloth and a symbol of a country.

Symbolism: In a general sense, the use of imagery so that one object represents something else. The *cross*, for example, is a symbol of Christianity; the *lion* is a symbol of courage.

In literature, symbolism is the use of objects or actions to suggest ideas or emotions. In Shakespeare's *Macbeth*, for example, Lady Macbeth's attempts to wash her hands symbolize her desire to cleanse herself of guilt. In *Hamlet*, Yorick's skull is a symbol of man's mortality.

Symbolism is also basic to the allegory. (See **Allegory**.)

Symposium: A Greek word meaning "a drinking together" or "banquet." Because such meetings were characterized by free conversation, the word later came to mean discussion by different persons on a single topic, or a collection of speeches or essays on a given subject. One of Plato's best-known dialogues is *The Symposium*.

Symposium Club: See **Transcendentalism**.

Synaesthesia: The use of terms usually applied to one sense to describe the sensations of another; the response of several senses to the stimulation of one. In Edith Sitwell's poem, *Aubade*, for example, the light is described as "creaking." Synaesthesia is also apparent in such phrases as *hot colors* or *blue notes*.

Syncopation: A temporary displacement of the regular metrical accent in music and verse, typically caused by stressing the weak syllable.

Syncope: A cutting short of words through the omission of a letter or syllable. Syncope is distinguished from elision in that it is usually confined to omission of letters within the word, whereas elision usually runs two words together by the omission of a final or initial letter. *Ev'ry* for *every* is an example of syncope. (See **Elision**.)

Synecdoche: A form of metaphor in which the part mentioned signifies the whole. A good synecdoche is based on an important part of the whole, the part most directly associated with the subject under discussion. For example, *The factory employed 500 hands*. In this case, *hands* is a synecdoche for *persons* or *workers*.

Synonyms: Words in the same language with the same or similar meanings. For example, *sharp* and *keen* are synonyms. (See **Antonyms**.)

A synonym can also be a word or expression generally accepted as another name for something. For example, *Shakespeare's name has become a synonym for excellence in playwriting.*

Synopsis: A summary; an abstract; a résumé of the main points of a composition or argument. Usually, a synopsis is given in complete sentences and is, therefore, more connected than an outline. (See **Précis.**)

Syntax: (1) The arrangement of words to form phrases, clauses and sentences; sentence construction. (2) The patterns of such organization and construction in a language. (3) In grammar, the function of a word, phrase or clause within a sentence.

Synthesis: The combination of two or more elements into a unified whole. Synthesis is the opposite of analysis, which involves detailed consideration of the separate elements or parts of a work.

Synthesis is also the outcome of the dialectic process: thesis and antithesis combine to produce a synthesis. (See **Dialectic.**)

Syzygy: From the Greek word meaning "yoke," a term used to describe the combination in verse of two feet into one metrical unit; for example, *iambic trimeter* instead of *hexameter.* Phonetic syzygy is complex alliteration, such as that used frequently by Gerard Manley Hopkins.

T

Tableau: (1) A stationary, silent grouping of performers in a theatrical production for a special effect. (2) An elaborate stage presentation consisting of dance, pantomime or ballet in impressive settings.

Tail-Rhyme Romance: A metrical romance in which the tail-rhyme stanza is used. (See **Tail-Rhyme Stanza**.) The term is especially applied to the group of romances (including *Amis and Amiloun*, *Athelston*, *Horn Childe* and some twenty others) that have a tail-rhyme stanza of twelve lines, made up of four groups, each with a short "tail" line, such as *aab*, *aab*, *ccb*, *ddb*.

Tail-Rhyme Stanza: A stanza of verse containing, among longer lines, two or more short lines that rhyme with each other and serve as "tails" to the divisions or parts of the stanza. The form developed in medieval times and is known in French as *rime couée*. Charles Lamb's *Hester* is a more modern example. (See **Tail-Rhyme Romance**.)

Tale: A simple narrative. Formerly, no real distinction was made between the tale and the short story; the two terms were used interchangeably. Tale, however, is a more general term than short story, since the latter is applied to a narrative that follows a fairly technical pattern, and the former denotes any short narrative.

In poetry, Chaucer's *The Canterbury Tales* are examples of tales. Irving's *Rip Van Winkle* is a prose example.

Tanka: A type of Japanese poetry similar to haiku. (See **Haiku**.) It consists of thirty-one syllables, arranged in five lines, each with seven syllables, except the first and third, which have five syllables.

Taste: A basis for critical judgment of a piece of literature, founded upon personal appreciation rather than upon logical laws or established standards of criticism. Cultivated taste is based on an intelligent understanding of the history, culture and character of the form being judged, as well as on a sensitivity to the author's mood and intent.

Tautology: The use of superfluous words; unnecessary repetition of words that do not add clarity or force. Phrases such as *the modern politician of today* and *necessary essentials* are tautologies. (See **Pleonasm** and **Redundant**.)

In logic, a tautology is a statement that is true by virtue of its form. For example, *He is either alive or not*.

Telescope Word: See **Portmanteau Words**.

Telestich: A poem in which the last letter of each line, when taken in order, forms a word or words. (See **Acrostic**.)

Tenor and Vehicle: Two essential elements of a metaphor. The tenor is the subject and the vehicle is the figure of the comparison. For example:

> O'er the earth there comes a bloom
> Sunny light for sullen gloom

In this case, *bloom* is the tenor and *sunny light* is the vehicle.

Tension: A term introduced into contemporary criticism by Allen Tate. Tension refers to the integral unity of a poem, a unity that results from the successful resolution in the work of the conflicts of abstraction and concreteness, of general and particular, and of denotation and connotation.

The term results from removing the prefixes from two terms in logic: *intension*, which refers to the abstract attributes of objects, and *extension*, which refers to the specific object named by the word.

Tercet: A stanza of three rhyming lines. The term is also used to denote either one of the two three-line groups forming the sestet of the Italian sonnet.

Terpsichore: See **Muses**.

Terza Rima: A three-line stanza form borrowed from the Italian poets. The rhyme scheme is: *aba*, *bcb*, *cdc*, *ded*, etc. The following stanzas, from Browning's *The Statue and the Bust*, provide examples of terza rima:

There's a palace in Florence, the world knows well,	*a*
And a statue watches it from the square,	*b*
And this story of both do our townsmen tell.	*a*
Ages ago, a lady there,	*b*
At the farthest window facing the East,	*c*
Asked, "Who rides by with the royal air?"	*b*

Testament: As a literary form: (1) a will, often characterized by humor and satire; (2) a document that bears witness to or affirms a belief. Wills and testaments of the first sort were part of the popular literature of the sixteenth century in England. Humorous examples include *Jyl of Breyntford's Testament*, *Colin Blowbol's Testament* and Humphrey Powells' *Wyll of the Devil* (ca. 1550). More serious literary testaments include the *Testament of Cresseid* by the Scottish poet, Robert Henryson (1430-1506), and the love complaint, "The Testament of the Hawthorne," in Tottel's *Miscellany* (1557). The second type of testament is represented in English literature by Thomas Usk's *The Testament of Love*, written about 1384. A more recent example of the type is Robert Bridges' *The Testament of Beauty* (1929).

Tetralogy: A series of four related plays, novels, etc. In ancient Athens, each contestant in a competition for tragedy submitted four connected plays: three tragedies, followed by a satyr play. The satyr play was a kind of burlesque in which a mythical hero appeared as a ridiculous person or buffoon, with a chorus of satyrs (half man, half beast). Today, the term is applied to any group of four connected works.

Tetrameter: A line of verse consisting of four feet.

Tetrapody: A group of words or a line of verse containing four feet.

Tetrastich: A stanza of four lines; same as quatrain.

Thalia: See **Muses.**

Theater of the Absurd: A term applied to drama that reflects the attitude that the universe is without purpose and that human life is futile and meaningless. Under such circumstances, man's existence becomes absurd. In both form and content, the theater of the absurd portrays human beings as isolated from others. Often, there is no conventional plot, dialogue or character motivation. This formlessness and apparent irrationality are an expression of the absurd predicament of man, whose existence has no reason. Among the dramatists who have written this kind of play are Beckett, Ionesco, Pinter, Albee and N. F. Simpson.

Theme: The central or dominating idea, thesis or meaning of a work. Usually, the theme of any given work can be stated quite simply. For example, the theme of Plato's *Republic* is *justice*.

Thesaurus: A collection of words and phrases; a dictionary of synonyms, antonyms and other related words. A widely used English thesaurus is Roget's *Thesaurus of English Words and Phrases*. The word is derived from the Greek *thesauros*, meaning "treasure."

Thesis: An attitude or position on a problem taken by a writer or speaker with the purpose of proving or supporting it. In university circles, thesis has the special connotation of a paper written as a requirement for a degree. (See **Dissertation.**) For thesis as a term in prosody, see **Ictus.**

Thesis Novel: See **Problem Novel** and **Sociological Novel**.

Threnody: A song of death; a dirge; a lamentation.

Title: In literature, the name attached to a written work. Usually, a title is intended to attract attention and arouse the reader's interest. Most modern titles are brief and specific. Typically, they are drawn from the setting of the literary work, the name of a character, a central image or a literary reference.

Tmesis: The separation of parts of a compound word by the insertion of another word, as in *what person soever* for *whatsoever person*.

Tome: (1) A volume forming part of a larger work. (2) A large or scholarly work.

Tone: A term sometimes used in criticism to denote the mood of a piece of writing. This mood is established by the quality of the speech sounds used. Short staccato sentences, for example, are used to show excitement and action; long, ponderous sentences for slow movement and dejection. Certain colors are associated with certain emotions (i.e., red with passion and anger, yellow with jealousy and green with envy or hope). The total effect of word sounds and associations sets the tone of the writing.

Tonic Accent: See **Atonic**.

Tour de Force: A French phrase meaning a "turn of strength," writing that is notable as a demonstration of the author's skilled technique and ingenuity. Sometimes the term is used in a derogatory sense for writing that is merely clever, rather than sincere.

Tract: A pamphlet, usually on a religious or political topic, that strongly supports a particular point of view. Often, tracts are distributed free for propaganda purposes. The Oxford Movement was also known as the Tractarian Movement because tracts were widely used by both sponsors and opponents of the movement. (See **Oxford Movement**.)

Tractarian Movement: See **Oxford Movement** and **Tract**.

Tragedy: A serious play or narrative in which the hero becomes engaged in a conflict, experiences great suffering and is finally defeated and dies.

The classical conception of tragedy, as defined by Aristotle in his *Poetics*, involves a hero of noble stature whose fortunes are reversed as a result of a weakness (or tragic flaw) in an otherwise noble nature. Othello's tragedy, for example, is the result of his jealousy, and Macbeth's, the result of his high ambition. The effect of dramatic tragedy, according to Aristotle, is to arouse in the spectator feelings of pity and fear in such a way as to produce a catharsis or purging of these emotions. (See **Catharsis.**)

In England, tragedy began in Elizabethan times. The chief influences, in so far as dramatic tradition and theory were concerned, were classical: the *Poetics* of Aristotle and the tragedies of the Roman philosopher, Seneca.

In the latter part of the sixteenth century, however, playwrights paid less attention to classical restrictions, producing dramas that varied widely in form and structure. These plays culminated in Shakespeare's tragedies. *King Lear*, *Hamlet* and *Macbeth* are usually regarded as the highest achievements of the English stage.

After the seventeenth century, few tragedies in the classical or Aristotelian sense were written. Eventually, tragedy came to be applied to any serious work that is tragic in tone and intention. (See **Classical Tragedy, Elizabethan Drama, Revenge Tragedy, Romantic Tragedy, Senecan Tragedy, Tragedy of Blood, Tragic Force** and **Tragic Irony.**)

Tragedy of Blood: An intensified form of the revenge tragedy, popular on the Elizabethan stage. The theme, borrowed from the Roman philosopher, Seneca, is revenge and retribution through murder, assassination and mutilation. In the Senecan plays, the violent actions were described by one of the characters. In the Elizabethan tragedy of blood, they were enacted on the stage, to satisfy the craving for morbid excitement of audiences accustomed to bear-baiting spectacles and public executions. The revenge plays, such as Kyd's *Spanish Tragedy* and Shakespeare's *Hamlet*, led to such later tragedies of blood as Webster's *The Duchess of Malfi* and *The White Devil*. (See **Revenge Tragedy** and **Senecan Tragedy.**)

Tragic Flaw: See **Hamartia** and **Tragedy**.

Tragic Force: The event or force that starts the falling action in a tragedy. The tragic force is either a separate event closely following the climax of the drama, or is identified with the climax itself. The escape of Fleance is the tragic force in Shakespeare's *Macbeth*, marking the beginning of Macbeth's misfortunes and leading to the overthrow of the hero in the resulting catastrophe. (See **Dramatic Structure.**)

Tragic Irony: A form of dramatic irony in which a character who is about to become a victim of disaster uses words that have one meaning to him and quite another to the spectator or those who are aware of the real situation. Othello's allusion to the villain who deceives him as "honest Iago" is an example.

Tragicomedy: A play that has a plot suitable to tragedy but which ends happily like a comedy. The action, serious in theme and subject matter, seems to lead to a tragic catastrophe. However, an unexpected turn of events brings about a happy denouement. (See **Deus ex Machina.**) In this sense, Shakespeare's *The Merchant of Venice* is a tragicomedy, though it can also be termed a romantic comedy. (See **Romantic Comedy.**)

In English dramatic history, tragicomedy usually designates the particular kind of play developed by Beaumont and Fletcher about 1610. Their *Philaster* is a typical example.

Characteristics of the tragicomedy include: an improbable plot, love as the central interest, rapid action, contrast of deep villainy and exalted virtue, the rescue of the hero and heroine in the nick of time, a penitent villain, disguises, surprises, jealousy, treachery and intrigue.

Examples of the type are Shakespeare's *Cymbeline* and *The Winter's Tale*. Fletcher's *The Faithful Shepherdess* is a pastoral tragicomedy. Later seventeenth-century tragicomedies are Massinger's *The Prisoner*, Davenant's *Fair Favorite*, Shadwell's *Royal Shepherdess* and Dryden's *Secret Love* and *Love Triumphant*.

Transcendentalism: A philosophy based on the belief that intuition and private conscience are valid moral guides.

In the United States, transcendentalism flourished from about 1835 to 1860, especially in New England, where it became a literary movement as well as a religious philosophy. Most of the New England transcendentalists were also interested in social reform. Leaders of the group included Emerson, Thoreau, Alcott, Fuller and Peabody. The Brook Farm experiment was one of the results of the transcendental movement. (See **Brook Farm.**)

Two documents expressing the views of the transcendentalist group were Emerson's *Nature* (1836) and Thoreau's *Walden* (1854). Members of this group were variously called the Transcendental Club, the Symposium Club and the Hedge Club.

Transferred Epithet: See **Hypellage.**

Transition: In a piece of writing, the passing from one subject or division of a composition to another. A good prose style accomplishes transition between sentences, paragraphs and chapters by proceeding smoothly and logically from one point to the next, so that the relationships appear clear and natural. Aids to transition include: (1) connective words (*further*, *then*, *first*, *second*, etc.); (2) phrases and clauses that show the relationship between two ideas (*consequently*, *for this reason*, etc.); and (3) terms that call attention to contrasts (*however*, *on the contrary*, etc.).

Travesty: In literature, writing that, by its tone, style or treatment, ridicules a subject essentially serious and dignified. Travesty is the opposite of the mock epic, in that the latter treats a frivolous subject seriously, while the travesty presents a serious subject frivolously. Cervantes' *Don Quixote* may be termed a travesty on the medieval romance. (See **Burlesque**.)

Treatise: A formal work in which conclusions are supported by the systematic examination of a body of evidence or principles. For example, David Hume's *Treatise of Human Nature*.

Triad: (1) A group of three. (2) The strophe, antistrophe and epode of the Pindaric ode. (See **Ode**.)

Tribe of Ben: A title adopted by the young poets and dramatists of seventeenth-century England who acknowledged Ben Jonson as their master. The chief of the tribe was Robert Herrick, and the group included the Cavalier Lyrists. (See **Cavalier Lyrists**.)
  Jonson influenced his followers to study and imitate classical writers, literary types (such as the ode, the epigram and satire) and ideas of criticism. In general, the group followed the creed: "Live merrily and write good verses."

Tribrach: A foot of three short or unstressed syllables. The tribrach is uncommon in English verse.

Trilogy: A literary composition, usually a novel or a play, written in three parts, each of which is a complete unit in itself. In drama, Shakespeare's *King Henry VI* (Parts 1, 2 and 3) is an example. In fiction, J. R. R. Tolkien's *The Lord of the Rings* trilogy is a more recent example. It consists of *The Fellowship of the Ring*, *The Two Towers* and *The Return of the King*.

Trimeter: A line of verse consisting of three feet.

Triolet: A French verse form. The triolet consists of eight lines and only two rhymes. The first two lines are repeated as the last two lines, and the first recurs also as the fourth line. The rhyme scheme is: *abaaabab*.

Triple Measure: In verse, a metrical foot containing three syllables, or a series of lines each with three metrical feet.

Triple Rhyme: See **Rhyme**.

Triplet: Three successive rhyming lines of verse. A triplet occurs in the fifth, sixth and seventh lines of the following stanza written by Swinburne:

> Here, where the world is quiet;
> Here, where all trouble seems
> Dead winds' and spent waves' riot
> In doubtful dreams of dreams;
> I watch the green field growing
> For reaping folk and sowing
> For harvest-time and mowing,
> A sleepy world of streams.

Tripody: In poetry, a line containing three metrical feet, or three feet treated as one unit.

Tristich: A stanza of three lines.

Trivium: See **Seven Arts**.

Trochee: A metrical foot consisting of an accented and an unaccented syllable, as in the word *happy*. The trochee is often used as the meter for the supernatural, as in the following lines from Shakespeare's *Macbeth*:

> Double, double, toil and trouble,
> Fire burn and cauldron bubble.

Troparia: A short hymn or a stanza of a hymn, sometimes used in odes.

Trope: (1) In rhetoric, figurative language in which a word or expression is used in a sense different from its ordinary meaning. For example, calling a shrewd man *a fox* is using a trope. In this sense, all figures of speech, such as metaphors and similes, are tropes. (See **Metaphor** and **Simile**.) (2) A verbal elaboration of the liturgical text of Roman Catholic church services. As early as the eighth or ninth centuries, musical additions to the Gregorian antiphons used in the Mass were permitted. Later, additions were made to the words of the antiphons. The elaborated texts were called tropes, or "amplifications of the liturgical texts." They were sometimes in prose, sometimes in verse, sometimes purely musical and sometimes in dialogue form. The liturgical and mystery plays of medieval drama developed from these tropes. (See **Liturgical Drama**, **Medieval Drama** and **Mystery Play**.)

Troubadour: An aristocratic lyric poet of Provence (southern France) in the twelfth and thirteenth centuries. The name is derived from a word meaning "to find," suggesting that the troubadour was regarded as an inventor and experimenter in poetic technique.

Troubadors were essentially lyric poets, occupied with themes of love and chivalry. Their poetry was important in the development of the ideals of courtly love and influenced the *trouvère* of northern France. (See **Courtly Love** and **Trouvère**.)

The lyrics composed by the troubadours were intended to be sung, sometimes by the troubadour himself, sometimes by an assistant or professional entertainer, such as the *jongleur*. (See **Jongleur**.)

Some of the forms invented by the troubadours are: the canso (love song), ballata (dance song), tenso (dialogue), pastorela (pastoral wooing song) and the alba (dawn song). Varied stanzaic forms were developed, including the sestina, later used by Dante and others. (See **Sestina**.)

Famous troubadours included William, Count of Poitiers, Bernard de Ventadour, Arnaut de Mareuil, Bertran de Born and Arnaut Daniel.

Trouvère: A term applied to one of a group of poets who flourished in northern France in the twelfth and thirteenth centuries. The *trouvères* were influenced by the troubadours of southern France. Most of their work was concerned with lyrics of love, although they also produced *chansons de geste* and chivalric romances. One of the most famous *trouvères* was Chrétien de Troyes (twelfth century), who wrote some of the earliest and best of the Arthurian romances. (See **Arthurian Legend** and **Troubadour**.)

Truncation: In verse, the omission of a metrical syllable at the beginning or the end of a line. When the syllable is missing at the beginning of a line, it is known as headless or acephalous verse. When the syllable is omitted at the end of the line, it is called catalexis.

In Swinburne's poem, *Nephelidia*, the first metric foot in the following line is truncated:

Life | is the lust | of a lamp | for the light | that is dark |
till the dawn | of the day | that we die.

(See **Catalexis**.)

Tudor: Of or pertaining to the English ruling family descended from Owen Tudor (Henry VII, Henry VIII, Edward VI, Mary I and Elizabeth I). The Tudors ruled England from 1485 until 1603.

Type Character: In drama or fiction, a character whose actions and qualities make him (or her) appear to be a representative of a particular class or a conventional type of person, rather than a complex human being. The *wicked stepmother* is an example. (See **Stock Character.**)

U

Ubi Sunt Formula: A convention, used in verse, which asks "where are" (in Latin, *ubi sunt*). The effect of the formula is to emphasize the transitory qualities of life. Perhaps the most famous example in English is Dante Gabriel Rossetti's *The Ballad of Dead Ladies*, a translation of a ballad written by the French poet, François Villon, in which the last line of each stanza is:

Mais où sont les neiges d'antan?
(But where are the snows of yesteryear?)

Generally, the *ubi sunt* query is placed in the opening line of a stanza or used as a refrain. In Edmund Gosse's *The Ballad of Dead Cities*, the three stanzas begin with these lines: "Where are the cities of the plain?"; "Where now is Karnak, that great fane?"; "And where is white Shushan, again?"

Ultima Thule: The farthest possible place. The phrase is often used in the sense of a remote goal, an ideal or a mysterious country. To the ancients, Thule was one of the northern lands of Europe, probably one of the Shetland Islands. In Latin, *ultima* means farthest. Thus, the farthest Thule was a remote and mysterious place.

Ultraism: The attitude and principles of those who push a principle or practice to radical extremes. In the twentieth century, ultraists in drama, literature and art attempted to transcend the ordinary limits of any one medium and sought the essence of experience. The language used by James Joyce in writing *Finnegan's Wake* is an example of the ultraistic mode. Expressionism, surrealism, the antinovel and the theater of the absurd are expressions of ultraism. (Each is defined in this dictionary.)

Understatement: A form of irony in which something is intentionally represented as less than it is in fact.

Unities: The principles of dramatic structure involving action, time and place. Renaissance scholars attributed Artistotle with establishing the three unities as rules for the construction of a drama. However, the only unity he specifically stressed was the unity of action. Tragedy, Aristotle said, is "an imitation of an action that is complete and whole and of a certain magnitude." A play should have a beginning, a middle and an end, and should include nothing irrelevant to the development of the single plot.

The unity of time was developed from Aristotle's statement: "Tragedy endeavors, as far as possible, to confine itself to a single revolution of the sun, or but slightly to exceed this limit." Italian critics of the sixteenth century formulated the doctrine that the action should be limited to one day. Some critics, however, favored the artificial day of twelve hours, and others favored the several hours that corresponded to the actual time of presentation on stage.

Of place, Aristotle said only that tragedy should be confined to a narrow compass. Later, this was interpreted to mean that the scene of the action should be unchanged or confined to the same town or city.

In England, the dramatic unities were denounced and defended for more than two centuries. When neoclassicism gave way to romanticism, they lost their importance.

Many English plays violate the unities. Unity of action, however, is generally recognized as an important requirement in serious drama. In two Shakespeare's plays, the *Comedy of Errors* and *The Tempest*, all three unities are observed.

Universality: A critical term frequently applied to a piece of writing that appeals to all readers of all times. Literature dealing with human characteristics that do not change with time or place may be said to have universality of appeal.

University Wits: A group of young men who came from Oxford and Cambridge to London in the late 1580s and became professional men of letters. They played a significant part in the development of the literature, particularly the drama, produced during the latter years of the reign of Queen Elizabeth I. The most important member of the group was Christopher Marlowe. Others included Robert Greene, George Peele, Thomas Lodge, Thomas Nash and Thomas Kyd. Some authorities include John Lyly, although Lyly was an older man and perhaps not personally associated with the others.

Upanishads: Ancient philosophical treatises or metaphysical commentaries on Hinduism. Written in Sanskrit, the Upanishads (meaning "sitting at the feet of a teacher") discuss the origin of the universe, the nature of deity and soul, and the relationship between spirit and matter.

Urania: See **Muses**.

Usage: The established or customary method of employing a particular word, phrase or construction. Good usage is established by the forms of language used by educated people and by acknowledged authorities. However, usage is not permanently fixed. Old word forms become obsolete and new forms enter the language. Dictionaries and grammars properly follow usage rather than set it.

Uta: See **Tanka**.

Utopia: A place in which social, legal and political justice and perfect harmony exist. Utopia, meaning "nowhere," was coined by Thomas More for the name of the ideal republic described in his book, *Utopia* (1516). Many philosophers and writers have presented plans for ideal commonwealths. Plato's *Republic* is the best known. Some others are Campanella's *Civitas Solis* (1623), Bacon's *New Atlantis* (1627), Harrington's *Oceana* (1656), Butler's *Erewhon* (1872), Bellamy's *Looking Backward* (1888), Morris' *News from Nowhere* (1890) and Wells' *A Modern Utopia* (1905).

V

Vade Mecum: An article carried and used constantly. The Latin phrase means "go with me" and, by association, has come to mean any book that is frequently used for reference, such as a handbook, manual or thesaurus.

Vanity Fair: A representation of the appeal of the devil. The term was first used by philosophers and later employed by John Bunyan in *The Pilgrim's Progress* (1678).

The term has been generalized to designate a city, world or civilization characterized by folly, vice and atheism. William Thackeray used the term as the title of a novel (1848) which he peopled with characters "living without God in the world."

Vapours: A word frequently used in eighteenth-century literature to explain the cause of eccentric behavior. Vapours were believed to be exhalations, produced by the stomach or some bodily organ, which rose to the head and caused depression, melancholy, faintness or hysteria. (See **Humours**.) As early as 1541, Sir Thomas Elyot wrote that "of humours, some are more grosse and colde, some are subtyl and hot and are called vapours." Heroines of eighteenth-century fiction were particularly subject to the vapours.

Variable Syllable: A syllable that may be stressed or unstressed in the scansion of a line of verse according to the particular demands of the metrical pattern. (See **Weak Ending** and **Wrenched Accent**.)

Variety: A quality of style, in prose or verse, that demands that the author avoid monotonous expression of ideas. Variety can be achieved by a number of literary devices, such as varying the structure and type of sentences used, shifting from narration to description, using figurative language, introducing dialogue into narrative and employing comic relief.

Variorum Edition: An edition of a book that has the comments, notes and interpretations of several critics, as well as variant versions of the text. The term is an abbreviation of the Latin phrase, *cum notis variorum* ("with notes of various persons"). An example in the field of English literature is the *New Variorum Shakespeare*, edited by Furness.

Vaudeville: A stage entertainment consisting of successive performances of unrelated songs, dances, dramatic sketches, acrobatic feats, juggling and pantomime. The word is derived from Vau-de-Vire, a village in Normandy, France, where a famous composer of lively, satirical songs lived in the eighteenth century. From these songs, later modified by pantomime, developed the variety shows known as vaudeville.

Veda: (1) From Sanskrit, meaning "knowledge". (2) Any of the four canonical collections of hymns, prayers and liturgical instructions that comprise the earliest Hindu sacred writings.

Vehicle: See **Tenor** and **Vehicle**.

Verbosity: The use of too many words; wordiness. (See **Prolixity**.)

Verisimilitude: The appearance or semblance of truth and reality. The term is used in criticism to indicate the degree to which a writer faithfully presents the truth.

Verism: The doctrine that literature should represent unadorned reality, no matter how ugly or sordid it may be.

Vernacular: The domestic or native language of the people of a particular country or geographical area. In the Middle Ages, books were written in Latin. During the Renaissance, writers began to use the vernacular for their work, as, for example, Chaucer did when he wrote *The Canterbury Tales* in English.

Vers de Société: "Society verse"; brief, lyrical verse, sophisticated in subject and treatment. *Vers de société* (sometimes called light verse) is characterized by grace, wit, ease of expression and polish. Often epigrammatic and satirical, it usually presents aspects of social relationships. Among the many poets who have written this type of verse are Alexander Pope, W. E. Henley, Austin Dobson, Hilaire Belloc, G. K. Chesterton, John Betjeman and W. H. Auden.

Verse: (1) A line of poetry. (2) A general term for metrical composition. (Poetry is usually reserved to indicate verse of high merit. See **Poetry**.)

Versification: The art and practice of writing verse. Like prosody, the term is an inclusive one and is generally used to connote all the mechanical elements that make up poetic composition. Some of these are accent, rhythm, foot, meter, rhyme, stanza form, diction and such figurative aids as assonance, onomatopoeia and alliteration. (Each of these is explained in this dictionary.) In a narrower sense, versification signifies the structural form of a verse or stanza, which is revealed by careful scansion. (See **Accent, Quantity** and **Scansion**.)

Vers Libre: See **Free Verse**.

Verso: See **Recto**.

Vice: An evil habit or wicked tendency. The Vice was a stock, buffoonlike character in many sixteenth-century morality plays. Often, the Devil appeared in the play carrying the Vice on his back. (See **Morality Play** and **Stock Character**.)

Victorian: In literary criticism, a term used: (1) to designate the literature of the age of Queen Victoria (1837-1901) or its characteristic qualities and attitudes; and (2), more narrowly, to suggest a certain complacency, hypocrisy or squeamishness assumed to arise from, and be characteristic of, Victorian attitudes.

Victorian literature is varied and complex, reflecting the changes in life and thought that occurred during the period. The religious and philosophical doubts and hopes raised by science, the social problems arising from the new industrial conditions, the rise of a new middle-class audience and new media of publication (i.e., magazines) are among the forces that colored Victorian literature.

The cautious manner in which Victorian writers often treated such matters as profanity and sex has been especially responsible for the common use of Victorian or mid-Victorian to indicate false modesty or empty respectability. Though justified in part, this use of Victorian is somewhat exaggerated and fails to take into consideration the fact that a large part of Victorian literature either did not exhibit such traits or protested against them.

Vignette: (1) A written sketch or short composition. It may stand alone or be part of a longer composition. Dickens' *Sketches by Boz* is a series of vignettes of London life and people. (2) A decorative design on a page of a book, particularly on the title page or at the beginning or end or a chapter.

Villanelle: A French verse form composed of nineteen lines divided into five tercets and a final four-line stanza. Only two rhymes are used, and the rhyme scheme is *aba, aba, aba, aba, aba, abaa*. The first line is repeated to form six, twelve and eighteen; the third line is repeated to form lines nine, fifteen and nineteen. Thus, eight of the nineteen lines are refrain.

Virelay: A French verse form (related to the lay) in which the number of stanzas and the number of lines to the stanza are unlimited. Each stanza is made up of an indefinite number of tercets, rhyming *aab* for the first stanza, *bbc* for the second, *ccd* for the third, etc. The virelay is rare in English poetry, perhaps because of the monotony of the rhyming. (See **Lay**.)

Virgin Play: See **Miracle Play**.

Virgule: A slanting stroke (1) commonly used in prosody to indicate the division of a line into feet.

viz.: Namely (an abbreviation of the Latin *videlicet*, meaning "to wit").

Volta: In a sonnet, the change in thought that separates the first eight lines from the last six lines. The term is derived from the Italian word *volta*, meaning "turn." (See **Octave**, **Sestet** and **Sonnet**.)

Vowel Rhyme: Rhyme in which the vowel sounds are the same, but the surrounding consonants are different, as in *time* and *nine*. (See **Assonance**.)

Vulgarism: A form of slang or colloquialism; a word, phrase or expression used only in coarse speech. For example, *kid* for *child*, or *kick the bucket* for *die*.

Vulgate: The popular or most commonly used, usually describing an edition of a book. The word is derived from the Latin *vulgata* (*editio*), "common (edition)." The Vulgate Bible is the Latin version written by St. Jerome in the fourth century. It is the authorized Bible of the Roman Catholic Church.

The vulgate romances are the versions of various cycles of Arthurian romance that were written in Old French prose (common or colloquial speech) in the thirteenth century and were the most widely used forms of these stories. The vulgate romances formed the basis of Malory's *Le Morte d'Arthur* and other later treatments. (See **Arthurian Romance**.)

W

Wardour Street English: A style strongly marked by the use of archaic language; an insincere, artificial expression. Wardour Street, in London, is a street housing many antique dealers selling both genuine and imitation antiques. Wardour Street English is a term based on the analogy of imitation archaisms in writing and imitation antiques in furniture, etc. The term was, for example, applied to William Morris' translation of *The Odyssey*.

War of the Theaters: A complicated series of quarrels among certain Elizabethan dramatists during the years 1598 to 1602. Jonson and Marston were the chief opponents, though many other dramatists, including Dekker and possibly Shakespeare, were involved. Among the causes of the quarrels were personal and professional jealousies, and the keen competition among the rival theaters and their associated companies of actors. Particularly important was the struggle for supremacy between the stock companies of professionals and between the companies of boy actors, the Children of the Chapel, who acted at the Blackfriars, and the Children of Paul's. (See **Public Theaters**.)

Weak Ending: A line of verse ending in a word that is stressed metrically, but would not be accented in normal speech. (See **Variable Syllable**.)

Well-made Play: A play that is logically and tightly constructed. At the climax and denouement, all the details of the skilfully contrived plot fall neatly into place. The term was introduced by the French playwright, A. E. Scribe (1791-1861). Henrik Ibsen (1828-1906), the Norwegian playwright and poet, followed the dictates of the well-made play in his dramas.

Whimsical: A critical term for writing what is fanciful or expresses odd notions.

Wit and Humor: Although neither of these words was originally concerned with the amusing or laughable, modern usage associates both wit and humor with this quality. Wit is primarily an intellectual quality and is expressed in ingenious phraseology, brilliant epigrams, clever comparisons, etc. Humor implies a sympathetic recognition of human values and deals with the foibles and inconsistencies of human nature.

Originally, wit meant knowledge and, in the Middle Ages, came to signify intellect. In Renaissance times, wit usually meant wisdom or mental activity. During the seventeenth century, the term was applied to the metaphysical poets to mean fancy, in the sense of inspiration, originality or creative imagination. With the advent of neoclassicism, the term took on new meanings to reflect new critical attitudes.

Humor was originally a physiological term. Later, it came to convey the meaning of eccentricity or individual disposition. (See **Humours.**)

Before 1800, both words were associated with that which causes laughter. The earlier connotations of wit remained; those of humor did not.

Women on the Stage: Although women appeared on the Italian and French stages during the Renaissance, women's parts in England were acted by boys. In 1656, the part of Ianthe in Davenant's *Siege of Rhodes* was played by Mrs. Coleman, and the tradition of English actresses is usually dated from this event. However, *Siege of Rhodes* was more musical and spectacular than dramatic, and Mrs. Coleman may have been employed in the entertainment because of her singing abilities. A few years later, with the revival of dramatic activities in 1660, women became a permanent feature of the English stage, although boy actors continued to play some feminine roles on the Restoration stage. Some women who early gained fame as actresses were: Mrs. Barry, Mrs. Betterton and Mrs. Bracegirdle (seventeenth century); Mrs. Susannah Cibber, Mrs. Prichard and Mrs. Siddons (eighteenth century).

Wrenched Accent: An alteration in the customary pronunciation of a word, that is, a shift in word accent, to accommodate the metrical accent in a line of verse. (See **Variable Syllable** and **Weak Ending.**)

X

Xanaduism: Research to discover the sources that have contributed to a work of art. The term is derived from the type of research that was done by John Livingston Lowes for *The Road to Xanadu* (1927), his book on Coleridge's poem, *Kubla Khan*.

Xenophanic: A term used to describe a wandering poet who writes witty, satirical verse. Xenophanes was a Greek poet who lived in the sixth century B.C., travelled widely throughout the Greek world and wrote verse satirizing Homer's and Hesiod's mythology.

Y

Yarn: A tale or story. Yarn is, literally, any spun thread, and "to spin a yarn" means, in informal English, "to tell a story." Usually, the implication is that the story is slightly improbable or exaggerated. Many of Robert Service's poems are yarns, and the stories written by R. L. Stevenson and Rudyard Kipling contain some fine yarns.

Yearbook: (1) A book or report published annually (see **Annual**.) (2) A school annual containing reports and pictures of the students' activities during one year. (3) Year Book: a book containing the annual reports of English common law cases adjudicated from the time of Edward II to that of Henry VIII inclusive.

Yellow Journalism: The use by journalists of cheaply sensational methods in an effort to attract readers or influence their opinions.

Z

Zeitgeist: The characteristic thought, preoccupation or spirit of a particular period. For example, the theme of death, dissolution and decay is evident in much of the literature produced by English poets and dramatists during the early seventeenth century.

Zeugma: See **Syllepsis**.

NOTES

NOTES